KT-132-727

We Remember
D-DAY

We Remember D-DAY

POWERFUL AND MOVING TRUE STORIES FROM

6 JUNE 1944

FRANK & JOAN SHAW

EBURY
PRESS

1 3 5 7 9 10 8 6 4 2

This edition published in 2014 by Ebury Press,
an imprint of Ebury Publishing
A Random House Group company
First published by Frank and Joan Shaw in 1994

The Random House Group Limited Reg. No. 954009

Addresses for companies within the Random House Group can be
found at www.randomhouse.co.uk

A CIP catalogue record for this book is available from
the British Library

The Random House Group Limited supports the Forest
Stewardship Council® (FSC®), the leading international forest-
certification organisation. Our books carrying the FSC label are
printed on FSC®-certified paper. FSC is the only forest-
certification scheme supported by the leading environmental
organisations, including Greenpeace. Our paper procurement
policy can be found at www.randomhouse.co.uk/environment

MIX
Paper from
responsible sources
FSC® C016897

Printed and bound by CPI Group (UK) Ltd, Croydon, CR0 4YY

ISBN 9780091941574

To buy books by your favourite authors and register for offers visit
www.randomhouse.co.uk

Contents

Introduction

The invasion force launched on D-Day was of a size never seen before and likely to never be seen again. There were more than 6,000 warships, transports and landing craft, including six battleships and twenty-three cruisers. In the air were more than 11,000 combat aircraft, 2,300 transport planes and 2,600 gliders. In the armada would be three million men, of whom over 150,000 landed on D-Day alone. Never again would an operation of this size be contemplated let alone undertaken.

To defend Holland, Belgium and France the German commander in chief in the west, Field Marshal Rundstedt, had thirty-eight infantry and ten Panzer divisions, plus seven reserve divisions in the Pas-de-Calais and three in Normandy. It was a formidable force, but he had only a handful of destroyers and torpedo boats, and only 497 aircraft. And eighteen of the thirty-eight divisions were stationed in the Pas-de-Calais because Rundstedt was convinced that was where the invasion would come. There were only nine divisions in Normandy.

However, to supplement these forces there was a defensive system of minefields, fortifications, machine-gun nests, mortar batteries and mined obstacles. It was a daunting defence system – for example on the beaches alone there were 1,400 obstacles and mines to the mile! To deal with all this was the job of 'Hobart's Funnies', the name given to various armoured vehicles adapted by Major General Sir Percy Hobart of the 79th Armoured Division. These included bulldozer tanks which could clear the beaches with impunity, the Crocodile flamethrower tank, which could incinerate anything within a range of one hundred and twenty yards, and the Bobbin tank, which was adapted to lay a roadway over sand or soft ground. There was also the Crab tank with whirling flails at the front, which literally exploded a ten-foot wide path through the minefields, and the Flying Dustbin tank, which could fire a forty-pound shell three times a minute to smash concrete strong points. But most important of all for a landing from the sea were the Duplex Drive (DD) amphibious tanks, fitted with twin propellers that could 'swim' ashore independently.

However, there was a problem. Many of the obstacles of the Atlantic Wall were just below water level at high tide. They would rip open the bottom of any landing craft like a tin opener. To avoid these the landings would have to take place at least three or four hours before high tide so that the 'hedgehogs', as they were called, could be seen. But because of the need to start the assault at dawn, this meant there were only a few days each month when the tides were just right at first light.

The original date had finally been set for 5 June 1944 but wind and heavy seas had forced a postponement. But then Group Captain Sir James Stagg cautiously forecast that for the evening of 5 June and the morning of 6 June conditions might improve sufficiently for a short period to allow the operation to proceed. But if the forecast proved to be wrong...? Well, it didn't bear thinking about. On the other hand the troops had already embarked and the navy had sailed, only to be recalled. Not to proceed now would mean a delay of at least two weeks, with all the enormous problems of refuelling and resupplying. But most of all the security risks would be horrendous. Too many people now knew not only that the invasion was imminent, but also where the attack was to take place.

A meeting of the commanders was held at 21:30 on 4 June and another at 03:30 on 5 June. The decision rested with

General Dwight Eisenhower, supreme allied commander. He had asked for the views of his commanders. Air chief marshals Tedder and Leigh-Mallory were apprehensive. 'Chancy,' said Leigh-Mallory. Two votes against. Admiral Sir Ramsay said they should proceed. General Montgomery was asked. His answer was crisp and precise: 'I would say – go'. Two votes for! Eisenhower sat for some minutes, silent and alone with his thoughts. Then he spoke the words that were to go down in history. 'OK – let's go.' It was a momentous decision. The invasion fleet headed to 'Piccadilly Circus', the assembly area just south of Isle of Wight, and then along the ten channels swept clear of mines by twelve flotillas of minesweepers of the Royal Navy. During this period the weather remained foul and the troops suffered badly with the smaller craft, in particular in difficulty in the rough seas. But the bad weather had its advantages – the invasion fleet remained undetected because an attack seemed inconceivable and so all German air and sea patrols were cancelled! Total surprise was achieved.

Rundstedt's belief that the invasion would be in the Pas-de-Calais area had in fact been confirmed by Operation Fortitude, a calculated and complex deception started by the Allies weeks before D-Day. Thousands of dummy tanks, guns, planes and landing craft had been constructed and then sited in Kent and Sussex. The RAF bombed Normandy but concentrated its efforts on the Pas-de-Calais to add to the illusion. The deception of the German intelligence service succeeded beyond all expectations. For seven whole weeks after D-Day the German High Command remained convinced that Normandy was a diversion and that the real attack was still awaited.

But it had already started at 00:16 on Tuesday 6 June 1944. To safeguard the beaches on which the troops and supplies would be landing in a few hours' time, the bridges over the River Orne and the Caen Canal at Bénouville had to be captured and held to prevent a German counter-attack on the invasion flank or the bringing up of reinforcements. A detachment of the Oxfordshire and Buckinghamshire Light Infantry led by Major John Howard landed in three gliders bang on target and within fifteen minutes had secured their objective. At 00:30 Corporal Ted Tappenden sent out the historic signal 'Ham and Jam' confirming that these vital bridges were now held by the airborne troops. They were the very first to set foot on French soil.

At Merville, eight miles away, the 9th Parachute Battalion followed shortly afterwards. Their job was to silence the Merville Gun Battery. Immediately things went wrong. At 00:30 the plane that was to mark the target for one hundred and twenty Lancaster bombers 'marked' the nearby village of Gonneville by mistake due to thick cloud. The result was that Merville was untouched but Gonneville was turned into a furnace by four hundred tons of bombs. Then the battalion lost the gliders carrying its heavy assault equipment and out of seven hundred and fifty men who jumped, one hundred and ninety-two were never to be seen again – drowned in the sea or marshes under the weight of their equipment. By 02:30 only one hundred and fifty paratroopers had reached the assembly point. But the job had to be done and so the attack went ahead and in a desperate hand to hand struggle the battery was taken. It was a fight without mercy as the figures show. One hundred of the one hundred and thirty Germans in the battery were killed. Sixty-six of the one hundred and fifty paratroopers were killed and thirty more were wounded. Amazingly, a carrier pigeon they had brought from England survived and so was sent off with the news that the battery had been captured!

Across to the west of Normandy on the neck of the Cotentin Peninsula the United States 82nd and 101st Airborne Battalions were landing. The 82nd was to capture both banks of the Merderet river to the south and south-west of St Mère-Église. The 101st was to seize the beach exits and the bridges over the river Douve north of Carentan.

The 101st landed nearest to Utah Beach but in an area of meadows flooded by the Germans. They had their own recognition system of mechanical 'clicking crickets'. Some paratroopers were captured and the Germans quickly recognised the significance of the 'toy'. Other paratroopers were lured into gunfire by the 'friendly' clicks of the now German held devices and the whole operation degenerated into a nightmare of confusion, saved eventually only by the heroism and sheer guts of those paratroopers who survived.

For the 82nd Airborne Division it was even worse. They lost more than sixty per cent of their equipment in the drop and were scattered for miles around St Mère-Église. Those who landed in the town came down through a hail of flak, but nevertheless, through grim determination they achieved most of their objective and even added substantially to the success of D-Day by cutting every telephone wire in the Cotentin they could lay their hands on!

While these events were taking place the Allied Air Force was softening up the defences for the invading troops. Between midnight and 08:00 on 6 June the air force dropped 10,000 tons of bombs on the invasion coast defences. At the height of the bombing, in one concentrated period, 2,000 tons of bombs were dropped in just one ten-minute period. In that same bombing period of eight hours, over 7,500 sorties were flown by Allied planes. On D-Day itself a total of over 14,000 sorties were flown; bombing, strafing, dropping leaflets and confusing radar. It is very often forgotten in our preoccupation with the army and navy that the Allied Air Force lost one hundred and twenty-seven planes on D-Day.

Before the bombings came to an end with the actual landings, the navy had arrived offshore with the invasion fleet and to the terror of the aerial devastation was now added the naval bombardment. The 16-inch shells from six battleships and twenty-three cruisers pounded the German defences. Then one hundred and one destroyers joined in, as did the rocket launchers mounted on landing craft. The devastation was terrible and continuous, and yet many of the fortifications remained operational because of the immense concrete protection that can still be seen to this day.

The seaborne landings were timed to begin one hour after low water. But because the tide rises earlier in the west of the English Channel, the invasion started with the arrival of the 4th US Infantry Division at 06:30 on Utah Beach. As early as 05:30 two hundred and seventy-six Marauder bombers of the US Army Air Corps had begun to pound the coastal defences at Utah and the 4th Division soon had the beaches cleared with few losses. By 10:00 the first support regiment was ashore, and by noon the troops had made breaches in the anti-tank wall and were pushing inland to join up with the 82nd Airborne Division. All the defences in the area were quickly crushed and the beaches under control by the evening, by which time 23,550 men were ashore together with 1,700 vehicles plus supplies.

The contrast could not have been greater at Omaha Beach. There the 1st US Infantry Division landed shortly after 06:30 but with heavy losses. The landing craft had been launched twelve miles offshore and in the still rough seas many sank or lost their bearings and foundered on Rommel's mined obstacles. Out of twenty-nine amphibious tanks launched at Omaha only two made it to the beaches. When the second wave of troops went in at 07:30 they were pinned down on the beaches by German artillery and small arms fire. The beaches had still not been cleared of anti-invasion devices and the tide was now rising. To make the problem worse General Omar Bradley had refused to use Hobart's Funnies and so there was no equipment to sort things out. Two destroyers moved in to shell the German positions but the slaughter continued to the stage where abandoning the landing was seriously considered. It was not until noon that the Americans were able to make some progress and get inland off the now bloodied beaches. This was the most difficult of all the landings and by nightfall only a small bridgehead six miles wide and two miles deep had been established. But even that had cost 3,000 casualties.

The British and Canadian beaches were Gold, Juno and Sword, and here the sea was even rougher than at Omaha. The assault troops on all three beaches all came under heavy fire from German strong points, but the use of the specialised tanks so disastrously rejected by General Bradley at Omaha proved decisive in allowing the infantry to make rapid progress. On Gold Beach the 50th Infantry Division and the 8th Armoured Brigade landed at 07:25 in front of Ver-sur-Mere, Meuvaines and Asnelles. The nearby village of Le Hamel was garrisoned by a detachment of the crack German 352nd Division and it was here that the heaviest fighting took place. But despite this they fought their way rapidly inland establishing a bridgehead eight miles deep. No. 47 Royal Marine Commando reached its objective in the west, Port-en-Bessin, on D-Day plus two, linking up with the Americans at Omaha Beach.

On Juno Beach the 3rd Canadian Infantry Division landed at 07:00 and encountered strong opposition as they came ashore, but the 7th Brigade was established in Creully by 17:00. The 8th Brigade landed at Bernières and St. Aubin but there two heavily defended and fortified radar stations held out until 17 June, a truly remarkable achievement. However, a considerable bridgehead was established, even though one objective, Carpiquet, was not reached and a link up with the 3rd British Division on the left was not made.

On Sword Beach the 3rd British Infantry Division began landing at 07:30 between Lion-sur-Mer and Ouistreham/ Riva Bella. Its mission was to take Caen. But although the towns of Hermanville, Périers, Biéville-Beuville and Blainville-Crevon were overrun, a vigorous counter attack was launched by the 21st Panzer Division, which recaptured Biéville and then Périers. No. 4 Commando, which had landed at 08:45 quickly put the fortified position at Riva Bella out of action and by 13:30 had linked up with the airborne troops still holding the bridges at Bénouville. By nightfall the British and Canadians had established a combined bridgehead twelve miles wide and six miles deep, but Caen had still not been reached. But within five days the Allies had established a bridgehead fifty miles wide and twelve miles deep. Over 325,000 troops had landed with nearly 55,000 vehicles and over 100,000 tons of supplies. The Mulberry harbours, consisting of vast steel and concrete sections towed across the Channel and sunk off the beaches, then allowed the level of supply and unloading to be increased enormously, even though the Allies had still not captured a seaport. The contrast with Rommel's situation was stark – when finally released, his Panzers found themselves short of petrol and lacking essential air cover. Already it was effectively all over.

The rest, as they say, is history. The small but significant perimeter established on D-Day was pushed ever outwards. Some 3,000 British and Canadian troops had been killed or wounded, plus six hundred men of the 6th Airborne Division. Over 6,000 American troops were killed or wounded. Large though these figures are, they were substantially less than expected.

On 22 August 1944 the Falaise pocket was sealed and the Normandy campaign effectively ended. Over 50,000 German troops surrendered – the remnants of the German 7th Army and the 5th Panzer Army. They had suffered slaughter and destruction on a vast scale. On 19 August the escape route was only two miles wide and crossed by the River Dives. Although 30,000 German troops did escape, over 10,000 died and the carnage was so terrible that the Germans called it 'Das Korridor des Todes' – The Corridor of Death.

But let no one underestimate what a close run thing it all was. What if D-Day had been delayed by Eisenhower? What if the invasion had failed? These are now hypothetical questions, but if either of these events had happened remember that only one week later, on 13 June 1944, Hitler launched the first of his Vergeltungswaffen (reprisal weapons): the V1 flying bomb. Over 2,000 were launched, followed later by the bigger, faster and even more deadly V2.

If Eisenhower had put back D-Day and security had been breached then surely these weapons would then have been targeted not on London but on Portsmouth, Weymouth and Southampton. The effect on the troops, supplies, equipment and communications would have been catastrophic. If the invasion had failed, how many years would it have been before nerves would have been braced for a second attempt? And in either case, what even more horrendous weapons could by then have been developed by the Nazi regime?

For those of us living today it is all now hypothetical – but that very fact is a measure of the debt we owe, and will always owe, to all those men and women who played their part (however small) in the success of the D-Day landings. Remember that.

Frank and Joan Shaw

The First to Die

The very first Allied soldier to be killed on D-Day was Lieutenant Herbert Denham 'Den' Brotheridge from Smethwick. He was a platoon leader in D Company, 2nd Battalion Oxfordshire and Buckinghamshire Light Infantry (the Ox and Bucks), who were a formation within the airlanding brigade of the 6th Airborne Division of the British Army. He was in one of three gliders, each carrying thirty men, assigned the task of capturing the bridge over the Caen Canal to safeguard the flanks of the beachhead. Three other gliders carried the men who had to capture the nearby river Orne bridge for the same reason.

Den Brotheridge was in the first glider to land, along with Major John Howard, the commander. That glider came down very hard at 00:16 and embedded itself in a barbed wire fence, smashing the nose. The pilot and co-pilot were thrown out unconscious, and inside everyone else was momentarily stunned. Major Howard had his helmet smashed over his eyes and when he revived, he at first thought he had been blinded. One minute later the second glider landed close by without damage and both groups now charged together to attack the east end of the bridge. Even as they were running to do so the third glider landed just behind them.

Private Bill Gray, a Bren Gunner, later recalled Lieutenant Brotheridge saying, 'Here we go,' as their glider came in and then there was the most mind-numbing crash. The undercarriage was ripped off, and pieces of the cockpit flew back inside the glider. Nevertheless, within a few moments they were out, with Brotheridge leading his platoon in the dash for the bridge. The whole scene was one of chaos as ninety superbly trained and fit men stormed the bridge and the nearby German trenches and pillbox. Total surprise was achieved and the German defenders, some still asleep, were bewildered and disorganised in the darkness. Some groups attacked and cleared the trenches and the pillbox but Brotheridge and his group headed for the bridge itself and charged across it. Halfway across they saw a German sentry about to fire a warning flare. He was instantly cut down in a hail of fire and fell dead as his flare burst above, intended as a warning to the defenders of the Orne bridge about a quarter of a mile away. It was a brave but futile action. The German troops there had already been overrun. Moments later the same situation applied to the Caen Canal bridge. Within ten minutes of the landing both bridges had been captured.

After the crash of gliders, the firing of guns, the yelling of attackers and the general bedlam of the assault, an eerie silenced descended as everyone recovered their breath, sorted themselves out and tried to bring some order back to the situation. The objectives had been achieved in an unbelievably short time but now the adrenalin had to be brought under control quickly. Bill Gray later recalled looking for his platoon leader in the disciplined calm that followed, and then finding him lying outside the front of the Gondree café at the western end of the bridge he had so recently charged across. He had been shot in the throat and also hit by a phosphorous smoke grenade and his airborne smock was still burning. He died shortly afterwards, aged 29.

Lieutenant Brotheridge is buried in the Churchyard at Ranville, in Grave 43. Every year Major Howard, his commander on the raid, returns to lay a wreath on 6 June in memory of his colleague. He wrote to Lieutenant Brotheridge's wife shortly after her husband's death:

I am writing to tell you how badly the whole regiment feels the death of your husband. He was killed leading his men on the attack on the bridges, and it was very largely due to his dash and courage that the attack was successful. He was an officer we can ill afford to lose and was admired and respected by all the officers and men in the regiment.

The Canal bridge was later renamed Pegasus Bridge in honour of the shoulder flash of the 6th Airborne Division and in recognition of the courage and determination of those who had captured it that night. The precision of the landings at the bridge were recognised later by Air Chief Marshal Leigh-Mallory, Commander of Allied Air Forces, who said that in his opinion the event was the greatest feat of flying of the Second World War.

We Remember
D-Day

I was on HMS Scourge at Portsmouth ready for D-Day and it was with pride, and delight, that we learned we would be escorting the minesweepers clearing the passage for the assault on one of the British sectors (which proved to be Sword sector on the extreme easterly flank of the overall invasion area). We would thus be in the vanguard of the British invasion forces.

The one great worry on that Monday afternoon was that we would be spotted by enemy forces and we wondered how well we would be able to protect the army personnel and weapons in our care from a possible mass attack by dive bombers, or from the large fleet of U-boats thought to be based in the area. Air attack seemed less likely as the night closed in and by 10:30pm we had reached the minefield. All crew members not working below deck were ordered to the upper deck and for the next hour and a half – at a speed of only three knots – we made our way through the minefield with the sweepers. For most of that time loose mines were clearly visible in the moonlight just a few yards from our beam.

During the minesweeping we saw and heard ghostly shapes in the sky and guessed (correctly) that these were our airborne forces in gliders towed by 'tug' planes. Many silent prayers must have been said by the armada personnel as the men who would be the first to land in France passed over-head. Perhaps even now those who have survived may like to know that our thoughts and prayers were for their safety. Anyway, by midnight we had passed through the minefield and were not many miles from enemy territory. For an hour or two we guided some of the other warships through to

*Pilot Officer Adams
with James Hinton*

their bombarding positions before taking up our own off Ouistreham.

As dawn broke on D-Day the sea around us was alive with ships of every description – it was the most amazing and wonderful experience. It seemed incredible that we had come across the Channel without attack. Not quite true. One of our sister destroyers – HNoMS *Svenner*, a Norwegian vessel manned by Norwegians – was torpedoed in the early hours by a German E-boat in, apparently, their only attack of the day.

At 6:30am HMS *Scourge* commenced the bombardment of her first target – a German gun emplacement. It was quickly demolished! By this time every type of craft imaginable was making its way to the Sword beachhead, perhaps the most impressive being the multi-rocket firing craft. Their rockets, and the shells from the bombarding warships, passed over the heads of the British troops attempting to get a foothold on the beaches. The noise was quite incredible. As well as shelling enemy positions from close to shore, during the early phase of the assault HMS *Scourge* put down a mass of smoke screens to cover the troops landing ashore. For some reason it suddenly occurred to me that it was my grandfather's 74th birthday and I wondered how he would consider this great event off France as a present!

After the initial landings had been established, seemingly successfully, our ship spent the last three hours of the morning patrolling the eastern flank to protect our bombarding battleships and cruisers from any marauding E-boats and U-boats that may have been about.

This was then followed by more bombarding of our own targets and giving assistance where needed, such as shelling to set up 'clearways' for the Allied tanks and infantry.

At 10:40pm we resumed a patrol of the eastern flank, and within the next hour we twice became the target for enemy air attacks. The first sticks of bombs hit the water close to our stern, and the second string straddled our beam with three bombs falling on either side! No damage – but the bridge was drenched! I remember that at midnight I thought, 'Well, I don't know what's in store for you, but at least you've survived D-Day!'

On 24 June 1944 a second of our sister destroyers (S Class) was sunk by a mine, just as she was about to come alongside us off Ouistreham. HMS *Swift* went down in minutes with heavy loss of life, less than a cable's length from our beam. A terrible tragedy. I was twenty-one at the time and an electrical artificer on HMS *Scourge*, which was awarded battle honours for her part in the D-Day action. At the end of June 1944 we returned to Scapa Flow in readiness to continue escort duties on the Russian convoys until the end of the war in Europe.

A note about the pilot in my 1944 photograph. He was Sergeant Pilot (later Pilot Officer) Ronald B. T. Adams. He was in 174 Squadron and spent D-Day above me flying a Typhoon! Early on D-Day his squadron attacked gun positions in Normandy with rockets, all of which burst in the target area, and later that day it flew armed reconnaissance over the beachheads. There was so much bombardment coming up from the Royal Navy that Ronald later wrote to me to say their gunfire worried him more than the enemy's!

Ronald was shot down and killed in Typhoon MN977 on

24 February 1945 near Osnabruck after leading an armed reconnaissance in which a German train and railway tracks were successfully attacked. A wonderful and long missed friend.

James R. B. Hinton, Sherborne, Dorset

I was a signalman in the 6th Airborne Division and on 6 June 1944 I was just twenty-three years old, as were millions of others; just bairns really. Now, as we crossed the French coast, we were met by searchlights and a barrage of ack-ack fire. For most of us it was our first baptism of fire and tension was really high. Just when it was becoming almost unbearable an RA officer in my glider undid his safety harness, stood up, placed his helmet upside-down on the seat and sat on it. As he did so he hung on grimly to his safety harness as the Halifax towing plane and the Horsa glider bumped their way through the flak. We watched him in silent bewilderment as he rocked about on his upturned helmet. Eventually someone asked, 'Excuse me, sir, but why did you do that?' The Officer looked at him quite seriously and then said with a straight face, 'I don't know about you chaps, but I'm getting married when I get back to England and I'm not going to have my bloody chances ruined!'

His reply broke the tension in an instant, and I can honestly say we became fairly relaxed, eager and ready on our way down to the fields of Normandy and, although we didn't realise it at the time, into the pages of history.

About two hours later, after getting the dead and wounded out of the crashed gliders, unloading Jeeps, guns and stores, and attending to the general organised chaos of a moonlit Airborne landing, I found myself digging a slit trench behind the chateau in Ranville. Dawn wasn't very far away when a very 'angry hornet' zipped past my ear, leaves flew off a nearby bush, and I heard the crack of a rifle. Frantically trying to stuff my body into the six-inch depression, which I'd so far managed to dig, I realised a sniper had singled me out and that my war, barely two hours old, had suddenly become very personal! I was to find with experience that it remained so until VE Day!

I have returned to the cemetery at Ranville many times since then to pay my respects to those comrades we left behind who were not as lucky as me with 'angry hornets'.

Ted Hold, Sunderland, Tyne and Wear

No. 3 Troop 6 Commando spearheaded No. 1 Special Service Brigade on D-Day, 6 June 1944. Our landing craft leading the brigade was hit twice on their run into the beach; first on the bridge, then the water line, the troop having to disembark in deep water. The air resounded to the roar of the heavy naval guns, still pounding the defences. Planes roared overhead, and bullets churned the water as craft raced for the shore. Around them bodies of other troops bobbed lifeless in the foaming, angry, now reddened, sea.

Suddenly we came under attack from 'Moaning Minnies' screaming just over our heads. Only seconds' delay then the troop rushed forward again, each man carrying rucksacks containing approximately sixty pounds in weight of equipment, as well as personal weapons. Within minutes the gun defences were reached and the area reported cleared for the loss of only one member killed by a sniper. The troop was doubling forward again, across fields, through hedgerows, along main roads, as we raced for our next objective, Pegasus

Bridge, which we hoped had been held by the airborne troops who had dropped in on the area during the night. No. 3 Troop's orders were to pass through the airborne if the bridge was intact. If it had been blown and the airborne wiped out, we were to attempt a river crossing in order to achieve the final objective of the day. On the outskirts of Bénouville, spasmodic firing indicated that the battle for the bridge was still in progress. At the incline in the road the bridge was a welcome sight with the airborne troops kneeling down either side of the bridge, engaged in a fierce sniping battle. We had been moving fast before; now in full flight we charged down the road and without a single pause thundered over the bridge to cheers, and shouts of 'snipers ahead' from the airborne forces. Possibly taken by surprise by our sudden appearance, the German snipers melted away and we continued our advance.

Our next task was to attack the German Headquarters at the crossroads at Bréville and hold this strategic position, in order to disrupt communications. No. 3 Troop moved quickly through Amfreville en route for Bréville. Suddenly everywhere was quiet; a strange uneasiness, as we came in sight of the chateau, which was the German headquarters. Captain Pymane led a section round the rear, while the rest of the troop made a rush through the gates of the chateau, across the orchard and into the large house. The Germans could not have anticipated our arrival. Steaming cups of coffee on the table, the radio still playing and the HQ was ours!

From the rear of the house heavy gunfire indicated that all was not well with our patrol section. We took up positions in and around the house to prepare for the anticipated counter attack, which commenced immediately. At that moment a runner came in to report that Captain Pymane had been killed and the rest of the patrol had suffered heavy casualties and were pinned down by sniper fire. No. 3 Troop was now cut off; the Germans had managed to surround the chateau but were beginning to suffer heavy casualties from the determined attacks, which they made time and time again as they attempted to retake their headquarters. Soon the roadway around the chateau was filled with the dead and wounded Germans, but still they came on. Our heaviest retaliation weapon was a two-inch mortar. The Germans retaliated with a battery of 88mm guns firing over open sights, their shells crashing into the house and passing through

the roof. Other shells crashing into the tops of the trees in the orchard; every salvo resulting in more and more casualties. Radio reports coming in indicated that the rest of the brigade was involved in heavy fighting and no help was available. The orders were for No.3 Troop to hold out at all costs: nothing had to get past the chateau and crossroads at this stage.

Then came the order to cut all radio communication until we were contacted. No. 3 Troop's last request was to evacuate if possible the wounded and dead, a request answered by the sudden arrival of a lorry driven by two airborne boys at high speed into the orchard. The wounded and dead were loaded as quickly as possible into the lorry, which sped away at top speed as we gave it covering fire. The remainder of the troop then took advantage of a sudden lull in the attacks to gather together all the weapons and grenades left behind and prepared for the final assault as night began to creep in. The lull did not last for long, then the attack was on again, this time without the heavy shelling so our casualties were light.

Evening was drawing in, the important position had been held against impossible odds. Suddenly the sky was filled with the roar of planes, flak, searchlights, and heavy ack-ack as the German defences went into action drowning the chatter of our own rifles and Bren guns as we beat off further determined attacks. Then the attacks suddenly ceased as the illuminated sky was filled with gliders and planes of the airborne forces. Our radio crackled into life ordering us to withdraw if possible and to re-join the brigade and No. 6 Commando, who were now dug in and had established a holding line with the other commandos at Amfreville behind us. This order was carried out by a tactical withdrawal, the wounded and walking wounded being assisted by a covering section bringing up the rear to ward off any sudden attack.

There was no jubilation as we arrived at Amfreville. Every other troop had suffered heavy casualties in carrying out their individual tasks, but none more than No. 3 Troop. Their toll for taking and holding Bréville on their own for that all-important period and disrupting the German HQ had been a total of twenty-two killed, twelve wounded seriously. Others suffered slight wounds but still continued the fight to hold on to this vital and strategic position whatever the cost, knowing that they could not expect any assistance as the rest of the commando brigade were carrying out similar important tasks vital to the success of the Bridgehead.

Clifford Morris, Lancing, Sussex

O n D-Day I was a prisoner of war in Stalag Luft 1 at Barth on the Baltic coast. I had been flight engineer of a Stirling of 196 Squadron, which crashed in France whilst on an SOE [Special Operations Executive] arms drop to the French Resistance.

We had a radio in the camp, which obviously was concealed from the Germans, and the news that was received from British Stations was circulated daily very discreetly. The Germans certainly suspected that the radios existed but were never quite sure.

However on D-Day the news was much too important to be written out and passed around. It was relayed verbally to the first group of people and they simply exploded into a

demonstration of joy, which was repeated and repeated and went round the camp like a shock wave. Within minutes of the reception of the BBC morning news a parade of prisoners had been created and it started to move round the inner perimeter of the camp in a skipping, jumping, waving crocodile, which lengthened continually as the news flashed from hut to hut. The men were banging cooking pots, tin plates, Red Cross boxes – anything that would make a noise!

Not unnaturally the German guards were quite astonished by this wild demonstration because the invasion had not been reported on German radio. It was of course asking too much to expect the prisoners to keep their mouths shut and so with great glee they announced to the guards the news that the landings had taken place. This was at first treated with some scepticism by the guards, but as the demonstrations continued they came to accept that it was in fact genuine. Much later in the day German radio did broadcast the news and confirmed what we had been saying for some hours! The result was that the Germans at last had actual proof of what they had long suspected – that we were in contact with Britain by radio. But who cared!

Gordon 'Bert' Hemmings, Birkenhead, Merseyside

We were taken out from Folkestone harbour in commandeered fishing boats, a detachment to each boat, and introduced to the large 6,000 ton concrete Phoenix caissons. They were to form the outer wall of the Mulberry harbour to be assembled at Arromanches in the coming June, after each section had been floated and towed across the Channel by sea-going tugs. We didn't know this at the time.

On the way we noted that the caissons, each over seventy metres long, thirty feet high from the water level, were dotted along the coastline, each laying about a quarter of a mile offshore and had Bofors guns mounted upon a central tower. We climbed from the fishing boat onto a lower ledge of the caisson and then had to climb twenty-five to thirty feet up a vertical iron-runged ladder to reach the top and deck. I remember that there were one or two members who were too scared to make the climb, which was understandable, and they had to be roped up.

Once on the top we found that the caisson was hollow, divided into about sixteen compartments, each compartment filled with water to the level of the tide at the time. (When it had been positioned the seacocks would have been opened allowing the sea to flow in thereby allowing the caisson to sink on to the seabed.) We found a small deck at each end with a catwalk leading down the middle of the caisson to the gun tower. We were to live on these monsters for a week at a time to get used to them. The designers had made a small concrete room at one end with a small window for any gun crew to shelter in. We found that sleeping was impossible there and we all had claustrophobia, preferring to bunk down underneath the gun tower. Equipment on the caisson was found to consist of many ropes, a generator for pumping out the water when the time came to 'float', several lifebuoys and signalling lamps.

There had been changes over the years and our detachment was now made up of Sgt Wallace Newcombe, Cpl Bottomley, Jack Capstick, Jack Crabtree, Bill Farrell, Tom Hannan, Arthur New, Alf Holmes (the cook), Ulingworth, Bob Beldon and myself. Bob was to become a good friend who I was to maintain contact with after the war.

Eventually our big day arrived. First, two Royal Engineer sappers and two Royal Navy ratings came aboard to accompany us across the Channel, the engineers to man the generator and 'pump out', and the naval men to assist in the positioning of our caisson at Arromanches. Also to join us were about three men from our battery headquarters, again just for the crossing. I remember that two of them I knew were Ernest Martin, an orderly, and Fitton, a clerk. Sadly both of them were soon to lose their lives.

We were off, but it was to be a long and very slow journey. I do remember seeing ahead another of our detachments on a similar caisson making about the same knots, and the tug towing it was dwarfed by the concrete hulk behind it. At this time there was little roll, on account of our weight, and the journey seemed quite smooth. The weather was deteriorating though and at night we huddled in blankets under the gun tower with hardly any sleep.

The next morning there was bad luck for us when one of the two steel hawsers between the tug and the caisson snapped, so we were being towed with one line at a slightly off-straight angle, and the weather getting rougher, as were the seas. We estimated that we were midway over the Channel. The worst thing was that we were taking in water because of the high seas and the angle of our course. We signalled by Morse lamp to the tug's crew and we had the reply that 'she looked OK'.

The tug was perhaps sixty to seventy yards ahead and rolling heavily, and even from our high position on the caisson we sometimes almost lost view of her. Our other detachment's caisson had forged ahead and out of sight.

After a worrying day, darkness fell and we were taking in more water. The caisson now had a list to starboard and I remember that we moved anything of weight to the port side and even bedded down on that side, though it made no difference. Credit to the sergeant and the corporal who had been signalling all night at intervals to the tug towing us and to any other ship that came in sight.

The next day a British naval frigate, obviously in answer to our SOS calls, came as near to us as she dare. I will never forget our cheers and joy to see her. I am sure that each one

of us expected a miracle and to find ourselves magically winched into the safe and warm quarters of the frigate, but it wasn't to be and impossible in those seas. The crew of the frigate fired lines by rocket towards us but they failed to land a line near enough for us to catch owing to the high seas. The frigate was rolling and heaving in the swell, more than we were, and moving with us about sixty yards to starboard. I remember that they made about six attempts on this dark cloudy rainy day without success, and then they gave up. Sailing in our sight for an hour, and continually exchanging signals with the American tug, the frigate was eventually to sail away.

Reaching the Normandy coast, still listing badly, we saw through the rain and mist a mass of vessels, which would be at the half assembled harbour. Still in contact with the American tug by lamp we were made to understand from the captain that it was not possible to land us owing to the weather and seas, and that we were a danger to other shipping. We were to spend another night at sea and were towed up and down the coast well away and out of sight of any other craft. Morale was low and everyone was getting frightened at this stage because of darkness falling. Tempers were frayed at the assumed attitude of the American tug's crew who seemed to have no interest in our plight. The water in the caissons chambers was deeper at one end than the other and the list was getting worse. There was nobody to communicate with and the tug crew were now ignoring us.

We had all worn our life jackets for the last forty-eight hours. Two of the lads were too scared to even speak and just sat huddled up in blankets. I was scared myself and most of us realised the strong possibility of the caisson going down during the night. A feeling of helplessness. Some of us took it in turns, in pairs, to walk the catwalk to the far end and check the water level by torch. It was always reported higher. By 3am in the morning I remember agreeing with Jack Crabtree that we 'jump together' as we were certain now that the caisson was doomed. Most of us thought that it was best to get down to the lower platform that ran the full length of the caisson and which was only eight feet above normal sea level. So we climbed down in turn that twenty-seven feet of iron runged ladder and positioned ourselves on the highest corner. I remember that some of them must have been too scared to climb down such a ladder in those circumstances because I only remember being aware of about eight of us on the lower ledge. Sergeant Wally Newcombe was there, signalling to the last.

According to a letter that I wrote to my mother a few days hence, the caisson actually went down at 3:30am. At that particular time on the caisson I remember seeing in the distance the far end of our lower platform go under water, at the same time aware that our end was getting higher. It was obvious that the thing was going under so I jumped.

I seemed to go a long way down in the water for a long time and when I surfaced I remember thanking God for a large wooden beam that had appeared from nowhere. I slung my arm over it and called out to two bobbing heads nearby. It was Jack Crabtree and Alf Holmes and they joined me. I saw nothing of any caisson and no other heads in the water though there was still a heavy swell.

As the hours passed Jack's condition got worse. He was an older man and had swallowed too much water. I was determined to survive and trod the water continually to keep my blood circulating and to avoid any cramp.

At dawn a fishing trawler suddenly appeared and spotted us. It was commanded by a Sub-Lieutenant Brown and had been engaged in laying smoke screens off the beaches and was returning to its homeport in England. I remember being pulled in by a boat hook and lifted aboard by the crew, and then nothing except drinking rum and put into a bunk with warm blankets below decks.

The first thing that I noted on waking up was a mess table top covered with our personal possessions that had been dried. The vessel was rolling and pitching but I couldn't have cared less. I was alive and safe. We had been picked up about six o'clock according to the crew and were heading for Portland Bill and Weymouth Harbour. The captain and crew were super and gave us all fifty cigarettes.

In dried clothes, with a meal inside us, and in the calm waters of Weymouth Bay, I went on deck with Alf Holmes and Arthur New to find the covered bodies of Jack Crabtree, Fitton, an engineer and one other. I had survived the ordeal with only a very stiff shoulder and bruising.

Eventually I learned that my other close pal, Bob Beldon, had been picked up by a US transport ship, downgraded and hospitalised; that Hannon, Martin, Fitton, both engineers, one of the sailors, and two others had drowned.

With Bill Farrell and Alf Holmes at Aldershot we luckily saw on the first day a truck bearing our battery's colour and emblem, 416 Battery, 127 LAA Regiment, RA. It was learned that it was our rear party ready to leave for Normandy. Wishing to be reunited with our own unit we saw the CO and quickly found ourselves at Tilbury Docks, joining a small party of our battery headquarters, and boarded an American manned LST [Landing Ship, Tank] heading back for France, and Arromanches.

Mick Crossley, Bradford, West Yorkshire

I was a flight sergeant engineer on a Halifax bomber MZ513 LK-K. The pilot was Squadron Leader Geoff Watson and the rest of the crew consisted of Flying Officer Hall the navigator, Flying Officer 'Paddy' Hefferman the bomb aimer, Flying Officer Bert Onions and a Polish flying officer whose name I never knew who was the mid-upper gunner. Flight

Sergeant Goode, or 'Goody' was the rear-gunner. We were all second tour aircrew. I myself had done a tour of thirty ops with 76 Squadron with a crew that were all new to operational flying.

On the morning of 5 June, Geoff Watson caught me as I was going into the sergeants' mess and told me we were on ops that night. 'This is it – what we have been waiting for.' 'The Invasion?' I asked. 'I'm pretty sure,' he replied, 'although it's not official.'

When we attended the briefing that night we knew he was right. The target was the gun battery at Mont Fleury. It didn't worry us. It was, so we thought, a case of nipping over the French coast, drop the bombs and get out again. We took off at 02:31 and were over the target two hours later without incident. I was in my position under the astrodome, from where I could see all that was going on all around us and above us. I remember I was watching an aircraft above us and slightly ahead and to port releasing its bombs. I was about to warn the skipper when I heard Paddy say 'bombs gone' and almost immediately there was a terrific bang to port. Turning my head I saw lots of burning bits and pieces floating in the air. The aircraft rocked violently and we lost height. I looked out and saw a small hole in the port wing, out of which a flame was spurting, like a blowlamp flame. I reported this to the skipper who told the navigator to give him a course for home. When he had the course he told us 'I'm going to dive to blow the fire out', which he did, but when we levelled out the flame was larger and more fierce. Soon the flames had spread and were coming from under the trailing edge of the wing. By this time we were well out into the English Channel and the skipper was holding the plane in a sideslip to starboard to keep the flames away from the fuselage and the fuel tanks.

At last it was obvious that it was hopeless and the skipper suddenly told us to bale out. I clipped my chute on and picked up my dinghy in its pack and went down to the escape hatch by the bomb-aimers position. Bert, Paddy and the navigator had gone. I assumed Goody had gone as well because as rear gunner he could turn his turret forty-five degrees and fall out backwards! I had noticed the Polish mid-upper gunner walking down towards the pilot when I left him.

I had baled out once before but that was from 11,000 feet and over the south coast of England. The aircraft had been severely damaged and almost impossible to land. This time it was over the sea and it was very dark. I remembered a pal of mine from another aircraft just a few days earlier saying that if you had to bale out over the sea you were as good as dead. However, where there's life there's hope! With some difficulty, because of the dinghy pack I had clipped on to the back of my harness, I dropped through the hatch.

As soon as I could get my hand on it I pulled the rip-cord and looked up to see if it had opened. I could see the cords and the canopy at the end, but it hadn't opened and for a fleeting second I thought it had caught fire. And then it opened with a crack and a jerk, which caused the dinghy pack to come away from my harness and disappear towards the water. As I looked down I was surprised to see the waves and realised that the aircraft must have been very low when I left it. It was the burning plane reflected in the silk chute that had made me think it was on fire. I remember thinking that the pilot would have no chance but in the next second I was in the water and the waves were breaking over my head. The chute dragged me through the water at quite a speed and I kept trying to release it by hitting the release mechanism with my hand but the pressure on it was too great. Then I managed to pull the cords towards me a little and tried again, this time with success.

Now I had a different problem. I was being buried under tons of water and then being shot to the surface with every wave. During one of these immersions I saw a light and realised it was the torch that switched on when hitting the water. I grabbed it from its pocket and held it above my head shouting, whenever I broke the surface, 'Help, help'. There was no one to hear me, but it gave me hope, somehow. Just before I had hit the water I had seen a shadowy shape that could have been a ship of some sort and I kept looking around hoping. While bobbing around and spitting out water I kept thinking about my parents and what they would think and how they would take it when I failed to turn up.  As the thoughts churned through my mind, suddenly there was the ship I had seen coming towards me.

Men were looking at me from over the rail and I remember one of them threw me a lifebuoy but it was too far away. Then someone tried to grab me with a boathook as I bumped against the side of the ship and then I lost consciousness. When I came too it was daylight and I was lying in a bunk wrapped in a blanket. My mouth and tongue were as dry as a bone and I looked around for a drink. I called to a young man and told him what I wanted. He got an older man to bring me a drink and he told me I was on an LCT (Landing Craft, Tank). It seems they were waiting in position to land men and transport on the second wave of the invasion. I asked him for my clothes. He told me there were only my battledress tunic and trousers left, but he brought them and I put them on and felt much better. I asked about my Mae West and torch attached to it but he hold me they had been lost in getting me aboard. I was disappointed. I owed my life to them as I was a non-swimmer! He told me I was very lucky to be picked up as the crew had been told not to stop to pick up survivors, but they were towing a rocket barge which had sprung a leak and had a crew of two and they had had to stop to take them on board. It was while doing that they had seen my chute being blown along with the wind and then my torch-light. What a coincidence!

For some time I had heard distant bangs and also noises like stones hitting the side of the craft and I found out they were mortar bombs being fired from the enemy. I went outside and saw an officer standing on the deck and staring down. I went over and asked him what was happening. He told me the LCTs were bolted together in sections and it seemed this one was loose. He was worried how long it would hold. Then the engines started and before we could say anything we were heading for the beach at full speed. Fortunately it all went smoothly – I'd had quite an action packed night already! Vehicles and men were offloaded rapidly and soon we were heading back to England. Having thanked them again for pulling me out of the 'drink' I was transferred to another boat and after some food and another night's sleep I was transferred AGAIN to a submarine chaser and taken to Bognor Regis. After being questioned by a doctor I was taken to Nytimbre Transit Camp where I was delighted to meet Paddy and Bert. They were the only other survivors of our crew. They had been picked up by a French Destroyer. We all arrived back at 578 Squadron on 10 June where we were given fourteen days' leave, which was very much appreciated – and needed!

All my family met at my brother's house. It was a very emotional meeting – lots of tears and lots of laughter. During my leave I received my Commission, and on 4 July Paddy Hefferman and Bert Onions joined me at 578 RAF Burn where we went on to conclude our second tour of operations. I received the Distinguished Flying Cross in December 1944.

Bill Middleton, DFC, Boston, Lincolnshire

D-Day – the memories come flooding back! I was seven-teen years old and doing voluntary work in the YMCA in Duke Street, Woking in 1944. It was opposite the Astoria cinema. All service people could come in and get light snacks and drinks at very low cost – even for prices in those days! A Mrs Davies was in charge. Every Wednesday we had games, like dressing up from parcels of clothes and there were some great fashions. I won once – a bar of chocolate! I often worked cutting sandwiches – all sorts – with a Miss Cohen, a little old lady who I later found out was a JP but we worked well together. She seemed to like me being with her and we changed places every now and then, or sometimes I had to go into the muggery (washing up for hours). No nice washing up liquid in those days – only soda. But the mugs had to be kept coming.

I was on duty on the night of 5 June when we received instructions to start packing sandwiches in greaseproof paper. Amazingly no one asked any questions or 'why?'. Then we noticed the doors were locked and a policeman was stationed at the back entrance. But even then it didn't seem odd because we all knew him. We were just told to keep making the sandwiches.

Then! Then! The other doors were opened and the room was suddenly crowded with young Canadians, soldiers from all regiments you could imagine. We were run off our feet. Everything was free – tea, coffee, cakes, even our sandwiches. I was put on the serving counter during that long, long night and I was tired out when suddenly I saw a big tall soldier stood there – a company sergeant major. It was my big brother from the Royal Engineers!

I just ran to Mrs Davies in wild excitement and she was very kind and told me to leave the counter to be with my brother. My brother cuddled me, held me tight to him and then playfully clipped me on the chin and said, 'Keep your chin up love, I'll see you soon.' It was the look on his face and the tone in his voice – I knew now something big was on but I daren't ask.

When they'd finished I was given permission to stand outside on Maybury Road which runs alongside the station. A very, very long road. As far as the eye could see there were trucks, armoured cars, Jeeps, tanks – it seemed there was no end. But it was the silence that struck me. All whispering – uneasy feelings. It's difficult to describe but it's real.

Then the trucks began to move off, carrying my brother with them. I waved, I cried and I prayed for all those young men, some not much older than me, all moving off in the blackout. To where? Southampton is only fifty miles away but I didn't work that out. I was just numb, as if all thoughts had stopped forming.

Afterwards I joined the ATS and my brother came back ten months later, wounded in action. He died in 1988. He was a peacetime soldier; saw service in India in 1935, went through Africa and then on to D-Day. I often wonder if we were the last to see, talk to, and serve those servicemen that night as they set off? I was near the Arch in Woking later when buses came through carrying sick and wounded servicemen. I ran alongside just touching hands that were hanging out from windows. The buses went very slow. They were returning prisoners of war – just glad to be home and touch a loving friendly hand. God bless them all.

I've just remembered – those sandwiches were filled with dried egg, Bovril supplement, anything Mrs Davies could get her hands on! Funnily enough, after hours and hours of work, I don't remember ever being tired. The YMCA building was pulled down years ago. The whole town has been ripped apart since. I'm glad I'm in my old age now – I don't like all these changes. Life was better as it was!

Mary T. Turner, Woking, Surrey

I was in the Hampshire Regiment and I had not been on a ship before and had never been to another country when we set off to France shortly after D-Day.

The ship berthed alongside a floating timber platform; there had been nothing to eat or drink since we had left Aldershot the morning before but there was a huge cauldron of food on the forward deck and we discovered this contained a sort of salad mayonnaise – no one was interested! So each man was given five fruit drops and we went ashore to move inland in single file.

There were empty houses along the top of the beach with structural damage and doors and windows missing. This was Arromanches. Everyone assembled in a field surrounded by hedges and trees and here an officer gave us some advice. Not to make tracks, which could be seen from the air, and not to associate with ladies on the continent as they were different to English ladies and for the sake of ten minutes it wasn't worth the risk!

A water truck soon arrived and we made tea in our mess tins. The tea was a cube containing tea, sugar and milk heated by a white methylated tablet but it didn't really work. Gunfire could be heard constantly as we moved inland again to the outskirts of Bayeux. Buildings were damaged and an elderly Frenchman shook his fist as we passed. Our twenty-five-pounder guns were firing constantly and the shells passing overhead could be clearly heard followed by explosions forward.

In a field there were many makeshift graves containing German soldiers; their bayonets had been fixed to rifles and thrust through the bodies with helmets hanging above. Boots and other parts of the bodies were still showing above the ground. We finally joined the 1st Battalion Hampshire Regiment in the 50th Division resting in a field. The field had high hedges around all sides. My pal Bill Muttitt and I were not too welcome as newcomers and rookies. This unit was from North Africa and there had been casualties.

We rested there overnight and next morning everyone assembled just to the edge of a wood of small trees. There appeared to be hundreds of chaps all milling around. To our front was a distant view with ground falling away down a hill and rising quite steeply to the skyline. There were trees in the distance and the fields were bound by neat hedges. We could hear gunfire to the right and left but here it was quiet and a beautiful day with blue sky and warm sunshine. A long single line was now forming right across the field and everyone began to move forward. A Sherman tank was moving forward to our left. Gun and mortar fire now began from forward of our position and there were explosions in the field. Some were quite near to us. We veered to the right to an opening in the hedge and at this point a soldier began to shout and run around in distress. An officer said to me to stay with him until he settled, then to follow. I persuaded him to sit by the hedge and talked for a minute and he was soon all right. A cow, bleeding from several shrapnel wounds, was still grazing.

We continued uphill along the side of the hedge and each time there was sound of a salvo we fell flat. There were more wounded cattle. At the top of the hill we went back through the hedge and I saw Bill with other lads assembled behind another hedge with a house and road just ahead. One of our chaps was rapidly firing his rifle at three German soldiers who were running from the house with heads down. Explosions were continuous with trees and branches splintering just behind our position. Everyone was lying down in the shelter of the hedge. Bill and I were talking to a Corporal Baker who was lying between us. He then said, 'I've been hit,' and two stretcher bearers immediately cut his trouser leg to reveal a severe shrapnel wound to his knee. A dressing was applied and the bearers carried him away sitting on their clasped hands. There were more casualties and others helped with field dressings and began to carry wounded back.

A major now appeared; I believe his name was Anscombe. He told Bill and me to fire a Piat bomb into the upper window of the house as this could be a German observation post. I loaded the bomb and Bill fired the shot right through the window. The major now decided we should move left around the hedge corner and along another hedge leading to the road. He said, 'I expect you chaps are scared; I am too.' I now realised there were just five of us left here, the major, two other lads, and Bill and me. There had been no verbal instruction to advance and we were unaware of everyone retracing their steps back down the hill! Perhaps battle experience had been a lesson to everyone: if possible, to move away from the bombardment area. We had expected the position to be held until a further advance was ordered. The major now decided we should run down a small slope to the left to the shelter of a clump of trees; he would go first, then we would follow in twos. Shells and mortar bombs were still exploding and as the major was running five explosions appeared to knock him flat. However, he regained his feet and ran on to the trees and signalled to follow. The other two lads ran down followed by Bill and me. This move had surely saved our lives because the next salvo blasted along the entire length of the hedge we had just left.

The major now left to find a way back to our unit; he said we could follow or perhaps he would return. The bombardment continued and after about an hour the other two lads left. Bill and I decided to move out but it was difficult to know which direction to follow and we could have been wandering into front line troops of either side. After crossing fields, wading a stream and going through a wood, we were pleased to arrive at a road. We went to the left and amazingly found our unit resting in a field. There had been no food and a Canadian captain asked Bill and me if we would accompany him to find the cooks. We set off again and walked about an hour in the moonlight, as it was now dark. Everywhere was completely deserted. The captain decided to go on alone and said to wait until he returned. We were beside a sort of rubbish tip at the side of the road. The captain never returned and we eventually had a short sleep until dawn. Royal Engineers came along at first light clearing road mines and gave us a welcome mug of tea. We hurried back to the unit but breakfast had just finished and the cooks had packed away.

We moved forward to a new location and were proceeding in single file along a road with woods and just a few houses each side. Two British soldiers who had been killed were lying in a crawling position. A padre was there and he had placed a gas cape over the bodies. I remember as we passed the sunlight reflecting on their boot studs and there were flies buzzing above. Somewhere the relatives back home would soon be informed. A little further on a dead German soldier was lying awkwardly in a roadside ditch and on the right were more dead German soldiers. Suddenly from the woods on the left came a burst of Spandau fire. The bullets seemed to pass right through our column and two chaps dashed back down the road with the officer shouting for them to return but they kept going. Later we heard they had both been killed by a German shell. Bill noted that it could be safer from shelling when close to the front line as artillery from both sides did not fall in this forward area.

We now passed through the village of Villers-Bocage and continued on to high ground with open country. At this point we were again under heavy bombardment and we were told to dig in as this was the objective. We were tired, dirty, unshaven, thirsty and hungry; we had been without food for two days. Shells were exploding everywhere; it was a very open position. Bill was angry but nevertheless we somehow managed to dig a trench through stones and rocks with the entrenching tools and prepared to spend the night. The following morning the Royal Engineers discovered a German mine inches from the edge of our trench! At this point we were each given a mess tin of water, a little to drink and the remainder to wash our faces as we were smothered with white chalk from the digging. We now moved forward again and settled behind a hedge. This position was under shell and mortar fire and there were casualties in the field to our front. Stretcher-bearers with white flags ventured out from both sides to recover wounded. Small arms fire had stopped. We heard later that our stretcher-bearers had entered a house and met the German doctor.

Proceeding in file again next morning we entered a village, which had possibly been strafed from the air. There were dead horses and abandoned carts. No doubt an attack on a retreating German column. There were also damaged houses each side of the road. I discovered a Sherman tank, which had fallen into a deep concrete channel. The tank had come to rest on its nose and I wondered if the crew were still inside but we had to move on. That about sums up Normandy and what we had to do.

Ron Gladman, Minehead, Somerset

It was an amazing sight. From all sides came big ships, little ships, tin-cans, landing craft, amphibious ducks, all converging on the rendezvous, where we had to alter course – alter course to France. There were low clouds o'erslipping the darkened seascape, the salt spray made white marks on my cap, and overall hung a silence and a steadfast hope.

At half past four we went to 'action stations'. I thought it was just a run-through, so went up, ill prepared for the cold. That after-Oerlikon is a very drafty place in a breeze. But I surreptitiously inveigled a steward to bring up my oilskin

and sea boots, when he brought my cup of soup and a cheese sandwich for supper. Then, after this huge repast, I sat down, but became so cold, I had to rise again, and was still standing at one-thirty when he brought a cup of 'kye' (basic English!) and another sandwich – this time tongue. By now, we were sweeping, and had left the landing craft behind. All that could be made out was a flotilla just visible on each side of us, all bent on the same job. It was the silence that was so uncanny, broken only by reports of planes from the look-outs, who were kept very busy in that respect, and the thud of mines going off in the other ships' sweeps. There must have been much more tension on the bridge than down aft, for I didn't realise that mines had been cut, and that we had to keep a sharp lookout not to bump unexpectedly into one.

Expectancy grew round about three-thirty. We were still the leading ships – and now came the final and all important lap. The alteration of course order to sweep out the anchorage; the coast was not yet visible but I knew it was only eight miles away. We all knew it was close as we could see fires burning inshore from the heavy weight of our bombs – there was a continued roar overhead of our aircraft. Still we ploughed on, as daylight came inexorably nearer. Still no sound of gunfire from shore, save the 'ack-ack' of small arms and machine guns directed at our planes. Still no one seemed to see us or our sweeping lights or dan buoy lights, which seemed higher than Piccadilly Circus on Armistice night. Yet every flash of gun from shore made one expect a nearby splash, denoting a shell, and every falling flare seemed to illuminate us far better than the flares. The seconds ticked on, and the glimmer of a dull sun shyly peeped over the horizon. One's imagination ran away with one, and the Rattlesnake sounded like a runner all out for a speed record, who cannot become behind schedule, and however much out of breath must keep going. Now we could see the dim outline of coast. We must be visible. Never have I felt so conspicuous, not even as a veiled fairy in The Merry Wives at the Old Vic! We could see the cruisers approaching for the first covering bombardment. The last dan buoy was in sight and up came our protecting destroyers, whom we hadn't seen all night, but had been close at hand and on the lookout for E-boats and U-boats. We felt rather like naughty dogs who having found their opponent rather bigger than expected, run up to their mistress and cower behind her skirts while she beats off the Alsatian. So behind the cruisers we went, and peeked out from between them as they started shelling. One felt very safe then, and with an air of complete detachment could survey the results of one's handiwork as the first landing craft infantry crept forward. More and more ships were arriving, and it was funny to hear on the 8 o'clock news that, 'The Germans report that cruisers and battleships are shelling the coast of Normandy' – and there was I on the spot saying, 'Yes, aren't they?'. After the first landings, or 'touch downs', my memory of what happened is rather vague – we just sailed happily up and down the anchorage, taking an interest in all the doings of various craft, peering with binoculars at them. It was difficult to see much owing to the smoke screens of our landing barge.

For the next few days we were kept pretty busy. At all times there was invariably activity when we returned to our anchorage. There were planes continuously falling, every one coming through endless tracers, which were now well established shore battery. We saw them bring down two German planes in two minutes. In the area in which they were hit, there was hardly a space not covered by great balls of fire, and exploding onions. One night, when I was on watch, we had a nasty shock, when the sound of a shell –

that ominous whine – passed right overhead, and seemed to fall very near the other side. At the time the Captain thought it was a splinter, until people down below came up on deck, as they had heard an explosion under water, which sounded too close for comfort. I think it was one of ours though, which had failed to explode in the air at the proper time.

The above is taken from a letter sent by John 'Oscar' Warner, Deal, Kent to his parents on 12 June 1944

I am a captain in 22nd Dragoons, 30th Armoured Brigade. It's 07:15. We've landed and we're moving onto the wide sandy beach where Jock Stirling, my second troop sergeant, and the second flail are already beating up to the wall. I can see the Bridge AVRE [Armoured Vehicle Royal Engineers] moving through the beach obstacles behind them, when there is an explosion on the turret and the bridge falls uselessly. The AVRE tries petarding the sea wall without success.

I move up to the foot of a concrete ramp leading to the top of the wall and blow my Cordtex. Paddy Addis, my gunner, clears the barrel and I sight through it just as we did at Orford, and we fire HE at one corner of a railway steel gate blocking the top of the ramp. Aim at another corner. Fire! Another joint. Fire! Several times until the gate is a wreck. I back off to let another AVRE climb the ramp to push the wreckage away, but it tips over on its side, one track off the ramp; another AVRE goes up the narrow ramp and pushes the wreckage to one side – and sets off a mine which halts it on top of the wall.

I move up to the foot of the ramp, dismount to attach the towrope to the wreckage which we drag backwards towards the sea out of the way. The tide is coming in with the onshore wind. I signal to Jock and the 2nd Flail to go up the ramp to start flailing inland. It takes a few minutes as they have to line up carefully on the ramp whose foot is already under water, but they're up, and just as we are about to follow the engine dies. We're flooded. 'Bale out!' Almost before the words are out of my mouth, Dogger Butler, the co-driver, a tall gangling man, has come out through the turret past me!

We take pocketsful of grenades, the .3 Browning and ground mounting and several boxes of ammo, and cautiously, 'walking the tightrope' along the jib, step off the rotor into deep water. It's almost up to my neck and it's cold as it trickles inside my clothes. There are some bodies, Chaudières, I expect, floating amongst the debris and flotsam already bumping against us. Some are not dead but we have strict orders not to deal with any wounded: a distasteful order, which goes against one's instincts.

We struggle hard to help each other up and I leave my crew to set up the machine gun on top of the wall while I run to Jock's tanks, which have halted about fifty yards down the path. They have struck so many mines that they've stopped to replace some damaged chains. There are marked minefields either side of us behind thick barbed wire with 'Achtung! Minen' and the skull and crossbones notices hanging on the wire. The grass in these patches is burning fiercely and the smoke helps to screen us but makes us choke.

As I can't raise the other half of my troop under Sergeant Geoff Crew on Jock's wireless I run back to the sea wall and walk along the top cautiously in case of mines. I pass a Canadian soldier with no face left being comforted by a padre, and see Geoff flailing merrily with his half troop past the now famous house and about to turn left along the 'first lateral' road, which runs parallel to the sea. Relief that they too have made it safely to shore. Back to Jock who is once more flailing. I notice some German soldiers with their hands up near a house and a large Alsatian guard dog tied up outside it. The infantry are dealing with them.

We get a short breather with some tins of self-heating soup. Our first meal. But then I get a call from the Chaudières who have been held up by a minefield the other side of Bernières. I ride on the back of Jock's tank and we find a Bren carrier upside down, the crew killed by a mine. We flail a wide path round it. We finish about midnight, utterly worn out.

Ian Hammerton, Dartford, Kent

I was a fourteen year old grammar school boy living at Chiswick in West London. I was mad about aircraft, and was a Corporal in the Air Training Corps. In the week of 13 May 1944 there were numbers of Air Training Corps Squadrons (boys between the ages of fourteen to seventeen) sent to RAF Brize Norton in Oxfordshire for the spring camp. Brize Norton was training troop glider pilots. There were seemingly dozens of these enormous Horsa gliders being towed by Albemarle bombers operating a perpetual cab-rank of towing the glider to altitude, releasing it, landing, hooking up behind another Albemarle, and going through the same routine again. As each glider passed a point on the flight-line a dozen ATC cadets equipped with parachutes climbed aboard. Each flight took twenty minutes and I logged eight hours in the seven days I was there. It was called 'air experience' but we were actually giving these student pilots their first taste of flying the gliders with passengers aboard. With hindsight, obviously they were not fully trained less than a month before they were required to be operational! Everyone that we spoke to was quite certain that the invasion was imminent and even at fourteen I felt that I was making a contribution to the war effort, and proud that I was.

6 June was a normal school day and I had a paper round to do before I went to school. It was quite hazy at 7am and

as I set off on my round I saw sixteen Douglas Boston day-bombers, which were stationed at Heston, flying in formation coming back to their airfield at low altitude through the morning mist. It was unusual to see them returning so early.

I got back home from my paper round just after 8am and my mother said that there'd been an announcement on the 8 o'clock news that General Eisenhower was going to make an important announcement on the wireless at 9am. My father, who was a policeman in the Met and had won the MM in the artillery in the First World War, said, 'There's no doubt about it, the invasion has started, and there's a lot of poor boys not much older than you that have seen their last sunrise this morning.' This was said at least partly for my benefit because all I dreamed of was becoming a member of RAF aircrew as soon as I could. At school I walked into my form room and 'Ikey' Rees our form master told us that assembly would be as usual, but we would be staying on to hear Eisenhower's announcement. The head, Dr Carran, led us in the usual prayers, Miss Evans the music mistress played the piano while we sang 'O Valiant Hearts'. Then came the prayer for the 'old boys' serving with HM Forces. I was at the school for nearly five years, and I lost count of the number of times the head had to announce that an 'old boy' who had attended say between 1938-42 was reported 'killed in action' or 'missing on operations', or was a prisoner of war. My closest friend lost both his brothers who were 'old boys', one

before D-Day and one after. Then the head said: 'There is an announcement of extreme importance coming on the radio at 9am. The school will wait.' We waited in sombre silence. At 9am General Eisenhower made his announcement that the invasion had begun. After he had finished, Dr Carran said, 'The school will now pray for the old boys of the school, and all the other young men of Britain and the Allies who today are carrying the war to the gates of the enemy that God will keep them safe in the terrible days to come... Our Father...'

At mid-morning break we were all outside looking skyward. There were swarms of B17s, like silver specks in the sky leaving white vapour trails behind them as they formed up, and as I watched 'my' Bostons roared overhead going out again. This time I noticed that they had black and white stripes painted under the wings and around the fuselages. It was an aid to recognition, which we soon learned to call invasion stripes. Not long after D-Day the school was hit by a V1, and much of the roof went, then in September the first V2 to fall in England fell on Staveley Road, and the day after the manager of Smiths made me redundant as my paper round was Staveley Road and I had no customers left! But if I live to be a hundred I'll never forget 6 June 1944.

Derek W. F. Waters, Royal Leamington Spa, Warwickshire

My memories of D-Day are very clear indeed. I was a VAD at the Cambridge Military Hospital in Aldershot. All the Canadian troops in the area had been mustered at Crookham, obviously in preparation for action. I had already bid a sad farewell to my Canadian sweetheart, wondering if I would ever see him again. Every spare space in the area, even in the centre of town, was absolutely crammed with armoured vehicles, tanks, Jeeps and equipment. All through the night could be heard the constant rumble of heavy traffic as the vehicles of war moved out. On D-Day an uncanny silence hung over the town. Empty spaces – empty streets. When the casualties from Normandy started to arrive it suddenly became 'all hands to the pumps'. Even the 'up patients' were allocated tasks to assist, such as cleaning and washing up. Everyone had a job to do and had to make sure it was done. But they all joined in cheerfully, even the officers. The convalescent ranks had to be dressed in bright blue suits with red ties. It was certainly a colourful enough outfit! I never did find out if this was to keep tabs on them in case they became inclined to go AWOL (Absent Without Leave) or whether it was to enable recognition by civilians when they were out. But it was made clear to us that we were to be treated just as soldiers on the battlefield. Off-duty was virtually non-existent as we were on-call at all times. From D-Day, the 6 June, I did not have one day off until the end of August by which time I, and everyone else because we were all in the same situation, was suffering from exhaustion.

Blood for the wounded was in desperately short supply, and we healthy staff were relied on, indeed expected, to make our own blood available if needs be. I know I gave two pints within a few weeks. However by the end of June, as casualties from the war zone increased, we did start to get a few more staff, so that as the months went by things did improve.

For a while during that period I was allocated to the detention ward which was guarded by troops because the patients were German POWs, deserters and soldiers with self-inflicted wounds. This group who had self-inflicted wounds had almost always injured themselves from fear of being sent back to the front line. They injured themselves by swallowing anti-gas ointment, sharp objects such as safety pins, or by shooting themselves, almost always in the foot. That very often led to gangrene and eventual amputation. Actually these men were, perhaps surprisingly, treated with a degree of understanding and compassion, though many of the peppery old colonels reckoned they should have faced a firing squad!

Many of the nurses had loved ones in the battle zones and were desperately anxious as news was received, especially of the fierce and bloody fighting in the Caen area. Nevertheless on the wards we had to 'press on regardless' as the saying was at the time, cheerfully and efficiently. One's own problems and anxieties were pushed into the background when confronted every day by those with shattered bodies and minds – the amputees and the blinded.

It really grieves me in this day and age to see the destructive self-pity over comparatively trifling difficulties, which now seems to permeate our society. Whatever happened to that intestinal self-fortitude and self-reliance so characteristic of the Britain I once knew?

On a final humorous note I have often been asked what VAD stood for. I expect many who have been reading this story will be wondering, although clearly it was something to do with nursing. The answer is it stood for Voluntary Aid Detachment. However you can imagine that the troops had their own versions! The favourites were:

Virgins Awaiting Destruction

Virgins Absolutely Desperate

Or, by those with a more charitable mind, and the one I of course preferred:

Virgins Adorable and Delightful.

But it's funny how one theme seems to be common to all versions!

Peggy M. Hart, Northampton, Northamptonshire

I was in the 22nd Dragoons, 30th Armoured Brigade. At this time rumour was rife about preparing for the invasion of Europe. We were equipped with a variety of all sorts of weird looking AFVs (Armoured Fighting Vehicles) and they all had one theme in common: all were connected with the destruction of land mines. We eventually ended up with the flail, which consisted of a jib fastened to the front of the tank. A roller was fitted to the forward part of the jib. Fitted to the roller were a series of steel chains, with a steel ball at the end of each chain. The object being for the roller to revolve and cause the chains to beat the ground in front of the tank, thereby detonating any mines before the vehicle passed over. As the tank crept slowly forward a lane was being made to allow the faster tanks behind safe access through the minefield, and continue any advance. We were far from thrilled at the role we had been selected to play, but we trained on and by the start of 1944 we settled on the type of tank we were to use, which turned out to be the American Sherman, all-purpose built and ready for the job of beating our way to the beaches at whichever place had been chosen to attempt the landings on the continent. I myself was a tank commander and troop sergeant and second in command to Lt Allen who was my troop leader. Each troop consisted of five tanks. Each tank was equipped with two machine guns loose, and one 75mm gun co-axially mounted with a further machine gun in a rotating turret. There was a crew of five men to each tank, being tank commander, gunner, wireless operator/loader, driver and co-driver who manned one of the machine guns at the front of the tank. Each regiment had three squadrons each with four troops as above. Regimental HQ had just three tanks without flails.

On 3 June we loaded as a troop on two landing craft, myself and another flail on one, and my troop leader and another flail on the other. Myself in the front tank and would be first off. Also on the craft were four Churchill tanks manned by Royal Engineers and each equipped with a different contraption to combat the different obstacles we were likely to encounter after landing. Owing to wretched weather the crews of the tanks (five to each tank, making a total of thirty men) spent most of the time in a small cabin at the rear of the craft, passing the time telling the odd story and discussing the task ahead. I recall one of the engineers had a mouth organ and we joined in a few singsongs. Rumours were afoot that the whole operation was being called off, but nevertheless at noon on 5 June we sailed out of the Solent into the main channel and were manoeuvred into the formation in which we were to land. The landings were scheduled to touch down at 07:00 on the morning of 6 June 1944. We were familiar with it as H-Hour D-Day. This meant nineteen hours in the most horrendous seas one could imagine. There was barely a man on our craft who wasn't suffering from violent seasickness from the word go. From what I learned later all the other LCTs were afflicted in the same way. All the men were so eager to get on firm ground that the German reception was of secondary importance! Sleep was impossible and although rations were in lavish supply very little was consumed. I do recall that my gunner, Johnnie Downs, was one of the few who proved to be a good sailor, and he spent the time heating tins of soup and pushing them in front of the sick ones (myself included) and for thanks he was given a roar of army-language or recipients running to the side of the craft to heave their hearts up. That more or less is the story of the crossing.

We unshackled the tanks at about 05:30 hours just as the rocket boats were delivering their deadly cargoes into what we hoped were the shore defences. We manned the tanks at 06:00 hours ready to beach. I think it was about 07:15 when we touched down on our return to France after almost four years to the date. The plan was that my troop on the two LCTs was to sail into the beaches preceded by the amphibious tanks. Unfortunately the rough seas were too much for the DDs [destroyers] and all were sunk before they could make the beach (unbeknown to us). So the cover from them to shoot us up the beach was missing. Our craft beached on Queen Red Beach, which was later identified as a small place called La Brèche. My troop leader and his second tank commanded by Corporal Rains on the left (incidentally the complete left flank of the entire landing) and myself in the lead tank followed by Sgt Johnson about fifty yards to their right. We each had to flail a lane of two tanks' width up to the beach wall, clearing these areas of mines. We were then to turn right and get under the cover of the sea wall, using our firepower to protect the following Churchills, which were using the lanes we had made. I should point out that owing to the flail action our gun had to face the rear whilst advancing at about 2mph up the beach, so you can see the disadvantage of not having the cover fire from the amphibious tanks was a terrible blow. We were more or less blind to anything to the front of the flail. The leading tank commander had to give orders to the following tank driver by tank intercom and using the turret periscope to the rear. Exploding a Teller mine had the effect of lifting the whole tank a foot or so off the ground. A somewhat eerie experience to the occupants of the tank and jarring to the spine.

That was the task and for my own part everything went according to plan except for the absence of the DD tanks with their cover fire. The beaches at the time of disembarking looked as deserted as an English holiday beach in midwinter, but within seconds of the touchdown they were transformed into a mass of vehicles of all shapes and sizes, men rushing in all directions and tank-craft ablaze before they had a chance to unship their cargoes. Some tanks that had landed were ablaze. I looked to the left through the periscope to see what progress the rest of my troop was making. My troop leader's flail was stopped on the water line and burning like a huge Bunsen burner. I felt very low at that time, and was half expecting to meet the same fate. However we were lucky and were able to complete our lane successfully. Once under the wall,

we managed to silence and destroy an enemy concrete gun emplacement which was situated on the sea wall immediately to our front. Why they had not given us the same treatment as my troop leader I'll never know. I also engaged a turret-like anti-tank gun emplacement, which had been causing no end of trouble and we found out later had been the gun responsible for the destruction of the troop leader's tank. This eased the pressure in our lane and our following Churchills went forward and made the first lateral and beyond exactly as planned. Once the vehicles got going through our lane, myself and Sgt Johnson continued to flail other lanes on the beach itself, thus making way for armour to surge through and get away from the by now congested area. There was very little close opposition from the sea wall as our infantry had by this time got in behind and put paid to anything in that area.

After we had made our section free of mines I, who automatically took on the role of troop leader, decided that we should get off the beach and onto the road beyond. The fields beyond had been mined. The Germans had conveniently put signs on the field perimeters: 'ACHTUNG MINEN'. Unfortunately, on the way to the road we had our flail gear put out of action. I think that during driving our flail over the beach wall it got entangled with barbed wire and jammed the roller. However, we used our 75mm and machine guns to good effect against various pockets of enemy resistance. It was mid-afternoon when we got onto the road and then another disaster. Sgt Johnson's tank, which had stopped flailing, struck a mine on the grass verge and had his track blown off, rendering him immobile. At this point I decided to investigate what had happened on our second lane and found Cpl Rains who was on foot and looking for me. He informed me that Lt Allen's tank had been hit almost as soon as he left the LCT. His tank had almost immediately brewed up and he feared that all the crew of five had perished. News which was shattering but half expected. Cpl Rains had made good a single tank width lane and from there engaged and destroyed the gun which had taken Lt Allen's tank. Unfortunately Cpl Rains tank had also lost a track coming onto the beach road. The time at this juncture was about 16:00 hours. All this time we had seen no sign of the Luftwaffe.

We managed to get Cpl Rains' tank mobile but Sgt Johnson's tank was more difficult and as dusk was descending I decided to take his crew aboard the two runners and take up a position on the outside perimeter of the mined fields about half a mile inland, using the tanks, which had plenty of firepower, as strongpoints against any counter moves by the Germans. The night passed without incident and most of the crews managed a little shut-eye, the first since the night of the 3rd in Gosport. Once again, where was the Luftwaffe?

During all this time we never encountered any French people so I can't say what their immediate reactions were. But a couple of days later when we set up harbour near Douvres-la-Délivrande, we were given a very friendly welcome. Although I did hear stories of odd ones that resented our intrusion on the nice peaceful life they had been having, but that is only hearsay on my part.

On the actual landings, my troop lost one tank and four men were killed. One man, who was gunner in this tank, miraculously escaped from the blazing tank and ran back and boarded the same craft he had left, and was taken back to England, suffering from severe burns from which he eventually recovered.

Our role from then until the Falaise break-out was to be loaned to various units, who had their progress hindered by minefields, and to use our guns to shoot infantry into enemy held strongpoints, as our flails were too cumbersome to use as standard AFVs.

For our part in the D-Day landings, myself and Cpl Rains were given an immediate award each of the Military Medal. Sgt Johnson was later also awarded the Military Medal for the attacks on the Channel ports. As our succeeding troop leader was later awarded the Military Cross this must have been a sort of record for such a small unit!

James 'Timber' Wood, MM, Rochdale, Lancashire

My memories of that day may not be exactly what you are looking for – but I will recount them anyway! I have relived the day many times in my memory and even now – fifty years on – I can remember it all very vividly.

It started for me on the evening of 5 June 1944. An ATS [Auxiliary Territorial Service] admin sergeant (aged twenty-four) attached to an AA Command Brigade Headquarters 'somewhere in Essex', I was called to the brigadier's office. Asked to re-affirm my allegiance to the Secrets Act, and aware of the assembly of much top brass, I knew it was going to be something big! And it was.

It was an operations order to be expressly despatched to all our regimental HQs, battery HQs, gun sites, searchlight sites and other radar and observation corps installations throughout our brigade area. The brigadier dictated, I typed, a staff major duplicated, other staff officers dashed around collating the pages for handing over to the waiting team of despatch riders – who I am sure were blissfully unaware of the major importance of their midnight mission. It was all rather light-hearted consid-ering the seriousness of the contents of the order!

My heart was thumping at the import of what I was typing. It was the final act of Operation Fortitude. It gave details of aircraft recognition marks, their flight paths on 'missions to nowhere' – a ruse to confuse the enemy. It told of bogus massive army convoys of troops and guns tearing around the Essex country lanes, presumably heading for east coast sea ports – only to turn around and re-run back to nowhere. Another ploy to distract the enemy's attention from the theatre of war where the real action was taking place. All gun and searchlight sites were to be double-manned – on red alert – in anticipation of reprisals – by sea or air – and so it went on for three foolscap sheets. And I realised there and then that Operation Overlord was now D-Day and the invasion of France was imminent.

We all sat for a while over coffee and I was asked to spend the rest of the night in the small guard hut – on my own – by the telephone, in case my services were needed again. Needless to say sleep was impossible – I lay on the bed reflecting upon what had just gone before, visualising our gallant troops on their hazardous mission, praying for their safety and an early end to the miseries that five years of war had already brought.

At breakfast on 6 June – it was a secret no longer. Over the radio came the news to the whole world that an invasion of France had been launched. For a moment in our mess there was a deathly hush – and then the loudest of loud cheers as the significance of the broadcast sunk home. D-Day – 6 June 1944 – most certainly a day to remember!

Joan A. Jackman, Chingford, Essex

I had volunteered for the Royal Navy in early 1940, before I was 18, and after training and experience in the Atlantic and the Mediterranean I came back to Britain in a troop-ship which carried the hardcore of those who were to go to Normandy.

I was drafted to HMS *Scylla*, in Portsmouth, the flagship for the invasion. This was a sister ship to HMS *Naiad*, which had gone down in the Mediterranean. Vice-Admiral Philip Vian had been rescued only after hours in the water. HMS

Scylla was a light cruiser, very fast, armed with 5.25 inch guns. She was fitted out with no less than fifty-seven wireless lines, to control all events. We became very tired as time went on, with so much to do, so as to be ready for sea.

One event greatly feared was that Churchill or the King might come down to be part of the events – we didn't have the time for 'show'. It happened that the King did come and we had to line ship as best we could. Vian walked as the last man of the inspecting top brass and he stopped at one tiny man who was very stout and bespectacled. Pointing to a large and colourful medal ribbon, the admiral asked, 'What on earth is *that?*' The little chap drew in a great gulp of air and said, 'Metropolitan Police, Long Service and Good Conduct Medal... Sir!' Vian said warmly, 'Well that's one bugger I'll never get!', and he laughed his way on. This man was always popular, because he *knew* his ships, he bitterly regretted their loss, he knew on Malta convoys how much water, fuel, ammunition, gun power each had. He would work one ship to death, covering, searching, running errands on the convoy strays, etc. Then, when there was just time and fuel left, he simply ordered, 'Go Home. Good Luck,' – and off she went, while the rest of us were fresh for the fight to come. He inspired great trust and he got it. He also sought out action; he led by example.

After delays due to appalling weather, the choice was made to sail out. As I recall, it would have been perhaps late night on 5 June 1944. Next morning, early, we heard a special broadcast from the Commanding General Dwight Eisenhower, USA. It was very long, full of words like 'Freedom', 'Democracy', 'Mankind' and so on, a full-blooded political speech. It eventually ended and the voice of Vian came on with a typical piece of terse naval command. 'You, hear me. When you are toothless old men, you'll want to be boasting about today – so bloody well *get on with it!!!*' A great cheer went up round the fleet. This was more like it!

It is not easy to set down the atmosphere aboard, but one

knew what every man felt. They had seen London bombed, Portsmouth on fire, Malta juddering under the onslaughts, convoys butchered for lack of air power, some had lost their wives, all had lost relatives and friends – and here it was – the great chance... This time, instead of pulling soldiers out of the water, we were going to put them ashore, and there would be no retreat. It wasn't like a film, there were no memorable words, but you could *feel* the lively, excited way orders were given, taken, carried out smoothly, men trained by hard knocks for just this special day. Never was there a cross word, a moment of panic, irritation, excuses... It was like a great team of sportsmen – but *it* was not a game.

The command came to start the firing. The ships called up were HMS *Belfast* and the old warhorse, HMS *Warspite*. The signal was sent in plain language to avoid all doubt – after all, the Germans were very well aware of our presence! Here is the signal that started it all: '*OPEN FIRE, FIRE AT WILL. DO NOT, REPEAT, DO NOT HIT THE WHITE HOTEL.*' The White Hotel, near Le Havre, still stands. It was needed for the gunnery bearing.

The bombardment was deafening. I had been off the coast for the El Alamein artillery attack, but Arromanches, with the 16-inch shells of the *Warspite*, the rockets from barges and all the other attacking guns, was unforgettable. It was as if every German soldier had his name on *something*.

We were always moving about. One young boats officer put up a life-long black when 'he', Vian, wanted to go near the shore to see what was going on(!) The admiral's boat was on the seaward side, with heavy waves thumping it against the stern. I was ordered to get it and bring it round, while the boats officer got the mother and father of a naval barrage...

Thousands of signals came in and went out. We had RAF and army signallers in our Radio Rooms, and a whole posse of recruited policemen to assist with decoding after a short course of signals. They had their own 'shop' and messages were rushed in and out for translation and sending off. The methods used were simply to paste signals that were 'finished' into a vast book, page by page. For this, a huge pot of glue was set up above head height, and mugs were filled from it by the dozen...

Well, we overstayed our welcome, and one night, with the troops well inland and our work nearly done, we went too close to Le Havre and hit a huge landmine set on the floor of the approaches. It took most of the stern off, but she steadied. We went to put on the emergency lighting, but the raw policemen, in the dark and with splitting heads, set off at a run to get above decks... Dangerous, because it was a single-gangway ship. No one knew what the true damage was, as yet. I remember bawling out at them, 'Stand still! Go Back! The lights will be on soon. This is a warship! There's no halftime and no bloody oranges! Walk back slowly, do it.' They did it and the lights came on; poor things, but our own!

At once, however, we heard a fearsome groaning... On and on... 'Mary, forgive me, it was just the once... Mary, I'm dying...' I put my hand down to where the man was lying, under a bench and in the dark. My fingers were sticky. I asked him if he was bleeding? 'Yes, 'course,' he groaned, and I got hold of a torch. Near him was the old glue crock, smashed in the mishap, and glue was all over him. The gales of laughter released all our tension and I set about getting the whole wireless room cleaned up, using sea water.

However, I had forgotten young Menzies, a Scot whose work was aft in the DF room, a steel box on the quarterdeck. I rushed out there, suddenly cold in the sea air, but refreshed by its cleanliness. Menzies was calmly sitting in his steel chair, with no power and not much air. His deck was carrying seawater, but I had walked it well enough. He said, 'Well now, I knew you'd come. Did you win the card game, then?' I told him shortly to bring out all code books for handing in, to bolt his door and return with me. He needed

a hand once or twice; he must have had the headache of a lifetime! He had been sitting directly above the mine.

Next day, soon after dawn, a US tug master sailed up to us and offered to tow us back to Chatham! The admiral and some others had gone aboard a merchantman made out as copy for the HMS *Scylla*, also with fifty-seven wireless lines aboard, so that the war went on. I think she was named the *Evesham* but I could have faltered in this respect. One event I do recall, and this turned upon the Geordie accent; we had a very simple call sign so that small ships like MTBs [Motor Torpedo Boats] and strangers could remember it. Soon after our dropout, a call came from *Evesham* to take it over. In plain English the inquirer said, 'Do you have a call sign? How to tell it without telling every German around? The answer came from an astute Geordie, Norman Box. He said, in his heaviest accent, 'Have we getten a call sign? Why aye, man! O'course we hev!' It worked. The wanted code was simply, 'YI'.

My abiding memory of D-Day was of a sea filled up with ships; all types, sizes, shapes, uses. All were represented. All were busy, bringing more troops or more supplies. Men were there by the thousand, again, all busy. It was a marvellous naval operation, the key to the eventual victory. I remember the line of bullet or shell holes that ran along one side of HMS *Scylla* when a single German plane attacked us as we lay still and helpless. It was soon seen off. And I remember the keen smell of the sea in the Channel that morning, after long days below deck. It was silent as we crept back to the white English cliffs, 'like wrongs hushed up'. I had never been to Chatham before, but I bought some red cherries there, to take home to a very special lady. They were bitter, she said...

The military cemeteries in Normandy speak out an eloquent testimony to the youth of many who lost their lives, especially in the Parachute Regiment. Ages like eighteen, nineteen, twenty, twenty-one; on and on the slabs go in the serried ranks. I found one small cemetery in a tiny settlement where German, French, British and others are buried together, not separated by nationality. Each grave is tended by one family, the flowers are very beautiful and it is very moving to see such tenderness.

Norman Green, Gatehouse of Fleet, Kirkcudbrightshire

I had been hard at work for a fortnight getting our vehicles ready and waterproofed and also our radio equipment for our landing. Our unit was sixty-five strong; wireless operators, linesmen, signal office staff, despatch riders, and drivers. We were all attached to 147 Brigade of the 49th (West Riding) Infantry Division and our battalions were the l/6th and l/7th Duke of Wellington's Regiments and the 11th Royal Scots Fusiliers.

On 5 June, we cleared the camp of all equipment and set off. My wife was expecting our baby in early June but owing to restrictions I had not seen her since Christmas. We arrived at our concentration area and were promptly marshalled behind barbed wire with armed sentries patrolling outside. After a briefing by the brigade major about our landing area (King sector of Gold Beach) I sought out the army chaplain and explained about my wife's imminent prospect of becoming a mother. He was extremely sympathetic and obtained a priority call to my wife's home for me. As the phone rang my heart was pounding and then my wife's mother answered. 'Harry, you've got a bonny baby girl. She was born half an hour ago and weighs 7lb 8oz. When will you be home?'

I stammered an excuse and said I would ring later. My heart sank as I knew that in a short while I would be on my way to Normandy. I wrote a hasty letter and to save my wife worrying I dated it a few days later, knowing that the green envelope wouldn't have a date stamp.

We sailed down the Thames and headed towards the Isle of Wight. As night fell, I fell into a deep sleep. My only thoughts were still of my wife and our baby daughter.

A huge thump on the metal deck woke me instantly, even though I was still in a daze. Bill Sinclair, a fellow wireless operator, shook me fully awake and in his Glaswegian accent shouted, 'Come on corp, we've been hit by a bomb; let's get on deck'. As we scrambled out bullets zipped off the deck from the Heinkel above and so we promptly dashed below again for cover! We had been hit by a radio-controlled glider bomb, which had cut through a steel cabin and now lay in the coalbunkers in the bowels of the ship. Would it explode? Did it have a time fuse?

It was still there in the cold light of early dawn off Arromanches. All we could hear now was the thunderous roar of the guns from the battleships, cruisers and destroyers that surrounded us. It was deafening, and added to it was the belching fire of a rocket firing ship a few hundred yards away to our left. Enemy artillery fire was falling erratically around the fleet. I picked up a small metal plate from the wreckage of the bomb and slipped it automatically into my pocket, and gazed sullenly at the unwelcome monster as it lay amongst the coals.

Fortunately we had a small detachment of Royal Engineers aboard and as daylight came we watched fascinated as they defused the bomb and swung it over the side on a gantry. A fussy destroyer saw us. 'Keep for inspection,' it signalled. 'Not bloody likely,' our Aldis lamp flashed in reply as it was released into the depths of the sea! Later as I climbed down into our landing craft to oversee our radio vehicle ashore, I made a stupid mistake and realised I should have stayed on the vehicle. I found that out as I walked down the ramp until the sea reached my chin! So what – I was ashore, alive and the father of a day-old baby!

But it wasn't all over. I should have realised that. By the end of June the l/6th Duke of Wellington's took a terrible mauling in the area of Fontenay, Cristot, Rauray and Hottot, and had to be replaced by the 1st Leicestershire Regiment. They stayed with us until the final defeat of Germany. The metal plate from the glider bomb became my mascot – and it still is! I was lucky; I came through it all and I am writing this on my 76th birthday. But it is really for my pals who didn't come through it and who are still in Normandy:

Signalman William Sinclair, the wireless operator who woke me, Signalman Reg. Thomas and L/Cpl's Hartley, Eric Dale-Thompson – all wireless operators, and L/Cpl Fred Sillitoe, despatch rider. God bless them all – I never forget them.

Harry A. Teale, Leeds, West Yorkshire

It was approximately 01:30 hours on 6 June 1944 when I stepped out of the belly of a Stirling bomber.

I felt the tug on my shoulders as my 'chute opened and my kit bag, which was strapped to my leg and was grossly over-weight, fell off and vanished into what was obviously an orchard below me. I then realised that something was wrong. There wasn't supposed to be an orchard below me and I was apparently going down in the wrong place! I managed to steer myself towards the corner of the orchard, as past experience had taught me that landing in trees by parachute can be quite painful.

I was at this moment oblivious to the sound of gun fire all around me, but on landing the sudden realisation of where I was and what was going on around me sent a short, sharp stab of terror up my spine. Here I was laying on my back in a field in Normandy, taking part in the liberation of Europe from the Nazis, with only a couple of hand grenades in my belt. All my equipment, including my rifle and ammunition, my Piat and food, were somewhere in the orchard and I was lost!

I had joined the 12th Battalion Paras in September 1943, having volunteered from the Royal Armoured Corps, where I had been engaged in demonstrating flamethrowers mounted in Bren carriers. But I was not happy with the idea of running around in a Bren carrier loaded with highly inflammable jelly. I was twenty years old and looking for some adventure and a bit of excitement, but did not fancy the idea of being blown sky high in a Bren carrier and the prospect of parachuting appealed to me.

The training was hard and rigorous but very thorough. We had been well briefed on the D-Day landings and knew exactly what we had to do.

I scrambled out of my harness, got to my feet, and took stock of my surroundings. Although it was dark the sky was aglow with light from the fires in the coastal towns that were being bombed by the RAF in preparation for the main landing force due to assault the beaches at daybreak.

I could see the orchard a short distance away and thought of my kit bag. I could see figures all around me and they all seemed to be going in the same direction, so I joined them hoping that I would eventually reach my allotted position. It was just breaking daylight when we approached Ranville, having been dropped some four miles from the DZ [drop zone].

I was re-equipped, given a Piat, and had been joined by the other two members of my section. So, fully equipped we made our way to Le Bas de Ranville and took up our positions in the corner of a wood.

A Piat and three men may not seem much of a deterrent to German Tiger and Leopard tanks but on the contrary is quite capable of disabling a tank when used efficiently. However, the main objective was for the three of us to make contact with the pilot and co-pilot of a glider which contained a Jeep, five-pounder anti-tank gun and limber, and within an hour of us setting up our position a Jeep, gun, and limber joined us and as a crew of five we became an even more efficient anti-tank section. In fact after a while a Tiger tank came down the field in front of us and promptly received two shells from us. One in the belly and one in the turret.

Things were pretty hot up until then with machine gun fire and mortar shells landing all around. A great many lads had been killed or wounded but so far we had been lucky and in the early afternoon we had been called back to base for a short rest period.

We spent the next few days taking up various positions. All the time under mortar and machine gun fire, but our defences were sound and we held our ground, thus preventing the enemy getting through to the main assault taking place on the coast.

On the fifth day, during a heavy mortar attack, the young lad, who had joined us just a few days before D-Day, was killed. This upset my mate and me considerably as we were just getting to know the lad. He was only eighteen and quite a jolly little bloke.

We assembled in the church at Amfreville and shortly

after were ordered to take up positions outside. There were just the two of us at this time as no replacements were available. I carried the Piat and my pal Bill carried the shells. We left the church and immediately came under extremely heavy shellfire. We got across the road when Bill took a lump of shrapnel in his leg and went down in a ditch. I could see he was out of action so I took the shells from him, saw that the medics were with him and went through into an orchard. I explained the situation to a nearby sergeant who told me to stand by while he tried to get me some replacement. I was standing under a tree in the orchard when suddenly there was a great bang, a huge red flash and a great cloud of dust.

I knew no more until three days later when I came to: I was at Portsmouth dock on board a train heading for Shotley Bridge Hospital. My small part in the liberation of Europe was over, but I was proud to have been part of it all.

George Price, Stockton-on-Tees, Co. Durham

I was in the 79th Assault Squadron. We were the first wave in on D-Day and the first to land on the beach.

Our Churchill tanks were fitted with special guns for putting out pillboxes and the hatches were sealed so that we could go in the sea. We were supplied with survival packs and French money. We were in the leading landing crafts and when we left England the sea was rough and nearly all of us were seasick. As we neared the French coast there was gunfire and two of the ships went up in smoke.

The rocket firing landing craft fired their rockets. As we were the next to go all the crew got in the tank through the gun turret, I was the first in to start the engine.

The first two tanks that went down the ramp off the landing craft were flail tanks. They went up in flames. It was not a very good sight to see your mates on fire trying to get out of their tanks. The flail tanks were to clear the mines. I was driving the third tank, which was an officer's tank. When we came down the ramp you could see mines everywhere on cross pieces about two feet off the ground, and pillboxes further up the beach. The officer told me to pick my way through the mines as best I could. That was alright for the ones you could see. Just before I made it up the beach we hit a mine and it blew the bogey  off, but the track held. One of the crew put the windsock up. The officer and sergeant in our crew had been killed. Over half of the squadron had been wiped out. I drove the tank behind a sand dune; there we unsealed the driver and co-driver hatches. By then the commandos were with us. Then the major came and took charge of our tank as his had been knocked out.

We then went along the road and came under some small arms fire which our gunners returned. We came to a bridge over a canal; there was a pillbox and Germans on the other side. As our gun had only a short range the major decided to cross the bridge. We had just started to cross when the Germans blew the bridge, the section we were on held so I was able to reverse off. The commandos took charge over the bridge.

The major told me to drive the tank into an open space so that we were clear of the houses, and to stay there as he had to go. The tank engine was running warm so I got on the back of the tank to unseal the engine covers. I had just started when I heard an aeroplane. I thought it was a Mustang until I saw it release a bomb. The bomb was coming straight at the tank. There was nothing I could do but to lay down on the tank covers. All my strength went and a funny feeling went all over me, but the bomb just cleared the tank and exploded in front of it. I had to lie there for some time until my strength returned. I then got back into the driver's seat and we stayed there all night. There were bombs and shells exploding, small arms fire and houses on fire all night. We pulled back next day to get repairs done and re-group. That's how it was for me the first twenty-four hours of D-Day.

Eddie W. D. Beeton, Cambridge, Cambridgeshire

For us D-Day came too late; my brother, nicknamed Loulou, had been arrested on 25 May 1944. As he was taken away by the Gestapo, he whispered 'mauvais' or 'Anglais' to his wife Christiane. She did not know for sure.

We had been involved with the Resistance from the earliest days. Loulou, who was a Belgian officer like my father, had been taken prisoner of war on 10 May 1940. Mother had been a Belgian refugee in Britain during WWI and had delayed leaving for London to the last moment as she wanted to know where he was and by the time we decided to go it was too late. So we stayed in Brussels. German planes laden with bombs and flying low were on their way to Britain. As a ploy to divide Belgium, the Germans released the Flemish prisoners and as Father was Flemish, Loulou came home in September, having joked with the camp officer about his place of birth being Bexhill-on-Sea. Both Father and Loulou decided that it was their duty to resist and in order to do so efficiently my brother joined the flying brigade of the Rationing Control Authorities. That way he had access to the various places forbidden to Belgians. We were working with Edith Bagshaw, a British lady who had married a Belgian and who was a member of Secret Intelligence Service (SIS).

By November 1940 we had begun a life of danger. We lived in Brussels in a large house, which was a 'safe house' as there were plenty of young people coming and going.

Loulou had his work as a British agent and Father directed the Provincial Department of Food. We worked at home helping both with various nitty-gritty tasks required by their work, writing on false identity papers, de-gluing and re-gluing rationing stamps, preparing bandages and parcels for the 'réfractaires' and generally helping to do the dull part of their Resistance work. Loulou's specific job was to liaise with the various groups within the Resistance: collecting money and arms dropped by parachute, organising the many informations required and deciding upon how to best inform SIS. Altogether his task was to smooth the relationship between the many factions of the Resistance so as to facilitate and establish a sound working state for when the landing would take place. As a sideline we harboured Jews, forced labour evaders, wanted killers, etc. In July 1943 William Alan Poulton of the RAF came to the house, proudly brought to our safety by a non-English speaking Loulou. We collected another two: Vincent Horn RAF, and Robert J. Hoke, US Air Force. There were no safe routes to send them back. In January 1944 we were contacted by a man who said, and proved, he had a 'line' to get the boys back. He was the infamous De Zitter; a German agent, and the creator of the infamous 'ligne Zero'.

Edith was arrested at the end of January. Loulou was offered to be taken to Britain but felt the end was near and wanted to be there then. When the Gestapo came it was very quick. None of the leisurely and thorough searching as they had done before. They simply took his valuable stamp collection, as they always took what they fancied, and left with him.

We learnt of his arrest the same afternoon. All we could do was to hide everything possible. We had dynamite; we buried it in the garden. We stopped having anyone visiting. We spoke to no one. We were in terror of my sister's children being interrogated as more of our work would be known. We were still in a state of shock when we learnt of

the Allied landing through the German-controlled radio –
we did not even dare to listen to the BBC so D-Day found us
not only devastated but powerless.

I remember making my way that day to the hospital where
I worked as an auxiliary nurse to avoid deportation to
Germany. I had been so distressed by Loulou's arrest. Then
suddenly a feeling of utter joy overcame me. At last there was
a tangible end, we would be free and together soon. Mother

took the whole day to understand
the full implication of the events in
Normandy. She found a great calm
and proud hope restored her spirit:
we all knew Loulou had had a
hand in the landing and she
rejoiced in the anticipation that he
would soon be there to triumph
when four years of oppression
would end and our reward would
come with freedom.

Mother received a typed card
from a place called Buchenwald, telling us that Louis Thiryn
had arrived there. The simplicity of the printed form reas-
sured us as we knew where he was. We did not understand
its awfulness. We learned of Loulou's death in the cruel
shifting operated by the Nazis on their slave-labourers. He
had been used to work at the V1 and V2 plant at Dora-
Mittelwerk and the SS had not wanted them to be alive when
the Allied troops finally reached them.

What must be quite understood is that what we endured
– and we were privileged – must never be allowed to happen
again. Even if my brother had survived the message should
be the same. It took great emotional stress to write my story,
as even after fifty years I mourn my brother.

Claire Keen, Caersws, Powys

I was in the United States 29th Infantry Division from its induction into federal service. If you've read Joseph Balkoski's account of the division in Normandy – *Beyond the Beachhead* – you know that I figured prominently in that decisive World War II campaign.

I was then Captain King, 175th Infantry Regiment, Maryland National Guard, and the Commanding Officer of K Company, the leading unit, or 'point', for the 29th Infantry Division. And, as Balkoski noted, 'Company K seemed to get all the dangerous assignments'. Not the least of these was the crossing of the Vire river and the capture of Auville, a critical linking point for the widely separated Utah and Omaha beachheads.

I had led Company K in the final assault on Omaha Beach on D-Day plus one. I then moved my troops up the coast road, marching for fourteen hours, and captured the port city of Isigny. While in the city's main square rounding up prisoners – Cossacks who fought for the Germans in exchange for rations and keeping their horses – I was handed a special assignment from the division commander, Major General Charles 'Uncle Charlie' Gerhardt. He ordered Company K to advance three miles to the river

Captain King being decorated by Field Marshal Montgomery

Vire, secure its bridge and seize the town beyond: Auville-sur-le-Vey.

I remember nobody had the faintest idea what we were up against. We owned the air, but intelligence reports on ground forces were nil. For all we knew, the Germans could be preparing to counterattack with several armoured divisions.

When we arrived at the Vire just before dawn, we found the Germans had blown the bridge. We had no boats or bridging equipment and we were down to one hundred and fifty effective troops. So we moved to high ground, organised a perimeter defence and waited for reinforcements.

We didn't have to wait long. But instead of additional support, we were handed a new order by General Gerhardt himself: Cross the Vire in broad daylight and storm Auville!

It seemed like Balaclava and the 'Charge of the Light Brigade' all over again! We would be completely in the open, no cover for our flanks and no protection at the rear, facing an enemy of equal force occupying high ground. It was obvious it should have been a night operation, but my orders were to attack at 16:00 hours!

My maps gave *no* indication of the depth of the Vire. Even worse, the only approach to the river was across two hundred yards of open field strung in barbed wire!

Calling for a mortar barrage and fire support from four light tanks, I deployed my troops in a single skirmish line to make the Germans think I was leading the entire US Field Army. To suppress enemy fire, I ordered my men to deliver rapid fire from the hip without selecting a target! Gerhardt had said to simply 'walk across the river' and I tell you I was relieved to find that Uncle Charlie was right. The Vire was only knee-deep!

Halfway across the river, I called for a signal flare to move friendly overhead fire to my flanks and it was then that a German machine gun nest opened up and I took a bullet in both thighs. The men of Company K went on to seize Auville.

I recuperated from my wounds and returned to active service, serving in the Rhineland and Central Europe.

After advancing to the rank of major, I left active service in 1945, having earned the Silver Star, Bronze Star and Cluster, Military Cross and the Purple Heart. The latter two were for our crossing of the river Vire. All those who participated in that invasion, whether army, navy, air force, coast guard, marine or merchant seamen, officer or non-com or in the ranks, are part of a noble brotherhood from whom no other event nor time itself can take away the everlasting association. It was, indeed, one of those rare happenings that did and will forever stir the hearts of men.

John T. King III, Baltimore, USA

Not many twenty-year-olds were lucky enough to land on Sword Beach, at H-Hour on D-Day, 6 June 1944 without getting their feet wet. The 13/18th Royal Hussars in Sherman tanks and the commandos on Shanks's Pony were among the first ashore. The 13/18th Queen Mary's Own were part of the 27th Armoured Brigade. The flash on our uniforms was of a seahorse, more commonly known as the 'pregnant prawn'! It was expected that on landing the 27th Armoured would receive so many casualties that we would have to be disbanded soon afterwards. We were disbanded all right but fortunately without too many casualties at this point.

A and B Squadrons were in DD tanks, which had to swim ashore. C and HQ Squadrons were the lucky ones. They waded ashore! For the uninitiated the DD stands for duplex drive. Each Sherman tank was fitted with a propeller between the rear sprockets which drive the tracks forward, a canvas screen all the way round the outside of the tank. The bottom was also sealed to keep out the seawater. These Heath Robinson modifications turned a conventional tank into a floating vehicle.

A and B Squadrons had to drop off the tank landing craft into deep water, well away from the beach. They looked tiny in the water and very vulnerable in the rough seas. It was only when their tracks touched bottom and the screen was dropped that the enemy found they had to contend with a tank.

But now our years of training were over, no more firing on the ranges, no more cruising in an LCT around the north of Scotland in midwinter, no more paddling on the Norfolk Broads in a DD tank, learning the intricacies of the Davis Escape Apparatus. Had I volunteered for the tanks or the submarines?

As soon as we left Gosport, knowing this was no exercise, this time it was for real, out came the spanners, and the guard around the 75mm gun was thrown overboard. Let me explain. The gun recoils when it is fired and the guard is there to protect the crew from sustaining broken bones. On the practice range this is fine but in action if the three men in the turret had to make a quick exit, the poor wireless operator, who also loaded the gun, would have difficulty getting out, so the guard was fed to the fishes.

As most of us know D-Day had been postponed for twenty-four hours because of the weather, but some poor sods were already at sea and were left sitting it out, somewhere in the Manche. Seasickness was our main concern. Even the sailors were sick. But on seeing land at first light our spirits picked up. The adrenalin was flowing and we wondered with some apprehension what was awaiting us. Our main aim was to get ashore and off the beach as soon as possible. If only we could get our tracks on dry land. The enemy were of secondary consideration. HMS *Warspite* was alongside us sending broadside after broadside on to the enemy positions and as we passed the *Warspite* I thought, 'now it's our turn. God help us!'

A few kilometres inland – let's forget about the killing which was what we had been trained to do – our tank found its way to a small farmhouse. The farmer was pleased to see us. He was free and we had not damaged his property – not yet anyway. He produced a bottle of home brew and five thick glass tumblers. All the contents of this bottle were divided equally among the tank crew. This clear liquid may have looked like water but it turned out to be Calvados. It put fire in the belly as it worked its way down! In my best schoolboy French all I could say was 'Santé, Monsieur. Vive la France'. For the remainder of D-Day this tank crew felt remarkably brave! We learned the meaning of Dutch courage.

Fifty years later, now an OAP, not quite so young and innocent, I know that Calvados with age takes on a slight brownish tinge and can become quite smooth and pleasant. Our arrival on D-Day must have been rather premature. This bottle had not had time to mature. Perhaps it had only been distilled the week before! But as far as our tank crew was concerned it settled our stomachs and was much appreciated.

Matt 'Jock' Lamont, Prestwick, Ayrshire

I was eighteen and a student at London University, but Queen Mary College had been evacuated to Cambridge, so at 9am on the morning of 6 June 1944, I was at King's College and trying to get absorbed in a heavy French classic. I was sitting on a window seat in a room of the Fellows' Building, where Miss Aitken – QMC librarian – had been allowed to set out essential books. There wasn't much room for readers, so the window seat was much in demand – providing peace and quiet, and possibly a cup of weak wartime tea from Miss Aitken.

There was another reason for wanting a good place to work. Call-up regulations put the pressure on all students – girl entrants of eighteen were only allowed two years for their degree course instead of three, and were called up immediately after their final exams. I was lucky in that I was an under-age student, just seventeen when I started, and would be allowed the full three years. But to work hard was the in-thing. Failure in intermediate examinations meant instant call-up. There was a staggering imbalance of the sexes. In the schools of medicine, dentistry and theology, hardly a woman was to be found among those hearty and healthy young men. But elsewhere, most of the men were either medically unfit for service or were not British. Our French department of about fifty had just six men, four Belgians, a noisy and self-opinionated Dutchman and a quiet, witty Englishman with a weak heart.

The spring of 1944 buzzed with rumours in Cambridge – our Belgians became reticent and mysterious for no clear reason. The town was full of American GIs and airmen. They were friendly and known for their generosity, but at night they terrified us girls in the blackout. They could come upon us silently in their rubber-soled boots and try to start up an acquaintance with the invisible females! We never walked alone, but then they usually roved in twos and threes. (On the other hand the tramp of British Army boots was a wonderfully reassuring sound!)

Just after 10am that morning Miss Aitken's cup of tea appeared beside me. Almost at once the library door flew open and an excited male voice called, 'We've landed! It was on the news!' For a few minutes there was a babble of raised voices, then normal silence returned. A few students had rushed out to find out more, if they could. I went on with the heavy classic, but it was impossible to concentrate. Instead of the students in the hot sunshine of the quadrangle, I saw men in battle-dress storming up the hot sands of the French beaches.

I was facing in exactly the right direction to see what was going on in Normandy, could I have moved away all the buildings and hills between myself and France. So I sat and tried to use a mental telescope.

With youthful optimism I discounted failure of the plan and danger to the troops. Surely all possible safety measures had been put in place? This was, we all felt, the beginning of Germany's downfall. We were quite sure that all would be well, but we wanted every scrap of news about progress.

It happened that this was one of my two weekdays for having a meal at my digs rather than at the British restaurant. Rations were tight. I suspect that the food saved by my three days out was redirected to help feed the man of the house. There were three in the family, Father (mid-sixties), daughter Joan (twelve), and the lady (early-fifties), who was excessively house proud. She would cover the kitchen linoleum with newspapers, even though our slippers stood just inside the back door, and she counted the number of times that her students went up and down the stairs. She usually had two girls at a time, but she had complained that two were too much to cope with, so I was 'sent as a lamb to the slaughter'. I heard of this only when I myself complained – on D-Day! – and asked for a change of lodgings. (I got the change and went to a proper study-bedroom in a luxury home on Grantchester Road.)

Meals were served punctually – ferociously so. We – Father, Joan and I – always hoped that we would have finished eating by the radio news time as Mother insisted that we stand to attention while the National Anthem was being played. We were allowed to sit down again while the band went through the Anthems of the Allies, which was just as well. I believe it eventually took something like twenty minutes to get through them all.

At the end of the morning lectures, I cycled back up Hills Road to my digs, hoping to hear the one o'clock news, but when I arrived home, my excitable landlady was sitting on a stool in the kitchen, very flushed. 'You haven't got any dinner today! I couldn't bother with it. I keep thinking about all those poor boys in France!' The daughter came in. Same reply; and we both felt *very* hungry. Then Father appeared. He was unflappable. In his hand he held a bright, new galvanized pail. 'Look dear! I've managed to get you one at last!' Mother glared at him. 'Damn you and your pail!' She flung her apron over her face, burst into tears and left the room.

Unperturbed, Father enquired about dinner, then calmly made a fry-up of chips, an egg each and a single sausage shared between the three of us. For all of us quiet prevailed for once on D-Day!

Phyllis S. Bowles, Great Yarmouth, Norfolk

I had returned with my brigade from the Middle East to train on specialist tanks in Suffolk. All the tanks had peculiar names and were called Hobart's Funnies after General Hobart, the divisional commander. I had around three months' intensive training on this equipment and, when it was finished, I was declared proficient on the flails and flamethrowers. We were moved to Worthing. The town had been evacuated and was almost all military. We were then engaged on stripping down every bolt and screw, access plates etc. on our tanks and refitting them after they had been coated in a special waterproofing compound. The tank tracks were modified with fabricated scoop extensions to assist in obtaining a better grip in sand.

Then we had word to move again, 'another exercise,' we thought, but not this time. This was different. We went into a large wooded area, with more military police than we had seen in our lives. Bell tents, equipment and men were everywhere. Loud speakers were giving out instructions: no one allowed out, no letters. All night long there was one long procession of units moving out with full kit. Then it was our turn. We were given our pay, which was all in French money specially made for the occasion, and an extra blanket, shaped like a sleeping bag, but in effect, a burial blanket – lovely thought – and a stock of paper bags for sea sickness!

Off we went, and in a short time we suddenly arrived at the seaside!!! There were boats as far as the eye could see; troops, tanks, lorries all embarking and moving out. I learned later this was Gosport and we were to be Strike Force J. We loaded up and secured the tanks and moved out of harbour and lay off the Isle of Wight for forty-eight hours. We were all very, very seasick. The flat-bottomed craft and the corned beef sandwiches, given to us by someone who had a sadistic streak in them, had taken its toll!

On the late afternoon of 5 June, we set sail. I was in B Squadron, 3rd County of London Yeomanry. Our sea sickness got worse and we felt that anywhere would be nice as long as it was dry land. Then, at first light, we were called together by our squadron leader, who said, 'Well lads, there is the coast of France. This is IT. Tank commanders will collect their orders, crews mount. God bless you all and a safe landing.' I can never forget these words. It was then that I knew fear. My seasickness had gone and my whole inside seemed knotted up.

We climbed into our tank, the navy lads wished us well and then we felt suddenly very alone. The hatches were shut, and the spare crews busied themselves putting the final seal on the hatches. We were now virtually in a steel tomb. No one spoke as the tank commander read out our orders, but thoughts were passing through our minds; 'will the waterproofing hold', 'have the spare crews done the job right after we closed the hatches', 'would we sink too far in when the ramp was dropped', 'what was waiting for us when we landed'? Our minds were in turmoil.

Then, as if he knew what we were thinking, the tank commander tapped me on the shoulder and offered his hand. We all shook hands in turn, but no one spoke. We knew that, whatever happened, we had a bond of friendship and we would support each other. It was a unique but calming feeling. Then radio silence was broken, the ramp was lowered and it was 'GO! GO! GO!' Into the sea we went. It seemed an age before we hit the bottom, which gave us an almighty shaking up. Had the bump dislodged anything? We had no means of knowing.

The lack of noise was eerie as the engine exhaust was above sea level, but we could tell the engine was still going and we were making slow but steady progress. Then, through the periscopes, we saw daylight. It was 7:30am and the beach was Juno, Courseulles-sur-Mer. I fired the electric detonators to blow away all the waterproofing on the hatches and guns. 6 June had begun, an event I will never forget as long as I live. Out of four tanks in my troop, two never came out of the sea.

Charlie Salt, Derby, Derbyshire

Leaning against the rail on that bleak morning of 6 June 1944, my eyes were riveted to the spectacle which had started to unfold bit by bit as the dawn broke, like the lights going up in a theatre. It was only half light when the first bright flashes could be seen, followed by the swish of 16-inch shells passing high over our heads to land ten miles inland. On the skyline, we could see the dark silhouettes of the great warships. As the landing beaches came into focus I thought of my comrades in the 1st Bucks Battalion (Ox and Bucks Light Infantry) we had lost at Hazebrouck on 28 May 1940. They had fought with such doggedness that according to at least one report 100,000 men had got away at Dunkirk who perhaps wouldn't have made it. Only ten officers and two hundred men got back from the Hazebrouck action, and they received a rare compliment from the enemy themselves. A German broadcast stated: 'The defenders of Hazebrouck resisted in a manner truly worthy of the British Army.' It had been a sad day for many Buckinghamshire families – now we're going back to avenge it.

I'm in the hold of the landing craft, in the cab, sitting behind the steering wheel, engine ticking over and my knees knocking. I can hear the aircraft overhead, bombs falling, shells and rockets going in from our own battleships and havoc on the beach. I can see nothing but the ramp in front of me, waiting for it to drop. With nothing in my stomach but that horrible feeling, a feeling indescribable, which has to be experienced to understand what it's like. I wasn't worried about the bomb or shell hole I might drive into, hit a mine, sink, drown or receive a shell in the cab or just break down. I was scared stiff. At a rough estimate I reckon I lost a stone in sweat, while waiting behind the ramp. I had imagined the worst, but when out in the open, I shall never forget the Canadian sergeant lying in the attention position to the right, and the headless British officer to the left as I drove off the ramp. We were the lucky ones. Many in more unwieldy craft had no alternative but to jump for it and get very wet – or worse; many were offloaded well out of depth and never made it to the beach, with the loads the infantryman was carrying holding them under.

On the beach were a lot of people on stretchers waiting for a return passage and also a lot of people who would not be needing stretchers. The dead for most part had been laid out in neat rows, as if still on parade. This was a practice, which the British seemed to adopt even at the height of conflict, unlike the Germans who were apt to leave their dead where they fell. Worse, sometimes they are wired to booby-traps so the tidy-minded medical orderlies, surely among the bravest of all, were liable to get blown up for their trouble.

My contact on the beach was the pioneer platoon, who were responsible for lifting mines and keeping a beach exit free from obstruction. I had with my load the tools to do the job, mine detectors and explosive charges to clear obstructions.

Battalion Bren gun carriers and anti-tank guns went in support of the 6th Airborne, while the remainder of the battalion prepared the supply dumps.

D plus one. 7 June.

At 12:00 hours, a single German aircraft chased by Spitfires flew low over the main lateral, which was crowded with traffic, and dropped a bomb. A DUKW carrying petrol was hit and the burning petrol flowed down into an ammunition dump, which began to explode. Stack after stack blew up with deafening reverberations and pieces of shell started to fall all over the beaches. Soon blazing petrol added a huge column of smoke and flame, which roared skywards with a mushroom of smoke. The explosions and fire were fully visible to our own troops and the enemy in the line, and must have been as disturbing to the former (who saw the ammunition vital for their attacks exploding in their rear) as they must have been gratifying to the latter.

Many ordnance experts hold the opinion that once an ammunition dump catches fire the only practicable thing to do is let it burn out and then to start stacking elsewhere. In this case they were strongly of this opinion, as the stacks were placed so close together. But anyone with even a nodding acquaintance with Lieutenant Colonel Sale knew that such counsels of despair were not good enough for him.

Soon after the first explosion had taken place he was in the dump rallying the staff.

The stacks had been covered with camouflage netting, which caught alight easily, the grass was so dry it burst into flame whenever red-hot fragments of metal landed and the result was that every stack that exploded started up a succession of new fires. Helped by a small band of officers which included Major Geoffrey Pepper, the DADOS [deputy assistant director of ordinance service], Captain Erdle of the petrol depot (who was very soon fatally wounded) and Major T. W. Butcher of No. 12 Ordnance Beach Detachment, and by a handful of pioneers, the commanding officer started to drag the nets from the stacks, beat out the blazing grass, drive out vehicles which had been abandoned by their drivers, and eventually, as more men were rallied, to demolish the stacks nearest to the seat of the fire so as to create a fire-break. For nearly an hour the party worked in this blazing inferno until Colonel Sale was hit in the stomach by a piece of flying shell and carried off unconscious to the nearest field dressing station. His place was taken by the second-in-command, Major Carse, and after a further two hours' hazardous work the seemingly impossible was achieved. The fire burned itself out and half the dump was saved, with the result that when an urgent call for anti-tank ammunition was received that evening from the 3rd British Division the call was answered and the ammunition supplied. But four hundred tons of precious ammunition and 60,000 gallons of petrol had been lost.

No. 6 Beach Group – 1st Bucks Battalion. The following vehicles were to be landed on the first four tides:

D-Day	Tide 1	1,510 vehicles
D-Day	Tide 2	720 vehicles
D +1	Tide 3	532 vehicles
D +1	Tide 4	118 vehicles

It was planned to land 2,200 troops and 1,500 vehicles in the first nine hours.

An average of 3,000 tons of stores were to be unloaded daily in addition to the troops and vehicles.

This was all *double* the highest tonnage ever previously landed by this method and if a proper beach maintenance area was not established, chaos would result.

Les Root, Gillingham, Kent

I was a (very) ordinary seaman at the time, a member of the crew of a fleet minesweeper, HMS Selkirk. The armament of each ship was minimal; I think only a twelve-pounder gun on the forecastle and Lewis guns at the Bridge extremities. So, they were no match, especially when sweeping with wires etc. streaming, with their top speed around twelve knots, to the enemy E-boats, which were heavily armed and with a speed of over forty knots.

Immediately before D-Day there was much activity on board. The ship bustled with life as guns, equipment and engines were cleaned and checked. The sweeping gear and winch were overhauled, and the ship's boat and Carley rafts were re-stocked with fresh water and provisions etc. ready for immediate use should we hit a mine... It became known that this was 'it', and I am sure that many a prayer was offered up.

Towards late afternoon, on the fifth (my twentieth birthday, and what a birthday!) we weighed anchor, hoisted our 'battle ensign', and in company with the remainder of the flotilla (by then, I think, depleted – while on lookout duty a few weeks previously, I had seen the explosion from a mine under one of our sweepers; and it could well have been that another was unseaworthy at that time because of damage), we left the bay. This was a repeat of the previous days activities when D-Day had been set twenty-four hours earlier. Then we had steamed well into the early hours before being recalled when we were about halfway across the English Channel!

At some point – I do not remember where – we reformed from 'line ahead' to our usual echelon formation for sweeping and would have had the usual signal: 'out sweeps, speed eight knots'. We set course for the point south of the Isle of Wight for the purposes of the operation known as Piccadilly Circus where a change of course was necessary to take us directly across the English Channel. Here was the area where all our shipping and invasion craft would come in the next twenty-four hours and for some weeks, to pass to the 'other side' through about eight separate swept lanes.

When sweeping normally, the only guns manned would be those needed to fire at and to sink or explode floating mines. We even had an elephant rifle donated by a loyal citizen! However, for this operation where attack was expected, we had to man our twelve-pounder gun and for the first and only time in my naval 'career' my action station was manning a gun. It was just as well we did not meet any E-boats!

We plodded on and on through the night. I cannot remember the state of the moon, but there was a degree of visibility to enable us to do our work. Nevertheless, we were constantly on the forecastle straining our eyes for the telltale wake of E-boats, and more importantly for any floating mines cut adrift by our sister ships ahead. A bobbing mine in the swell prevailing, at night, was difficult to see, and despite the lack of sleep in the previous forty-eight hours, we were all wide awake, for obvious reasons!

As usual when sweeping, we were each wearing cork life-jackets (similar to those worn by lifeboatmen – and better

than our standard issue), and on the forecastle we consoled ourselves with the thought that if we hit a mine, it would be almost under our feet and that the explosion would probably fling us into the sea where hopefully we would float until a returning ship could pick us up. (The orders were that no ship was to deviate from the outward course for any reason, unless sinking! The invasion was not to be held up.)

Amazingly, I think for us all, as the dawn began to break, we had had few alarms, but were still alive and well. We had survived! What is more our flotilla was still afloat and on station. It has been said that there are no atheists who serve at sea; my distinct feeling was that there were none on board that night. I cannot describe the feeling of thankfulness that appeared to come over everyone on board. I am sure it was not my imagination. The wonder of that morning those years ago, is still with me. I was in no doubt that the Good Lord had watched over us. And, I suspect, others felt similarly!

It was not long before ships and landing craft anchored in the area we had swept. From there, they dropped their smaller landing craft, which embarked their troops, and proceeded towards the beaches. At that stage, I think we were off Omaha Beach and Vierville, though once, I was called onto the Bridge and shown our position on the chart with Arromanches in the distance. It was probably Vierville, but the coastal town we saw from a distance through the haze and smoke looked just as one might have expected a small seaside place to look with buildings onto the front, some white. Some were obviously damaged or on fire.

Our own landing craft and ships were firing at the shore defences; there was much confusion and noise and fireworks!

To our mind, the most fearsome craft from a defender's point of view, were the rocket landing ships, which had batteries of rockets mounted where troops would normally be carried. The rockets were fired in awe-inspiring broadsides of fifty or more at the same instant, horizontally at the beach defences. A general view on board was that *we* would not wish to be facing such an armada!

Although our flotilla was to return time and again to the French coastline, our job for the present had been completed, and at some stage in the morning, we reformed into line ahead and turned northwards, back along the swept Channel we had so fearfully made in the dark!

As we returned, we saw more ships and landing craft than we had ever seen together previously. Convoy after convoy of ships and craft of all sorts were heading towards the 'other side' – all of them in the swept lanes from 'Piccadilly Circus' – and many of them making heavy weather of progressing through the rough seas!

So, we steamed back to Portland, still flying our battle ensign, so that ALL could see we had done our work! We all felt highly relieved, elated, proud, and thankful indeed! Needless to say, Weymouth Bay was all but clear of ships at anchor and Portland harbour was now easily navigable after the congestion of the previous days and weeks. On many of those ships and craft still there, frantic activity was in progress, with loading of landing ships continuing from the 'hards'.

We felt for the soldiers who soon would be on their way to the 'other side' in crowded ships or craft. They were going to have an uncomfortable voyage, and many of them would be seasick. For them it indeed would be 'the longest day'; for us it had been not only the longest day, but also the longest three days in our lives!

As I reflect back over the years I feel a deep sense of indebtedness to all my shipmates of the HMS *Selkirk* with whom I had the honour to serve, for they taught me what true comradeship was! Further I am even more grateful to the Lord who brought me through D-Day and life's experiences since!

Derrick L. Willcocks, Bexhill on Sea, East Sussex

I was with Coastal Command, 59 Squadron Headquarters at Ballykelly when we were told that the invasion had commenced. Soon our sixteen aircraft took to the air to carry out 'stopper' patrols at the entrance to the English Channel and over the narrow seas. The aim was to prevent a large expected force of German U-boats attacking, damaging and sinking the vital ships of the Allied invasion forces.

Our duty was to fly on parallel courses backwards and forwards covering the designated sea area once every hour, by day and by night. All told we flew in Liberator V FL990, 59 Squadron for ten hours of daylight, and six hours and ten minutes by night keeping watch with all the other anti-submarine aircraft visually by day and with our modern ten centimetric radar by night. Neither directly with our eyes, nor on the radar screen had any of us seen such a sight. By day we saw ships everywhere sailing in regular lines shown up through the mist and cloud by the white foam of their wakes; by night the usually empty cathode ray tube was a mass of orange blips – ship echoes from which we attempted to sort out any small splinter-like blips indicative of likely submarines. On the whole the weather was dreadful. High winds, mist and low clouds. A very bumpy flight for the nine man crew as we nosed along at about one hundred and forty knots at our normal patrol height of between five hundred to one thousand feet.

We did not see a U-boat. Firstly the Germans had been caught totally by surprise and the orders for U-boats to attack the invasion forces were not issued until the small hours of D-Day. A week too late! 'Wolfpacks' of U-boats ought to have been lurking in the armada path and not at

their bases. The density of the air patrols together with the naval submarine attack groups gave the U-boats little chance. Apart from the loss of the frigate HMS *Mourne*, the destroyer *Blackwood* and one tank landing craft, the only success U-boat command could claim was the sinking of three liberty ships and the damaging of another by torpedoes off Selsey Bill on 29 June. In one month, coastal command, in co-operation with the naval forces, had sunk eighteen U-boats of the forty-three found, and rendered harmless the others by being kept away from the convoys or by being driven back to their bases.

All told my squadron put in ninety-six sorties as part of the invasion protective air screen. It was a memorable task in the squadron history. Congested was indeed the right word for the sky. On that day the full strength of 171 Squadrons was in the air above the short stretch of French coast and the narrow Channel.

And that brought about for my crew one of the most unforgettable incidents of their operational tour. When aircraft collide there is no escape and collide we nearly did. Flying so low in darkened aircraft in such demanding weather conditions among so many other aircraft keenly searching for enemy targets, we had to keep alert. It was possible to mistake a low flying aircraft for a U-boat. The radar blips were small and very much alike. In any case collision even without such mistaken identity could have easily taken place. Whatever the reason on this night an aircraft of a sister squadron thought we were undesirable and not only nearly ran us down but switched on the powerful Leigh Light (anti-submarine searchlight) and possibly prepared to attack. Nearly blinded we weaved from the area at maximum knots! Worse, when we met later at the intelligence interrogations on our return to base the culprits did not even apologise!

So if any members of B-120 flying at that time read this perhaps they will recall what was possibly a mutually lucky escape.

Joseph E. Collins, Poole, Dorset

I served with the 1st Battalion, the South Lancashire Regiment in the 8th Brigade of the 3rd British Infantry Division. After two and a half years of tough and intensive training in Scotland, we were moved south to a wooded area in a place called Cowplain just north of Portsmouth in April 1944. We were all sealed in the camp with barbed wire all around the perimeter and the outside patrolled by security troops who wore green armbands to distinguish them from the assault troops. Later we were taken into a huge marquee and inside on the floor was a huge model of the beach we were to attack. It was codenamed Queen White, a sector of Sword Beach. There was also a strong point code named COD and a small village about one mile inland.

At 4:30am on Saturday 3 June we left our camp and joined the massive convoys all making their way to the docks for loading on to the assault craft. There were security troops lining the roads and streets to make sure we couldn't talk to the civilians but very often trays of beer were brought out from pubs for the convoys which the security troops couldn't do much about, and we also spent the last of our English money. At about 5:00pm we eventually loaded onto our LCT (Landing Craft Tank).

The docks and harbour at Portsmouth and Gosport were a sight to behold. Just one seething mass of assault craft all being loaded with young men and their machines of war to be then transported to their Day of Destiny. We were on board until we finally set sail at about 5:00pm in the early evening of Monday 5 June into a rough and unkindly sea. Our LCT, being a flat-bottomed craft, shuddered violently at every wave it encountered – and there were plenty! The voyage was a nightmare in itself. As we crossed the Channel in the fading light everyone appeared to be quietly having a long last look at dear old England and wondering to themselves what tomorrow's H-Hour would bring for them.

Conversation on board was very hard to make. Your mouth was so dry and you felt very self-conscious trying to hide your fears from one another. Most of the men in our battalion were conscripts, in their early twenties, and going into battle for the first time. And what a daunting task we had been given. We were to lead the assault. The two sacrificial infantry battalions assaulting Queen White and Queen Red were both north country regiments: 1st South Lanes and the 2nd East Yorks. They'd obviously chosen the dour men from the north! As we continued to plough our way through the heavy sea the senior officer on board our craft called us all together on the open deck and told us the named destination of our assault. Normandy! We would be on the extreme left hand flank of the whole invasion force.

Overhead we could now hear the drone of a large number of aircraft. The officer told us it was the Paras, going in to capture and hold the bridges on our left flank. We all wished them God Speed with all our hearts. About an hour or so later the same officer called us all together again for an impromptu church service of sorts – I can remember we sang the hymns 'Abide with me' and 'O God our Help in Ages Past' and that it was so very emotional for us all. Fleetingly the moon would appear and lighten the heaving sea, and I remember seeing the battleships HMS *Warspite* and HMS *Rodney* steaming past us in preparation for the bombardment of the beaches.

The streaks of dawn began to appear in the east. This was it! Looking to our right we could clearly see the vast invasion armada and I remember that our hearts were really filled with joy. In our briefing we had only been informed about our sector – now we saw all this support! Suddenly there were huge flashes and an unbearable noise as the whole fleet opened up, firing onto the landing beaches. It was a terrifying spectacle and one I have never seen repeated. We sat in our Bren carrier with our heads well down! After

about an hour of this bombardment I ventured a look over the top of our vehicle in the direction of France and for the first time I could just make out the coastline. But even then it was obvious that our craft was making its way steadily to a blazing inferno, which was our allotted beach.

Most of the troops on our LCT had suffered seasickness very badly but we were now making full speed ahead to the beach, which was shrouded in smoke and fire. Suddenly there was a violent explosion underneath the craft, stunning me. We stopped in an instant about one hundred yards from the beach. The naval commander immediately lowered the ramp and in no uncertain manner ordered the vehicles off. Not knowing how deep the sea was at this point a Sherman tank moved down the ramp into the sea and disappeared beneath the waves in seconds. Only two men escaped – the others drowned. Next off was our Bren carrier with its gun in tow, and urged on by the naval officer. The tracks of our Bren carrier stuck on top of the submerged tank and couldn't move at all. The sea at that point must have been some twenty-foot deep.

Being good swimmers my four pals launched themselves into the sea, but me not being able to swim at all stood at the barrier with ice-cold water up to my chest. I tore off all my equipment, including steel helmet and rifle, blew up my lifebelt to the full and, urged on by a burst of machine gun fire from the beach striking the water just in front of me, I offered a silent prayer and into the water I went! No words can ever possibly describe my feelings at this moment. The landings having been planned for low tide, I remember thinking that if my lifebelt holds out then the tide will eventually bring me onto the beach!

On the way in, an assault craft having discharged its cargo of troops was pulling away full speed astern to get away from the hell on the beach. One of the crew leaned over the side. I thought he was going to help me, but all I got was, 'Good luck mate'. Thanks a lot! I suppose I was in the sea for fifteen or twenty minutes before my feet suddenly touched the ground. So I waded through the heavy breakers and could see a number of men laid on the sand clear of the sea. I stumbled to the one nearest to me and was shocked when I got to him to see that his chest had been torn wide open. He had paid the full price without even firing a shot.

Having no weapon I took his rifle and bayonet together with his bandolier of fifty rounds of ammunition and his steel helmet and ran like hell to the cover of the dunes at the top of the beach. In these early minutes of the assault both the dead and wounded lay scattered about the beach, with no apparent sign of anyone attending to them. It proved to be an awful baptism of fire for us all. I lay on the sand dunes for a while, recovering myself and my thoughts – I had also swallowed a fair amount of seawater and was now violently sick.

A war photographer saw me and came over. He gave me a packet of cigarettes and told me he had got some wonderful film of the landings if only he lived long enough to get it back to England! I assume he did so as he shot the world famous photograph of the landings taken on Queen White during the early assault. I understood his worry at the time though – snipers were still taking pot shots from the houses on the seafront and the beach itself was still being heavily shelled and mortared by the Germans.

When I had recovered I moved off the beach into the side streets of a seaside village in search of my unit. Going along a narrow country track with hedgerows on either side, all alone, and not knowing whether or not I was walking into the enemy lines, there was suddenly a burst of machine gun fire through the hedge just in front of me. I fell flat on my stomach and as I lay in the ditch I spotted one of our tanks in the field. He immediately opened fire and silenced the enemy gun. As I looked along the track I could also see troop movements in the grass. Moving closer I suddenly realised it was my unit preparing for an attack on a small village so I re-joined them and within the hour the village had been taken.

By midday we had cleared the beach, destroyed the strong point codenamed COD and liberated the village of what I now know was Hermanville. But we had paid an awful price. One hundred and seven officers and men killed and wounded in those first few mad hours. The German 21st Panzer Division counter-attacked about four o'clock in the afternoon and at one stage reached the sea between us and the Canadians. They later withdrew after seeing the glider-borne troops coming in about seven or eight o'clock in the evening. What a wonderful sight they presented. The sky was full of planes towing gliders carrying troops to reinforce the Paras. Then came darkness and the German bombers came over instead, dropping hundreds of anti-personnel bombs.

No sleep at all that night! Weary – still wearing my sodding-wet battle dress uniform – I was still reasonably happy. I was alive! God only knew why, but I was, and that was enough to keep *me* happy!

Tommy Platt, Wigan, Lancashire

My ship, of which I was the navigating and gunnery officer, was the SS *Empire Moorhen*, an American 'hog-backed' cargo vessel of the First World War, at this stage having completed her life as a cargo-carrying ship now displaying, in very large figures, on either side of her bridge, the identification numbers 307.

She had previously been divested, at Glasgow, of all her cargo winches, derricks, and of everything else that would be of no further use to her during what was to be her future task, which, at this time, was not known to us. Explosive charges had been laid in two corners of each of her five cargo holds, and electric cables had been run up to her bridge, each one having been connected to the respective charges. We set sail, in convoy, together with many other merchant, Royal Naval and fleet auxiliary ships, towards the coast of Normandy, having very little idea as to what was in store for us. We arrived off Arromanches on the morning of D-Day, and dropped our anchor, in line astern of some dozen or so other block ships (as had been designated in our sealed orders). Many others followed us, to their respective charted positions.

After a short while, we were boarded by the wrecking officer and his party, and, without further ado, the afore-mentioned cables running to the bridge were connected to a

plunger, the trigger was pressed and Number 307 sank gently onto the bed of the English Channel, in about two and a half fathoms of water, close inshore at Arromanches beach.

I noticed flashes coming from the spire of a church just behind the beachhead and then I noticed shells or bullets falling into the water close to my ship. By this time, several small oil tankers and other supply ships for the troops, had entered the artificial harbour made by the block ships, and they, also, were in line of fire from the snipers. The missiles were getting too close for comfort.

On our starboard quarter, there was a large Royal Naval landing craft – apparently at that moment doing nothing of any vital importance. I signalled to her, on the Aldis (daylight signalling) lamp, and told her what I had seen. Within a very few moments, she had manoeuvred onto the beach to get as close as possible to the church (which was out of range of my four Oerlikon guns). Then she fired! Only two or three rounds, as I remember. Then it was all over! The spire disintegrated, and, of course, the firing ceased.

I, and some thirty of my crew members, remained on board Number 307, the two upper decks of which were clear of the water, for a further two weeks, during which time, in addition to being on continuous action stations, we had several encounters with attacks by German planes. I had a grandstand view of the two-way journeys of the Thousand Bomber raids. I was also able to watch the flashes and hear the guns during the Battle of Caen, watch our Paratroopers landing behind the beachheads and watch (with pride and concern) the embarkation of our brave soldiers and marines on to the beach. I think that this latter sight was the most moving of all my wartime experiences (which were many!). I felt proud to be British, and my prayers went out for all those brave men and women (for very little praise has been publicised for the forces' nurses and other female participants who were very much involved in the landings) who were fighting for peace.

When I eventually arrived home (in Higher Tranmere, Birkenhead) – we were taken from Number 307 to Southampton on a returning landing craft – my father, whose interest was to keep press-cuttings concerning anything in which he thought I may have been involved, produced, amongst other things, a press photograph depicting a woman prisoner being escorted ashore at Southampton. The caption read that she, and others, had been captured whilst trying to escape from a church at Arromanches, which some two weeks' previously had been shelled by the Royal Navy, as it was believed that the said church was harbouring the enemy or its agents.

I still have the (rather tattered) Red Ensign, which I 'acquired' from the flag-staff of Number 307 as the landing craft came alongside to bring us back to England.

Just a note about the block ships at Arromanches. Virtually, it was a man-made breakwater, consisting of thirty-one merchant and other vessels (five more were added at a later date) manned by volunteer crews and scuttled in the approaches to Arromanches.

These vessels were of various categories – cargo, passenger and intermediate type ships which had been converted. Each vessel was armed with Oerlikons and/or other types of guns, for their own defence, should that be necessary.

The conversion consisted of the stripping-off of all unnecessary deck and engine-room equipment – derricks, some winches, capstans etc., mainly to reduce their respective draughts, but also to swell the country's supplies of scrap metal. Into each corner (bilges) of each hold of each vessel an explosive charge was fitted (by Admiralty personnel) and these charges were connected to the bridges of each respective ship by twin electric cables.

Lester Everett, Preston, Lancashire

I was in the 83rd Welsh Field Regiment and what I remember most about D-Day was the noise, the feeling of unreality and inevitability of it all. There we were, about two hundred in my unit, facing the most terrible ordeal in our lives and we were standing on the deck of an American ship, the SS *Frank Lever* watching the historic battle, possibly the greatest battle of all time unfolding before our eyes.

In front of us on the beach and by now inland we could see evidence of a fierce encounter between what we knew to be the 50th Division and the defending German stronghold on the beach and beyond, up the hill that leads from the shore to the relatively open country, behind the small resort of Courseulles.

Every few seconds the huge battleships standing farther out to sea thundered out a terrifying broadside shaking our ship as if it was a tiny cockleshell, the smaller destroyers darting in and adding their not inconsiderable voice to the proceedings, all manner of other vessels going flat out to ensure that they would not be left out of the party, and yet, in spite of the apparent chaos one felt that it was all going to a well designed plan, and that it was certain to succeed.

Standing on that deck waiting for our orders we might have been forgiven for thinking that this was a massive film set and that we would find it was not reality, but pure fiction. Suddenly our illusions were rudely shattered. Imperceptibly we had been slowly moving toward the shore and some of the empty landing craft were passing us and moving towards some ships lying farther out to sea. As they passed close to us and we saw the rows and rows of stretchers lying there we suddenly realised that these men had already paid a terrible price for the small piece of land that had been won back in the early stages of the battle. Then, all at once, the battle became a very personal fight. We had quickly been loaded into landing craft and we were off towards that very unfriendly shore to make our contribution to the invasion.

On reaching the beach we drove into about six feet of water, sitting on the back of seats, then up the now fairly well trodden track between the white tapes, up the narrow road for a couple of hundred yards, and into a field where I gave up my driving seat to another chap and went to find my own particular section, the signals unit. I had been temporarily attached to a gun crew because of the shortage of experienced drivers.

As soon as I caught up with the sergeant in charge of my group he told me to dump my kit in a radio truck and join a party setting out to establish field telephone contact with our forward observation post, some half a mile away. Because the few roads were full of traffic there was no chance of using a vehicle to run out the telephone cable as we would have liked. The radios were almost useless because of the close proximity of so many other units so we had to carry out the task manually, cutting across fields, and using hedges and trees to support the cable, and keep it up out of harm's way. After the link had been accomplished I was ordered to take a signals truck along some farm tracks to check that the cables were still in a safe position and to check that it had not become dislodged or badly damaged by the almost non-stop barrage of mortar shells, heavy machine gun fire and small tracked vehicles that were rushing about in all directions trying to make their way forward without using the main roads.

The cable at one point had been taken around a small clump of trees away from a well-used track and I followed it around checking as I went. I was so intent on making the line safe that I did not notice a destroyed German machine gun post at first, and as I came right up to it I saw that lying partly in the bushes and partly on the track was a German, obviously quite dead, and partially blocking the way forward.

I got out of the vehicle and walked towards him warily in case he was shamming and would suddenly start shooting at me, but I realised quickly that he was not in any way a threat to me, and started to make my way rather gingerly past him as if I might become contaminated in some way. I walked around a small clump of bushes until I was almost out of sight of him, then, remembering my training I went back to see if he had anything on him to identify his unit. He was lying partly on his side so I decided that I would have to move him to get into his tunic pockets and I was not very happy at the prospect. I looked around rather desperately to see if I could find any of my mates to give me a hand but there was nobody near enough to help me.

When we were coming through the shallow water on to the beach, and all the way up to the battery position I had seen dozens of bodies, but everything had seemed so unreal, as if it was happening to someone else, in another time and dimension, and being brought face to face with this situation was something my previous life had in no way prepared me for.

I was very aware at this point of the warnings we had received in training about booby-traps, but I did not think that there would have been time for the retreating Germans to have used such devices in this case, especially with one of their own men, although I did hear of many instances of this happening later. Failing to attract the attention of my mates I decided to drag him farther into the bushes and to try to establish his identity. After a bit of a struggle I succeeded in moving him into a better position and I took his paybook out of his pocket with the intention of handing it in at BHQ when I got back to base.

As I opened his paybook a photograph fell on to the ground. I picked it up and found it was a picture of the dead soldier with a very charming girl, obviously his wife, standing behind two beautiful little children, equally obviously his daughters.

I felt at that moment as if I had intruded into very private family grief, as if I had been personally responsible for that young man's death and that it was me and the thousands of Allied troops who were the villains in this terrible conflict. I sat down close to this former enemy. I no longer thought of him as being part of a nation that had enslaved almost the whole of Europe and by its dreadful example precipitating a Holocaust on a scale that the world had never even dreamed of.

I was brought back to earth and to reality by a voice calling me from a signals truck that had managed to find its way through the fields to where I was waiting.

'Everything OK here mate?' It was one of my pals, the signals sergeant. He had realised that I was a long way out and came to bring me back safely. I handed over the paybook I had taken from the dead man to the sergeant. His only comment was, 'That's one less of the bastards to bother us,' while the driver, a hard bitten cockney, merely walked back to the truck without giving the body a second glance.

I think their reaction might have been influenced by the fact that both had served in the Western Desert with the 8th Army and all of this was fairly routine to them.

For a short while after this incident I felt some sympathy with the rank and file of the German army especially during and after the Falaise pocket battle when thousands of their dead lay everywhere, even clogging the tracks of tanks and Bren gun carriers. But when stories of the atrocities in the concentration camps were proved to be even worse than most of us imagined I believe the whole attitude of those people I had contact with changed substantially. Instead of looking on the German soldiers as being just like us, fighting for what they believed was a just cause, by this time all Germans were evil, to be wiped from the face of the earth. Any feelings of revulsion when dealing with dead people soon went at the end of the war.

I was present when two large death camps were liberated and for some time after the war finished I was part of a transport unit engaged in clearing several camps over a wide area.

I have spent many happy hours in Germany on holiday and I love the country and respect the local traditions, but I have a terrible feeling that if another Hitler should emerge it could all happen again.

Eric Morgan, Newport, Gwent

My D-Day was on 5 June. It was a day I will always remember for the rest of my life. Me and nineteen other men under Major George Payne, plus twenty other men, all from 22nd Independent Parachute Company moved off to Harwell Airfield in Oxfordshire. The time for us to jump was 00:20 hours (H-6 hours 55 mins) from four Albemarle aircraft. Us forty men were among the very first of all Allied assault troops to land in Normandy but half of us were dropped by mistake on DZN, at Ranville, instead of on DZK at Touffreville four miles east of Caen and eight miles from the coast.

Our tasks were to set up the Eureka radio homing transmitter beacons for DZK and to prepare the flare path for the six Horsa gliders of the battalion group on the adjoining LZK. The 8th (Midlands Counties) Battalion was a new parachute battalion. It consisted of young men who had never heard a shot fired in anger. Commanding the battalion was Lt Col Alastair Pearson DSO and two Bars and the MC for bravery and leadership. The 8th Para Bn Group was an independent force of seven hundred and sixty men and the group's tasks were to capture and destroy three bridges over the River Dives in Normandy before 09:15 hours (H+2 hours). Two of them were at Bures and the other was at Troarn. After that they had to hold this remotest area of the airborne bridgehead to protect the extreme left flank of the Allied beachhead against any German counter-attacks.

At Harwell Airfield the time had come for us to go. Major Payne came round to say, 'Good luck. I know you will give them hell.' At the time the only hell was in my guts. I just felt sick and wanted to get it over with. We had blacked our faces and hands and looked more like chimney sweeps. We all got a mug of 'Sgt-Major' to drink before getting on board the Albemarle, a bloody awful aircraft. It carried ten men and we had to squeeze up tight to the top gunner, not like the Dakota, which was a lot more comfortable.

As we flew over the Channel the sky seemed to become

lighter, I could see the waves breaking on the shore. As we passed over the coast gunfire was making little red blobs in front of us but I could not hear a thing because of the engines. We were already hooked up just in case we were hit by flak, but so far no worse than flying in a thunderstorm. Someone said, 'Five minutes to DZ.' Red on. We all stood up, took up positions ready to jump. This was it. No turning back, no calling it off this time. Someone shouted, 'Good luck boys'. Green go. Out I went. Done it lots of times in training. Just like dropping on Salisbury Plains! The ground came up fast. I hit it with a bump and never saw it because as I came in lower the ground got darker and darker. Got out of my chute and looked around. Not a bloody person could I see, and I was too scared to call out in case a German heard me!

What little I could see was not like any of the models we had studied or the maps we had looked at for hours at our transit camp. Thought I saw someone move towards me. My Sten was already cocked with two mags taped together so I could reload without much trouble. It was a German. He fired as I rolled to my right and missed getting hit. I fired a mag of thirty-two 9mm bullets and got him in the guts and both arms and nearly cut him in half. I didn't feel bad about it, in fact later after seeing the number of lads in the Btn on 7 June that had been killed only wished it had been more at the time. Up came Tommy Green my pal, 'Got one then Frank?' He'd heard Sten-gun fire and came over to help out but could see I didn't need it. 'Have you seen Taffy Burt?' I said, 'No, and let's get away from here.'

Just then gunfire came from our right. I guessed it must be Caen. Tommy was doing a recce. When he came back I said,

'I don't think we are in the right place,' and then heard planes and down floated some Paras. A Sgt came running over. 'Seventh Battalion, mate?' 'No, 8th Battalion' I told him. 'Bloody hell, they've dropped us on the wrong DZ.' 'You're OK Sergeant. Us silly buggers have got to get to Bois de Bavent. This is Hérouvillete. You are not far from Ranville.' Just then it seemed like daylight. The Germans had fired up parachute flares and then opened fire on us with two MG 42s and small arms. The sergeant said, 'What shall we do – rush them?' I said, 'Not bloody likely. Let's outflank them from right and left and leave the Bren gun to draw their fire, then when we are forty feet away knock them out with 36s (Mills bombs).' Took half an hour to get in position. The two groups must have read each other's minds! Mills 36s fell down on them like rain. Then we went in to find eighteen dead Germans and not a live one in sight.

I then decided to try and reach Touffreville. Tommy said we'd never make it. 'Too many Germans about in this area.' We must have been four miles from DZ, so on we went. After about a mile we had a bit of luck and met up with a patrol from 8th Battalion led by Sgt Fred Baker from our own B Company. Said to Fred, 'Don't mind if we tag along do you?' We heard later only one hundred and forty men had reached the RV out of six hundred and fifty. A lot had dropped in the River Dives and drowned, also many killed and wounded. CSM Jones in a stick from 4 Platoon was saved when their Dakota was hit by 88mm and caught fire. At the time he was standing in the door waiting to jump so he did! He was found by the French Resistance and got back to England via Spain!

The rest of the parachutists were killed. Fourteen men from 4 Platoon B Company, five men from B Company HQ. Two of the men were Cpl Smith and Alen Humphries, both mates of mine. Also the aircrew from 233 Squadron were killed. We do know that they are all buried in a collective grave; VB 1-22 in Ranville War Cemetery, Normandy.

We soon reached DZK. Six Horsa gliders of battalion group were supposed to land on the adjoining DZ but only two did. Then we saw Dakota aircraft, thirty-seven in number, from 233 and 271 Sqns. Only one hundred and thirty jumpers landed on or near DZK because of flak.

Two lads from Btn Signal Platoon were captured by the Germans when helping the Pathfinders to set up flare path for gliders on LZ. Privates Arthur Platt and Tom Billington were executed shortly after capture on a farm track just outside Touffreville, each with a bullet in the back of his head. Their bodies were left face down in the hedgerow at the side of the track, and were discovered next morning by a French woman from Touffreville, Mme Yveline Langevin. On 10 June when the 51st Highland Div arrived nearby, their bodies were taken by the Germans to a field near Démouville about two miles away and buried there to remove any incriminating evidence from the scene of the executions.

Arthur Platt's grave was found when the area was captured in July. His body was exhumed in September 1945 and reburied in Ranville War Cemetery. Tom Billington's grave was never found as it was probably blown to pieces in the very heavy bombing and shelling which took place in the area at the start of Operation Goodwood on 18 July. He is commemorated by name on the Bayeux Memorial opposite Bayeux War Cemetery.

Major Tim Roseveare, commander of 3rd Para Sqn. RE had been dropped by mistake on the DZN at Ranville. He commandeered an ambulance, Jeep and trailer, loaded them with explosives, and with eight men on board raced through Troarn and blew a gap of twenty feet in the bridge there at 05:30 hours. On the way from Touffreville to Bures a lance-corporal by the name of Stevenson and four men of the anti-tank platoon, armed with Piats were left where the lane crossed the main road from Troarn to the coast.

At 06:30 hours they knocked out the six armoured half-trucks that we had seen. They killed three Panzergrenadiers. The others ran away and reported back that a large British force had ambushed them, so no more enemy attacks were to make up the road on D-Day! In reality a small force of Nazi Heavy Panther tanks could have probably swept along the same road straight through to the bridges over the river Orne at Ranville and over the Canal at Bénouville.

They could have wiped out the small airborne bridgehead as only seventeen anti-tank guns had been flown in intact by 03:30 hours for the whole divisional area. Fifteen of them were 6-pouriders, which were too small to knock out Panthers, leaving only two seventeen-pounders capable of doing it.

A lot of men who had been dropped in the wrong areas managed to re-join the battalion group and by the evening our strength was about three hundred and fifty and we were surrounded by the Nazis for five days. We had done all that was asked of us.

Frank Ockenden, Rye, Sussex

I was in 76th Highland Field Regiment, RA, 3rd British Infantry Division. The morning of D-Day was dull but dry and the sea was slightly choppy, but we in our landing craft had been at sea so many times that no one, as far as I can recall, was seasick. At dawn it was time to get settled in my tank.

This was something to which I was not looking forward to with any joy. It was originally planned that I would go ashore on my motorbike in a dry landing but it had been decided that I should land early, and there would be a deal of water to go through between the ramp and the beach. As we had found it impossible to stay upright on a bike in anything more than about two feet of water, I was provided with a light two-stroke bike, which was roped to the turret of a Sherman tank and I would travel inside as co-driver and machine gunner. After I was installed in my seat the hatch was closed and then sealed with water proofing material, making me a virtual prisoner until such time as I could be released when dry land was reached.

Sitting in my seat, the wait seemed endless, my vision restricted to what I could see through my periscope and that meant the rear end of the tank in front. I did not feel at home in those surroundings. Although I did not actually suffer from claustrophobia my world was that of the motor-biker; the open spaces where I did my job as a surveyor and where I was not confined. Here I was shut in in a thirty ton steel monster, not even free to leave unless someone outside let me out!

I do remember the noise of the engine, the smell, peculiar to a tank, a mixture of engine oil, petrol fumes, camouflage netting and sweat, and I do recall the thought that if the tank was hit I would fry because I couldn't get out.

Eventually there was a shudder and I knew that we had grounded and a few seconds later the tank in front moved off and we followed down the ramp. I still couldn't see the beach and suddenly the periscope was below water. After a few minutes the view became clearer and I could see the beach and the houses beyond, exactly as in the photos I had studied back in England. I thought that they would have been flattened by the preliminary bombardment or by the RAF but they still looked more or less intact and one or two appeared to be occupied by riflemen who fired intermittently at our men on the beach. Soon we were stationary on the beach, the route ahead blocked by other tanks and vehicles as the beach exits had not been cleared.

I could not see much through my periscope but eventually the houses immediately in front were cleared and someone got out of the turret of the tank and released my hatch. I climbed out and jumped to the beach where I was very sick! And I couldn't blame my breakfast.

Only impressions are left of what the beach was like but it

was very noisy and there was smoke from burning vehicles, tanks and landing craft. Lots of debris lay around but it didn't seem all that frightening – at least not as bad as I had thought it would be now that I was on dry ground.

There was the odd shell landing on the beach but nothing close and further inland I could hear the sound of machine guns and mortar fire. The navy was firing over our heads and the shells of the heavy guns sounded like a train going through a tunnel.

I spotted our MO Capt Kelly, and went to speak to him, and as we were chatting a shell went overhead and I looked to see it burst a few hundred yards away. I turned back to the MO to see that he was flat on his face. He looked up somewhat sheepishly but this was his first experience of shellfire and he hadn't yet learned to recognise the sound of an 'over'. Some casualties then appeared and he got busy and from then on did a splendid job regardless of what was happening around him.

The first thing was to get my little two-stroke bike down from where it was perched behind the turret of the tank and the crew were glad to get rid of it as it restricted the movement of the turret. I got it started and moved off to my rendezvous with – I hoped – my two pairs of surveyors who were due to land from two other landing craft. Another two pairs were due on D-Day plus one.

I recall that I had not gone far when I passed

John McFarlane on left

the first dead Germans I had seen. In 1940 we had been going back all the time and never saw the results of our efforts. These men didn't look particularly frightening or aggressive but then they were dead and I was soon to learn better.

Dust soon became a problem as a result of the movement of so many vehicles over a parched countryside and my bike stopped with dust in the carburettor. I stripped and cleaned it but it happened again and again. I was beginning to become frustrated, especially when I stuck again on a crossroads, which was being shelled systematically, when along came the tank on which I had landed. The adjutant was aboard and seeing my predicament he waved me aboard and I abandoned my almost new bike for the comparative safety of the tank.

Soon I met up with my surveyors and we started with our task of surveying gun positions. This was a somewhat hazardous occupation as there was no fixed front and in any part of the beachhead there was still a sprinkling of Germans and they did not all want to surrender. As I no longer had my motorbike our sole means of transport was two Jeeps and as they were laden with survey equipment, personal equipment, food, petrol, water, mines, grenades, ammunition, picks, shovels etc., I travelled mostly on the bonnet. On one occasion I was booking readings for Gunner X who was on the director (theodolite) when bullets, twice, went whistling past our heads. He did not move a muscle and carried on with his readings, so I likewise carried on as I felt I had to show an example. It was not until later that I found he had earlier been partially deafened by a shell burst and had not heard the bullets! I discovered a German hiding in the hedge at the side of the field where we were working. He had been wounded and this probably accounted for his poor aim.

As the morning progressed the nucleus of an RHQ gradually formed but I discovered that our duty sergeant with the sergeants' mess truck had failed to land. In fact it never did and all our carefully acquired stock of spirits etc. was gone forever.

Rumours were rife during the afternoon and Tiger tanks were reported, although in fact there were no Tigers in Normandy. It became clear, however, that an armoured attack was imminent and in the absence of the duty sergeant I had to see to the deployment of our meagre resources for the defence of RHQ. I posted a man with a Piat (Projector Infantry Anti-Tank) on each flank and then had a walk round to check the Bren gunners and others in our small defensive position. On my return to the first Piat I was informed that the gunner had brought with him only practice ammunition! I had to order him to stay where he was, tell no one, and if necessary fire what he had until I returned with something more lethal. Fortunately the attack was beaten off before it reached our position and although armoured cars reached the sea between our division and the Canadians, they lost many tanks and we won the first round against the 21st Panzer Division.

Their arrival at the sea near Luc-sur-Mer coincided with the dropping of a brigade of the 6th Airborne Division on the west side of the river Orne and the Germans, believing they were being cut off, made a hasty retreat.

And so the day wore on and as it did, it became obvious that the main objective of Caen was not to be realised. Everything was behind schedule and there were pockets of resistance in our rear. I was surveying positions that would never be used by our guns, which were busy firing in support not only of our own Division but also of the 6th Airborne holding the bridge over the Orne. Darkness began to fall and it was time to get back to RHQ as I couldn't see to work anyway.

When I got back I found that my two Jeeps were no longer with us and when an hour later they had still not turned up, decided to take my other two men and their Jeep and go and look for them. By now it was pitch dark and I ran into crossfire with tracer all over the place. The question now was did I risk what I had in the faint chance of finding my missing pair, and I opted for home. The missing pair turned up next day having dug themselves in for the night until things had quietened down!

John 'Mac' McFarlane, Scone, Perth

Landing Craft Tank 645: Commanding Officer: Charles Summers, Lieutenant RNVR. First Lieutenant: Bryan Wyatt, Sub Lieutenant RNVR.

I have kept a copy of my log book and together with what I remember I have laid out the events as they happened.

LCT 645 was attached to the American Command based at Dartmouth where we loaded up with a contingent of the US Second Army with the following equipment and, personnel:

6 half-track vehicles, 6 anti-tank guns towed by the half-tracks.

10 Jeeps, one of which towed a trailer with radio equipment.

70 US personnel of varying ranks from a major downwards.

Monday, 5 June 1944

04:30 hours: Weigh anchor and proceed to sea.

07:00 hours: Form up in convoy in accordance with previous orders.

10:00 hours: Exercise action stations.

17:40 hours: Spot and report floating mine on port beam. Progress very slow, about five knots. Steaming southward.

18:00 hours: Minesweeper escort on fire on port quarter.

21:00 hours: Close up to action stations. All seems quiet and convoy is still steaming slowly. The Channel is brilliantly lit by marker buoys showing up in the gathering dusk.

22:40 hours: Note spasmodic firing to the south.

23:30 hours: More firing ahead. Tracers. Probably on French coast.

24:00 hours: Firing ahead now more concentrated. A myriad of lights dropping from the sky. Reminds me of Guy Fawkes Day!

Tuesday, 6 June 1944

H-Hour: Destination Utah Beach. Gunfire to the south is now continuous but there is little interference with our convoy which is proceeding through swept channels lit by buoys.

04:15 hours: There is now a constant stream of aircraft – bombers, fighters, gliders.

05:45 hours: We arrive at the transport area and the coast of France is now visible.

06:30 hours: *H-Hour arrives.* An ear-splitting bombardment from the capital ships further out to sea begins. Smoke screens are laid. The air cover is continuous and a heavy smoke now covers the coastline.

09:50 hours: We weigh anchor and form up in the 24th wave for Utah rendezvous area.

10:30 hours: Leave rendezvous area for line of departure.

11:30 hours: Leave line of departure for the beach. On the way an LCI, coming off the beach and about a cable's length on our starboard beam strikes a mine and sinks. There is no time to pick up any possible survivors. The bombardment from the capital ships is still deafening.

12:00 hours: Utah is now clearly visible and ruined buildings can be seen. A lot of gunfire is in evidence in the adjoining Omaha Beach. There is a two hour delay in unloading on Utah.

14:00 hours: We beach on Utah!

NOTE: As we beach there is now an ebb tide and the US major in command is repeatedly warned by me to disembark in five minutes otherwise LCT 645 will remain beached. He promises this will be accomplished. Unfortunately this does not happen and I am forced to threaten the officers with a .45 revolver. Whether they are scared to disembark into three feet of water or frightened at the sight of the burning vehicles on the beach I shall never know. Anyway by the time they do disembark the craft is, as I feared, high and dry and we have become sitting targets for the enemy. I order 'finished with engines' and we all take cover in the mess deck and engine room.

Utah Beach looks a shambles with broken-down tanks, burning and exploding vehicles of all kinds. The enemy mortar and 88mm gunfire is extremely accurate although the beached landing craft appear undamaged. Perhaps the enemy think the craft are abandoned and if the ships' company remain out of sight doing so will help confirm this. My other concern is that because the beach has a number of deep ridges and with the craft 'drying out' and the weight concentrated at the stern and being possibly unsupported there is a danger of breaking its back. This actually does happen on a future beaching on drying out. After floating off and a calm trip to the UK, two railway lines are welded to the catwalks and LCT 645 continues in service. One LCT did break in two completely but the skipper managed to get the bow section towed to port. Fortunately for us, on D-Day the craft remains seaworthy.

16:00 hours: A US private who is badly wounded in the arm and leg, limps aboard. We treat him as best we can and later transfer him to a medical boat. Sub-Lieutenant Wyatt and my coxswain manage ashore during a lull in the bombardment and examine other two LCTs on the beach. One is full of corpses wrapped in blankets and the other is still stacked with explosives, but nobody in charge.

19:00 hours: Our craft is now afloat. A Rhino ferry packed solid with American personnel is unloading alongside. (A Rhino ferry is a huge floating platform composed of articulated linked tanks with two large engines and rudders at the stern. They are used for transferring personnel from LST to shore.) The four seamen remaining cannot start the engines and request a tow. Although anxious to get out of the danger zone quickly I take pity on them and after three attempts I manage to get a line secured and proceed to leave the beach. They appear grateful and give us the thumbs up on reaching the assembly area at 21:00 hours.

Charles Summers, Symington, Ayrshire

On D-Day, 6 June 1944, I was a petty officer serving in HMS *Emerald* a light cruiser, operating off Gold Beach in company with other cruisers of the 10th Cruiser Squadron. The other cruisers in our sector were HMS *Ajax*, HMS *Argonaut*, HMS *Orion* and the Dutch cruiser *Flores*. The ships remained on this operation until about 18 July except for returning to Portsmouth to re-ammunition, continuing to give support to the troops ashore at Arromanches and, later, on the assault on Caen.

As we turned south on 6 June, the weather improving, I went on deck. In the grey light I could just make out our companion ships in line ahead. The captain, Captain Wylie, gave the order for battle ensigns to be run up. Just at the same instant, over the ships intercom, there came softly the Emerald's [Emerald City supporters] signature tune 'The Wearing of the Green'. I never hear that tune without thinking of that moment we headed into battle.

At about 5:00am we turned broadside onto the shore and literally all hell was let loose as we opened fire, all the ships almost at the same time. There was a wild cacophony of thunderous sound that anyone who wasn't there cannot begin to imagine.

My action station was on ammunition supply at the aft end of the ship. A Junkers 88 bomber dropped a string of bombs over us. One hit the ship on the deck above me and ricocheted off the iron deck and exploded in the sea alongside us, almost lifting the ship out of the water. I threw myself down a companion ladder and landed on top of Charlie, a shipmate, who cushioned my fall! No one was injured and damage to the ship was minor. Our lucky day – the luck of the *Emerald*!

We had a grandstand view, after the initial bombardment, of the rocket ships going close inshore and opening fire. Surely the most fantastic fireworks display of all time! And then the landing ships going in loaded with troops and me thinking, 'I wouldn't be one of those lads for all the tea in China – thank God I'm in the Navy!'

After the landing had been going on for some time, I remember watching landing craft that had been shot up, some with crew members dead, floating down on the tide. And then, as the tide turned, floating back again. Dead Americans, from Omaha Beach, buoyed up by life jackets, floating by. A tragic picture etched in my mind of the human cost of this great operation.

One thing is certain – I will never forget 6 June 1944 or the following days, and I am sure that the same applies to everyone else who was there, whatever service they were in.

Ted Pitman, Christchurch, Dorset

When I sailed out in command of the destroyer HMS *Ulster* in Force G – officially on exercises – we all knew pretty well that it was the real thing: I personally had received a cyphered signal indicating that D-Day would be 5 June. As we steamed down the Firth in a depressing drizzle, I suddenly remembered it was my daughter's sixth birthday. I wondered if I should ever see her again.

As we steamed up the Channel on the afternoon of 5 June from every port and inlet on the south coast there poured out convoy after convoy of craft of every shape and size, sailing in accordance with the minute to minute programme of the vast operation. There were ships visible in all directions for miles and miles, and it seemed impossible that the enemy could not find out that the invasion forces were on their way at last.

About 6pm we in *Ulster* were passing close inshore along the Dorset coast. The English countryside was clearly visible in its perfect summer setting; among the checkboard panorama of grassland and crops, the farms and cottages showed up white in the evening sunshine. Little wisps of blue smoke rose vertical from their chimneys in the still, warm air. It was England at her best bidding us all farewell on this great adventure.

And just before dusk there happened something else that was typically English – the admiral made a signal to his ships in Force G, the ships who were to do the bombardment next morning. He knew well enough what we were feeling like; he knew if we could batter down the defences before our troops landed, their casualties would be reduced enormously; he knew also that we had no easy task, and that hundreds – if not thousands – of British lives depended on the accuracy of our gunfire. It was a great responsibility for us.

He might have made a long and platitudinous signal, but it so happened that he was a keen cricketer, and his message was short and simple. It read: 'Best of luck to you all. Keep a good length and your eye on the middle stump, and we shall soon have the enemy all out.' That was just the sort of signal that was wanted; the sort of signal that made every man say to himself: 'My God, we will.' It made us on board *Ulster* more than ever before determined to put up a good show. Personally, I thought it ranked with Nelson's famous signal before Trafalgar.

The excitement on board was intense; men spoke in whispers as though the enemy might hear them ninety miles away. The words of Henry V ran through my mind all night, 'Once more unto the breach, dear friends, once more...' as the minutes ticked by so appallingly slowly. It seemed an age before we reached the little green flashing dan buoys halfway across, where the swept channels through the minefield started. We glided past the first one, with an ML sitting patiently there like a policeman on point duty, and altered course five degrees to starboard.

Apart from the navigational problem, the thought of our task on the morrow weighed heavily on my mind. For the hundredth time I studied the orders under the shaded light of the chart table. We had to anchor literally within yards of our appointed spot, and then knock hell out of those forts: the forts whose photo I had gazed at so often in the last few days. Unless our shells dropped on those two pinpoints on the chart, we would fail in our duty.

If only we weren't mined first! For I remembered some words at the final conference: 'The destroyers will lead the way, of course. If the minefield hasn't been properly swept, it will be cheaper to lose a destroyer than a cruiser.' *Ulster* was leading one section of Force G. Slowly the night dragged on. Suddenly the sub lowered his binoculars and turned to me. 'Land in sight, sir,' he said quietly.

The tension on board was terrific, and as if to encourage us even more, a continual roar of aircraft passed overhead southwards – our own bombers going to play their part. The daylight seemed to come up much quicker now; on either side of us, the faint outlines of hundreds of ships could be made out, steaming placidly along in an orderly array according to plan. It was a magnificent sight, almost unbelievable in its imperturbability; it was sea power personified.

As we approached the coast we overtook several convoys of smaller craft and had a hectic few minutes weaving our way through them; we could not stop as the other ships were close astern of us. Some of these tiny craft were all over the shop, and we whizzed past with only a few yards to spare. I saw a brass-hatted officer stand up and shake his fist at me!

And then seemingly quite suddenly it was broad daylight; houses and forts on the coast ahead of us were plainly visible. A lighthouse, yellow in the light of dawn, stood there like a friendly finger to beckon us in. It was a perfect June morning quiet and still. On either beam the other destroyers were forming up in a long line and astern of us the cruisers were easing down preparatory to dropping anchor; they were going to fire over our heads. My watch showed five past five; not long to go now. The immediate problem was to get plumb into the right spot before anchoring.

'Nearly there, sir. Steer two degrees to starboard for three minutes.'

From the chart table the sub's voice was muffled, but he could not conceal his excitement. Other reports followed in quick succession.

'Main armament ready, sir!'

'Starboard anchor ready, sir!'

Once again I gazed at the typed orders beside me. The whole thing was working out fine to date.

'Turn to anchor now, sir!'

I gazed at the other destroyers. Yes, they were turning also. We were hunky-dory. I turned *Ulster* beam on to the beach, now less than three miles away, and we let go the anchor underfoot. It was to help keep the ship steady during the bombardment.

'Well boys,' I said, 'we've arrived.'

The director and the guns trained round. Ten past five, only a few minutes now. The silence was uncanny, almost disappointing. We had expected to be met with a hail of gunfire, and a rain of bombs, but nothing had happened. It was like a peacetime exercise, but all the same, I found myself shivering violently. It seemed very cold at anchor. Half a minute to go. My heart was thumping like the proverbial sledgehammer.

'STAND BY!'

As I gave the order with my eyes glued to my stopwatch, my thoughts flashed for just that brief interval to my little country home, four hundred miles away. Five fifteen; all would be quiet there, too. My wife and little girl still fast asleep upstairs in their bedroom, and David the Sealyham downstairs curled up in the kitchen chair. Outside in the garden with the Lake District hills all round, it would be fresh and cool, the birds cheeping in the apple trees, and the old tabby puss gazing at them enviously as she picked her way daintily across the dewy lawn – the same perfect June morning, I could see it all.

'OPEN FIRE!'

For one hour and ten minutes we fired without ceasing, in

one long, magnificent and exhilarating roar. At intervals throughout,
the signalman touched my sleeve
and held up a signal for me to read.
Halfway through, he showed me
one that has been made many times
in British Naval history...

'Engage the Enemy More Closely.'

At that signal all the destroyers
weighed anchor and moved closer
inshore, each one led by their own
individual minesweeper in a single combined line. We were
firing as fast as we could now, almost point blank at the
shore defences. The assault craft, full of soldiers, were
passing us on their way into the assault; we could see the
men in them, crouched down, ready to spring ashore. In one
boat a man was standing up playing the bagpipes. For five
minutes, just ahead of them and just before they landed,
there was a tremendous shower of rockets onto the nearby
beach defences from craft specially designed to fire them,
and then on Gold Beach, at half past six on that June
morning, in the centre sectors of that great assault, the
British armies returned to France. One of the greatest
moments in history – one the whole free world was waiting
for – had arrived at last.

From the bridge of the *Ulster*, we had a grandstand view
of the whole proceedings, and it was a magnificent and
impressive sight. We ceased firing just then, and moved out
to seaward to wait the air attack that never came. We
anchored, and a small craft came back alongside with some
men that had been picked up from the sea. Doc Johnston
dealt with them quietly and quickly.

Up on the bridge we looked at each other, not knowing
what to say. The bombardment was over; we had done our
best. I picked up the telephone to the director tower.

'Bertie?'

'Yes, sir.'

'Pass to all positions from the captain. Well done, everybody.'

'Aye, aye, sir. Thank you, sir.'

I could hear the message being relayed to all the guns, and a muffled cheer came up from B Gun's crew.

After a short interval we relaxed somewhat, and some of the crew went to have breakfast. Up on the bridge there was a great silence among us still up there. It was only then that the strain and excitement of the last twelve hours began to tell. The sub crouched over the chart, grey with fatigue, and the signalman leant against the side of the bridge, struggling to keep his eyes open. Perched on a couple of chairs beside the compass, and blinking stupidly like owls disturbed in daylight, the officer of the watch and I listened as best we could to the progress of the battle ashore; the crackling messages in the RT set were like a running commentary of some great event. I was so utterly weary that I just could not think about anything.

It was five past eight when number one came up to take over the forenoon watch.

'Well, it's on the news, sir – the folks at home will have got their thrill all right this morning.'

The folks at home! I could see them in my home, I could see them in a million homes, I could picture the excitement and the jubilation everywhere, the calling out of windows to friends passing, the chatter between complete strangers in trains and buses...

'We've landed!'

Even more vividly could I picture the receipt of the news on secret sets in a million homes and places still under the heel of the hated Nazi... Then number one's voice broke in on my thoughts once more.

'It looks as though we've managed it all right, sir,' he added quietly.

I will never forget the intensity of that moment on the

bridge of the *Ulster* just then. I was overwhelmed by a surge of emotion that swept into oblivion any trace of weariness. It was a moment when the memories of every past triumph, every thrill of accomplishment, and every glow of happiness combined in one great brilliant flash. It was the most wonderful moment of my whole life. But outstanding in that surge of emotion was heartfelt thankfulness and pride. Thankfulness to the Almighty for granting us the victory, and pride in our service and our native land.

But although the initial landing had obviously gone more or less according to plan, there was no time to sit back and congratulate ourselves. The 'build up' ships were streaming in, and they had to be protected both by sea and from the air; the enemy soon started to hit back hard.

Ulster was one of the many destroyers that endeavoured to form a steel ring to seaward of the beaches to protect the ships from E-boat and U-boat attacks. These patrols, particularly at night, were no picnic as they were on a line parallel to the beach, and hence at right angles to the stream of incoming and outgoing traffic. By day we moved up and down, awaiting calls for bombardment of targets ashore through the co-operation of army spotting officers. This was another typical instance of the value of sea power; for while the German positions were still within our range, bombardments from seaward were carried out continuously. For several days after D-Day, the cruisers and battleships were able to send salvos of heavy shells far inland on to such targets as concentrations of enemy troops or tanks.

I personally shall always consider that 6 June 1944, was one of the greatest days in the history of the Navy, the British nation, and even of the whole free world and I shall always remember with a glow of humble pride one paragraph in the orders for Operation Overlord. It read as follows:

'It is the primary duty of the Navy to ensure that the

Army is landed safely on the shores of France. Regardless of any difficulties encountered, or losses sustained, this will be done.' It was.

William 'Spoons' Donald, DSC, Keswick, Cumbria

I had been a qualified House Officer at a teaching hospital and within a few weeks of donning uniform I found myself posted to Oxford, to join the RAMC and a military hospital, which was forming up in the examinations schools building. However, very soon I was sent with a small unit from the hospital to the Isle of Wight for a couple of weeks to train on amphibious three ton trucks (DUWKs), commonly referred to as 'ducks'. We learnt how they could be loaded with stretchers bearing wounded soldiers and how to unload them efficiently. We were also shown how these vehicles could be driven down a beach into the sea and then 'swum' out to mount the bow ramp, let down into the water, of a landing-ship anchored off the shore. It was an ingenious but quite hazardous procedure. If the DUWK when loaded failed to hit the ramp dead centrally and at reasonable speed it was liable to topple over or slither down the ramp depositing its luckless and helpless human cargo into the sea. However, once safely aboard and unloaded, the casualties could be simultaneously treated while in the process of being transported to base.

After training at Oxford and Southampton we were yet again moved by the same mysterious organisation which had recently so taken control of our lives. This time we ended up on board an American Landing Ship, Tanks (LST), (Medical) anchored in Southampton water. This vessel, a sort of roll on, roll off ferry with a lift to the upper deck like an aircraft carrier, was already fully loaded with a miscellaneous collection of vehicles ranging from armoured half-tracks and bulldozers to ordinary trucks and staff cars. Deep at the rear of the cavernous vehicle hold was our 'theatre' tent, neatly concertinaed back against the rear wall but containing our main medical and surgical equipment and ready to be pulled out once all vehicles had been unloaded.

The units on the ship were all from the 50th Division, to which we were being temporarily attached as a sort of sea-borne field ambulance. Including the American naval crew there were possibly three hundred men on board waiting in cramped accommodation to hear exactly what was going to happen next. At last we were informed that we were due to start unloading our vehicles by Rhino float onto a strip of beach referred to as Gold, next to the village of Le Hamel on the Normandy coast, at H+2 hours the next morning. Our emotional tension was not lessened by a twentry-four hour delay because of the weather, but real fear was subdued by growing confidence in the mighty organisation we saw assembling all round us. This confidence even grew as we finally set sail, towing the most enormous raft I had ever seen, into a wet, windy, grey Channel. Before darkness concealed everything we saw many strange looking vessels including what looked like floating castles, and others like colossal cotton reels. When allowed back on deck in the grey light of next day's dawn we gazed out on a massive collection of ships of war, transports and landing craft of all shapes and sizes. A mile or so away the grimly grey coastline in front of us spewed up a few columns of smoke. Suddenly a shattering explosion from behind us, followed by the tearing sound of a shell made me cringe and reminded us of the business in hand. A war ship had loosed off a salvo over our heads at some invisible target well inland. Next time it happened I was better prepared.

Very strangely, at about this point a naval launch approached us, thumping its way through the choppy seas in bursts of spray, and soon a notice was given out over the Tannoy that a naval chaplain had come aboard and would shortly celebrate Holy Communion on the fore deck. All were invited to attend. In those days I had not heard the saying that there are not many atheists in foxholes, and when I surfaced to present myself and gather sheepishly on the fore deck I was astounded to find that I had been beaten to it by well over two hundred armed men. The scene could not have been embellished even by Hollywood. The chaplain, in a fluttering white surplice over his uniform, was standing at the bow of the ship with landing craft heading for the shoreline behind him as a back drop.

Chris Bartley standing with his brother, a squadron leader in the RAF

Immediately in front of him there was a small table covered with a white cloth, anchored down by pieces of weaponry, on which there was a small silver cross, chalice, etc. And all around were the men mixed in with the parked vehicles. Tin helmets were reverently removed. Some found space enough to kneel at least on one knee. The words, sometimes blown away by the wind so as to be inaudible, of the hallowed prayers of repentance, forgiveness, humble access, and consecration were recited. Then the elements of bread and wine were shared out, and the men returned to their places of waiting, a little subdued, perhaps, but with a new degree of calmness. I personally knew that I had made my peace with God, at least for that day. I felt nothing now really mattered. What had to be, just had to be and that was that. It was a great feeling of release from the emotional tension.

What did come as a surprise was that among the early casualties and more seriously wounded were a number of foreigners, some clearly of Mongolian origin, in German type uniform. They had hunted, scared expressions and turned out to be TOD workers, captured in Eastern Europe or Russia and taken as slave labour to construct the Atlantic Wall fortifications. They spoke no known language and were unbelievably grateful for their lives being spared, their injuries being attended to and for the comfort of a single cigarette.

We all soon became absorbed in the work, and I was only half aware when one DUWK didn't make it up the ramp. There was even a team assembled for just that eventuality! Then there came a time when no longer did the DUWKs have to stand dripping in the steel hall while we unloaded them but the ship was able to run up on the beach for a few hours when the tide went out. A brief break from work enabled me to stroll ashore and walk, though with considerable caution, among the sand dunes for a breather. It was then I realised that we had indeed broken in to the Nazi empire and this was the beginning of the end of a nightmare; there was still a future and now a real hope of life ahead.

Even after we re-floated in the evening occasional DUWKs came aboard. Now the casualties of war predominated, but for the most part they had already been operated on at the beach dressing stations and it had been possible to get a number of the worst cases straight to the hospital ship anchored a mile or so out. So our work became mostly a matter of administering morphine, keeping drips going, renewing dressings and continuing the administration of sulphonamide and penicillin. This latter new and magic drug had been very scarce in civilian practice but was now freely available to any who were wounded.

Our own troops naturally tended to attract the greater part of our attention because it was possible to talk to them which some needed, particularly those from the Hampshire Regiment who had been caught by a flame thrower and concealed machine gun as they were clearing out Arromanches of enemy troops. The awful psychological shock of seeing their comrades die was as painful as their own burns and wounds. But all were astounded at the organisation and unbelievably gratified by the speed with which their needs had been attended to, and that they were safe. Only once did tension reappear. A single enemy aircraft suddenly swooped out of the clouds over the beach and every AA gun in the fleet and on land opened fire simultaneously. The noise for a moment was prodigious, and even the sudden ensuing calm was broken by an ominous pattering, like hail stones falling, of shrapnel on the steel deck above. Once it was dark the ship, now about half full of casualties, set sail back to Portsmouth. Around breakfast time we dropped our ramp on a 'hard', and a steady stream of ambulances drove straight into our steel hall, loaded our casualties and with great efficiency and speed were away. Meanwhile we were collared by medical brass who wanted to know all about the situation 'over there'. We were the lions of the moment, the centre of attention. It was impossible to repress a feeling of nonchalant superiority!

By the end of the afternoon we had been reloaded with further military hardware, and our used medical stores had been replaced in preparation for a return trip to the beaches. The glow of all this achievement soon tended to dim the memory of those emotions which had been circulating round that communion service thirty-six hours previously; although in fact they were never forgotten completely. They left a reminder that in the last analysis human flesh and human courage cannot supply all the answers. But the question remains why, although there may not be any atheists in foxholes, as the general commanding the United Nation forces in the recent Gulf War again remarked when being interviewed on the BBC, do humans so easily forget when immediate danger is passed.

Chris W. Bartley, London

I was a naval sub lieutenant aboard LCT 884, leader of the 24th Flotilla. I was nearly twenty. Our skipper was a Hull fisherman called Robinson, known to us as Robbie. As we cleared the Needles and put out to sea in the evening of 5 June, Robbie turned to me on the bridge and asked me to fetch him the sealed orders. I asked him for the key of the cupboard, as I knew he had it, but search as he might in his pockets, Robbie could not find that key, so I went out into the tank hold where there were four self-propelled guns, two command tanks and soldiers of the Hertfordshire Yeomanry. I asked in a loud voice, 'Any professional burglars on board?' Very soon a burly soldier with a figure not unlike that of a circus strongman came up and said, 'Whadya wont dun?' I told him and in about twenty seconds flat he had picked the lock and the sealed orders went to the bridge and a somewhat surprised Robbie!

On arrival off Gold Beach an hour before the first landings we bombarded the heavily fortified lighthouse at Ver-sur-Mer, after which a sergeant who was in charge of one of the guns came up to me, pointing to a porthole overlooking the tank deck and asked, 'Is that cabin yours by any chance?' I told him it was, whereupon he added, rather apologetically, 'I'm afraid you won't recognise it now.' I soon saw what he meant. The intense vibration of the guns had ripped everything off the walls except the bunk itself and deposited them in a heap on the floor. Just as I was recovering from this the naval cook came up and said, 'We haven't got a single whole cup or plate in the galley, sir.' He too had one vast pile of chippings!

The weather was disappointingly bad and it was obvious that the vehicles would have to drive off into several feet of water (there were a few Jeeps and a lorry or two as well as the guns and tanks). Their engines had been waterproofed with Bostik but there remained the human element. When cold water reached the sensitive parts of the driver's anatomy he instinctively took his foot off the accelerator, and probably stalled his engine. A sailor was therefore detailed to go round the vehicles and throw a bucket of water on to their laps prior to disembarkation, as his pal stood behind him asking, 'What did you do in the war, daddy?' (One of the many occasions on which I was glad I had not joined the army!)

Just as we began unloading I noticed a huge tank on a hill in front of us only a mile or so away. Knowing that our tanks were some of the first to land I realised that the one on the hill was no friend of ours. Soon one of his shells landed a few yards to port of us, with a resounding splash. His next landed a few yards to starboard. Where, I wondered, would number three land? We had a small RT receiver on the bridge over which came the unflustered voice of the beachmaster calling the cruiser HMS *Belfast* a mile or so to seaward of us. By this time all coding had been abandoned and he was using plain language. 'Hello *Belfast*, there's something on the hill behind me causing trouble, attend to it, will you please?' The accumulated gun smoke and early morning mist made it hard for him to see the tank. However, almost as soon as she received the message *Belfast's* huge guns 'spoke' with a vast broadside. The tank completely disintegrated in a swirl of dust. *Belfast* had very probably saved my life. When she came to her final resting place at the Tower of London I paid her a visit to thank her. There was, in addition, a nasty little German pillbox away to our left as we came off the beach. In this was, we assumed, an 88mm gun, which was doing a fair bit of damage. A series of LCMs (Landing Craft, Mechanised, capable of carrying one large vehicle), were passing across our stern. One received a direct hit on his port quarter, reared up, and went down like a stone. The next must have been carrying petrol, as he went down in a sheet of flame. I think *Belfast* must have 'fixed' this gun too.

Curious things happened on the way home which really should not have happened, leading to quite needless casualties – but the less said about them the better.

Dick Boustred, Hemel Hempstead, Hertfordshire

THE BEACH

She looks about four. Blonde, piquant and bubbling with merriment as she builds sandpies with her mother. A young father looks on fondly in between working on an elaborate castle. The mother draws the little girl to her and whispers something playful because she suddenly screams with tinkling delight.

Even as I watch this tender scene the little scream is transformed into the unforgettable, unforgotten clatter of metal on stone as tanks in a dozen monstrous shapes silhouetted against the rising sun mount the beach into the tiny resort waved through white tapes by crazily gesturing marshals, each tank with its tense phalanx of sheltering infantry behind. Offshore the big cruisers plumed in smoke, vomit, shells and rockets above the village. Behind, a cavalcade of scarred landing craft belch vehicles and men, some from flaming infernos, while smaller craft draw away with their inert packages of dead. Overhead the heavens thunder to the screeching solace of protecting planes.

An infantryman becomes a grotesque crimson mound of butchered meat by an avenging roadside mine. Blood spatters our tank's tracks. Rich green Normandy grass and golden buttercups are his shroud. The rest of his section stand up and move forward without a backward glance. That was the moment when the sombre image of death invaded my hitherto cheerful universe and fear became my fellow traveller. Fear. That dry feeling engulfing the mouth, the cold sweat running down the back, those icy fingers creeping up the neck. After that it never left me.

THE ROAD

It runs up the gentle shelving escarpment – straight and true like all good French roads. Fields of green corn and maize and vegetables stretch away endlessly on either side, lush and simmering in the early summer noon sunshine. Silent today except for a tractor lumbering down to the village with a load of hay.

This was the road stalked by selective death as it spat from superbly sited guns someone had forgotten to silence. Like toy ducks in some macabre fairground booth down went the six tanks as they nosed and probed out of the shelter of the grey dusty village. Hissing steam and resonant ringing echoes as each one exploded, armour-piercing shell destroying the men inside and igniting ammunition and petrol. Each one its fiery tomb as a few luckier crewmen escaped to scramble for the ditches under a hail of machine gun fire, stunned and sickened by the first blood of war. Each one now marked only by a large patch of smoke forming shimmering ringlets against the azure blue sky.

But today the tractor is alongside us now, the driver perched nonchalantly atop and whistling something from Abba, a Gitane clenched between his teeth. He wishes us a cheery 'ça va' as we pass.

THE ORCHARD

I found it after some searching, found it much as it was on the evening of that day. The same mellow-stoned farmhouse, flat-stoned limestone walls, lofty hedges, apple trees in blossom, lovely copse of elder and ash at one end, fat brown and white Normandy cows, larks high above.

Over that wall the mortars rained on the laagered tanks and resting crews, followed by stream upon stream of Spandau fire. Three of us were spared because we were foraging for cider in the cellar of the house. Stunned by blast we emerged to find rustic peace transfigured into a holocaust of dead and dying amid an inferno of burning tanks and exploding shells. Later we returned to the scene to claim and bury our dead amid the scattered detritus of their last moments. Here an abandoned diary, there a last letter home, an opened book of poems, a pair of socks.

THE BRIDGE

They'd counter-attacked that morning on the far side and we had to regain it. Men went forward but wavered before devastating crossfire. He was their leader and he knew with frightening precision what he had to do. White rose in buttonhole, wet from the morning hedgerow, he took a final stroll across. Men followed the ghastly signpost of his blood and secured the bridge once more.

But today it's Sunday. We watch some boys fishing by the lockgate. They use a stick with a four-way hook and just drag the surface with it. Not very expert but effective in producing a rich harvest of flailing mackerel quivering their pathetic last on the quay. I suppose we must have looked equally forlorn moving up the road on that tranquil June morning as the mist lifted from the canal and we got our first glimpse of the bridge standing four-square like some ghostly stranded battleship.

It's a tourist curiosity now. Well labelled and with a museum full of waxen images and the far unhappy shapes of long ago – Bren and Piat, mortar, and half-truck and Jeep. There's a restaurant there now where the dedicated hold reunions.

THE COUNTRY

The old desert hands said it was poor tank country. Certainly the small backyard fields with their high hedges and sunken roads were murder for us. Tiny orchards hid hostile guns. Tight little houses and streets saw bloody short-range tank duels with no room for manoeuvre or quarter. Church spires housed the deadly sniper, and the thick hard-going bocage – as tough an obstacle as the Argonne had been to our fathers – concealed the Tigers, which stalked relentlessly by day and haunted by night. Good for defence, bad for attack. Poor tank country indeed.

But, as Shakespeare's Henry V told his men, maybe many a poor sod still kipping in England would in retrospect envy us that day. The great ships with their marvellous names – *Warspite*, *Hotspur*, *Ramillies*. The proud old county regiments – Green Howards, King's Own Shropshire Light Infantry, 13/18 Hussars. But all this amid Normandy's golden ocean of June corn, swollen cattle grotesque in untimely end with legs in the air and corpses in pretty green copses with brown holes stitched in them and eyes shrivelled like raisins, blackened and bloated before they could be retrieved. Certain it is that none will forget the timeless suspense of watch by day (brew up, bale out were the watchwords then) or the fearful sleeplessness of laager by night with its cacophony of clattering tracks, the crackling matchstick noise of automatics and the fatal beauty of enveloping tracer. War's terrible beauty.

I suppose time has healed where once the monstrous roar of artillery drummed the ears. Today the air is filled only with the rustle of barley and the song of skylarks and no longer a gigantic abattoir filled with human and animal corpses crawling with flies, giving off that terrible sweet-sour stench which once smelt is never forgotten.

THE CEMETERY

I suppose it could be said that they lie in serried ranks. For us they do – Scottish Borderers, Black Watch, Hussars, Staffordshires. All the shires here up the quiet grassy track from the old village. A silent green patch with rows of white inscribed stones among neatly trimmed lawns and flowering shrubs. Headstones drilled in immaculately tended order, devotedly preserved by the Graves Commission and dedicated locals with a neat register of names on the memorial wall. Serried ranks of white.

But they weren't like that at all. Not the ones I knew in the Staffordshire Yeomanry anyway – lived with, fought with, hated, loved. Each was unique in his exultation and despair, in his foibles and passions, in his dreams and his nightmares. Yet common in not showing fear simply because they dared not. Common in knowing the indifference of folks back home unaware of the realities they faced. There was Topper; trooper extraordinaire, bank clerk and self-appointed toff, whose function was to fire the gun but whose real role was to relieve so many tense moments with his set of erotic cards acquired on what we all regarded as sophisticated and lascivious visits to pre-war Paris. 'Let's have a look at the pics, lads,' he would say as the flak began to beat against the turret. Then there was Ginger; driver, but also womaniser par excellence whose modest ambition was to remain alive long enough to be the first of us to confer his favours on the local talent. This, he constantly assured us from his vast experience, would be a source of heartfelt gratification on their part. 'You see they all like it these Frenchies.' And Jim; the wireless operator, whose war had interrupted the reading of Greats at Oxford and whose singular distinction of being the only one capable of reading map and compass extricated us from many a shambles.

These were my comrades, now lying in serene and holy stillness in the green embrace of pine and cypress and lawn and rotting apples. Tufts of white marguerites grow in the wall sheltering their resting place and nearby an elder bush is in blossom. They lie in quiet repose. Not I am sure in any kind of rank but in glorious disorder.

I wished now I'd stayed away because I could find no words for them. The chance path of a shell decreed that I should survive to have the privilege of fifty years coping with achievement and disappointment, satisfaction and frustration, sweetness and bitterness, this and that. Bonus years.

Neville Patterson, Newbury, Berkshire

6 June, 1944 was the day which changed the course of my whole life. At 2:00am on that morning almost fifty years ago I awoke to hear the drone of many aircraft flying overhead, the sound went on and on. There seemed to be hundreds of aircraft in the air and something told me there was a big exercise taking place. During the morning I heard the news on the radio – the invasion of Europe had begun and then during the afternoon of 6 June I received a telegram to say that my husband was missing. My husband (of just a few months) 1577461 Sgt Leslie George Knight flew in a Stirling aircraft as a bomb aimer from Keevil on that fateful night.

They were carrying twenty paratroopers to the Caen area and the Pegasus Bridge, but only twelve paratroopers were dropped

Nothing more was known of the aircraft or its *crew* and the eight paratroopers. After the war I met several of the men who were dropped and they told me the last words they heard from the pilot were, 'Heavy flak coming up.'

Although we were both only nineteen years old we were so happily married and looking forward to our first baby later in the year. At the end of May we had seven days leave together and as we said goodbye at the railway station, his last words, to me were, 'On my next leave we will look for a pram.' These were the last words he ever spoke to me.

Les and I had known each other from school days and after his two elder brothers had volunteered to serve in the RAF and both were killed in raids over Germany we hoped and prayed that Les would be spared.

Our daughter was born in late August 1944 and I named her Lesley in memory of the father she has never known, only seen in photographs. Some happiness did come from that sad time. Lesley married at the age of twenty and had two lovely daughters and they have both made me a very happy great-grandma. Lesley's father's name is on the RAF war memorial at Runnymede, for airmen with no known graves. To explain my signature at the end of this letter, in later years I married for the second time (to another ex-airman) but sadly after six years my husband died from a brain tumour.

Barbara A. Stones, Market Drayton, Shropshire

I was a Lieutenant RNVR in charge of G2 591 Flotilla on an LCA (HR). Our tiny open-decked boat, with its crew of four, butted into the Channel with sturdy purpose. It was dark, we were soaking wet and we hadn't eaten for twenty-four hours. There was a heavy swell and rough seas. It was an unpretentious vessel, low in the gunwhales and flat keeled. It was about the length of a living room and half its width but it somehow gave off an aura of naval heroics. In June 1944 the white ensign was flying bravely from many a strange vessel that went on to perform sterling deeds but the LCT Hedgerow was an exceptional craft which in post-war books on D-Day has largely been disregarded.

It was the smallest of its breed. It carried no defence beyond a Lewis gun but it bristled with armaments. Its task, allotted two days earlier at a briefing meeting, was to get up to the enemy-held beach in Normandy. There, irrespective of opposition, we would pull a switch. That one action would launch a barrage of spigot bombs onto the beach. In theory they would explode on the beach defences and detonate any mines. They would clear away entanglements and leave a safe gap through which troops, tanks and guns could be rushed ashore. It was D-Day, 6 June 1944 and the beach in military parlance was 'Gold'.

We were cold, wet, sick, miserable and hungry and we also knew that we would be the first to arrive at Gold Beach. We would have to launch our fighting action well in advance of the actual start of the invasion, and we would have to do it successfully. Through that gap would pour later that day troops, guns and artillery and supplies of the famed 50th Division composed of men from the East Yorks, Durham Light Infantry, the Green Howards and others. The battles which led the troops inland from Gold and the adjoining beaches of Sword and Juno would in fact represent the outstanding successes of that first day of the invasion. But we didn't know that at the time!

Our arrival was precisely timed. We were due to attack one minute before the rest of the invasion forces rushed ashore. That at least was the theory, and I still think the entire plan a masterstroke of planning genius, particularly landing at half-tide, but even the best laid plans can go awry, and ours did! By midnight the tiny craft – the smallest in the entire operation – were in bad trouble. The towing arrangements were proving abortive and most had cast off to make way under their own steam as best they could. They had already suffered casualties. One of my flotilla had been towed under with the loss of all crew. Another had returned due to a fouled propeller. A companion flotilla fared even worse. Of the nine vessels involved in that

flotilla I don't believe one made it to the beach. It was a rough passage with a vengeance.

I remember flak lighting up the night sky and the sight – oddly enough – was viewed with gratitude! It showed the proximity of land, even if it was enemy held. An aircraft was hit and slowly dropped to earth, a blazing ball of fire. Dawn came and my little fleet passed through the ranks of other ships to take up its allotted place at the front. I remember that the crews of cruisers and battleships, busy firing their guns at distant targets, nevertheless lined the rails of their ships to cheer them on. One had to show a brave front even though we were scared. I certainly was not conscious of the fact that we were on the threshold of any great event. We simply had a job to do and we wanted to get it over with so that we could get out of it!

The beaches appeared – the little boats lined up, lifting and dipping on the rough swell whilst the shells of the British bombardment dipped overhead to land on the shore. Some landed in the water nearby – 'fall shorts' from our own ships. At 'D minus 1', a minute before the official landings were scheduled, I made my run in. I was on time and according to plan although things had gone wrong for so many others. My crew shut themselves in the engine room. I pulled down the cockpit and navigated through slits in the armour plate. The tide was rising. It was just after 7am and there came a bad moment. My friend, Bruce Ashton, in the adjacent boat, was rammed by a following landing craft and went down. He and the entire crew were drowned.

And then it was time. I pulled a switch. My spigot bombs lifted into the air and fell on the beach ahead, exploding satisfactorily. I immediately pulled aside to make way for the following landing craft bearing tanks. I watched as one tank drove ashore up the cleared lane and moved upwards, its mine-exploding flails whirring. Two mines rapidly exploded. And then something odd. There was complete silence. The bombardment had suddenly lifted and there was no enemy response. It was an almost eerie moment. This, I felt, is what it must have been like in World War I in the trenches before an attack went over...

The silence was brief. Suddenly a tank exploded in smoke and flames as it took a direct hit from a German 88mm gun fired from an emplacement. It was all too clear there would be no survivors. A second tank also took a direct hit. Then a third tank moved in and silenced the gun emplacement. Whilst this was happening we were being fired on from a machine gun post just to the east of our landfall. Bullets were splattering the craft but caused no casualties. Another boat with heavier armament got a direct hit on the enemy gunpost and knocked it out. The post, it later transpired, was manned by Poles who had been recruited into the German army.

Twenty minutes had elapsed since the first of the assault troops of the 5th Battalion of the East Yorks Regiment had landed and rushed – many of them to their death – up the beaches. They were met by machine gun fire and shells and I watched, shocked, as one man fell and then stumbled into cover, never to move again. I was only one hundred and fifty yards away from the infantry action and saw how they dashed to a beach wall where German troops suddenly appeared and dropped grenades on them. And then it was time to pull out. It took us around three hours to get to a large landing ship which lay-to about four or five miles offshore. We were winched aboard and for me and my remaining crews, D-Day was effectively over. We had been thirty-six hours without food and were soaked to the skin and bone weary. I fell asleep and was in the Solent when I awoke. I felt we had done our job well, but my thoughts were with the 'pongoes' who were now ashore and fighting. That reminds me. When the Green Howards were issued with French letters as waterproofing for their rifles in the initial assault over the beaches, the general comment was, 'I thought we were to shoot them not f........ them!'

But there was to be one more D-Day experience for me. It was in the sixties and I was standing on the same beach that I had helped 'clear' about twenty years previously. I looked down at the sand and saw a tin helmet with a bullet hole through it. It was queer – it somehow just seemed to rise out of the sand. It was a helmet of the Green Howards who had landed in that sector. It was really quite strange – almost as if it were an act of God!

H. Michael Irwin, Gosforth, Newcastle-on-Tyne

Where does one start in recounting such a momentous day as D-Day? The 27th Armoured Brigade had been part of the 79th Armoured Division otherwise known as the 'Funnies' because of all the unusual tanks and devices, which were experimented on and developed and eventually played such a big part in the success of the invasion. I was in the brigade workshops which played such a big part in the actual development of these Funnies, but that of course is a different thing to D-Day and a completely different story. The 27th Armoured was equipped with DD swimming tanks, which were to be some of the first to land behind the AVREs on Sword Beach near Hermanville. We were to be the first workshops ashore on D-Day in order to keep the tanks in action.

But to start. On 3 June 1944 our unit moved to King George Docks on the River Thames and all our vehicles and equipment were loaded onto an old coal ship which had come down from Newcastle. Talk about being well looked after! We anchored along the coast near Southend, along with many other ships, which gave us a chance to get used to

the type of food we'd have to eat for the next month – Bully beef and some of the hardest biscuits ever made by man! There were also cans of soup, which were heated by lighting a candle set in the middle of the tin. We remained at anchor for two more days.

However we eventually set sail on Tuesday in a very large convoy and as we sailed through the Straits of Dover the Germans opened up with their big guns at Calais. Immediately three destroyers sped alongside the convoy putting up a smokescreen but despite this, three of our ships were sunk. With the dawn, back came our fighter planes and on the shore there were billows of smoke from the fierce fighting and the bombing. As we waited to get ashore there was suddenly a noise like an express train going over our heads and then there was a terrific bang. We learned later that it was one of the battleships further out to sea firing 22-inch shells at some target near Caen. At high tide our ship went full speed for the beach. We were still in about ten feet of water, so we then had to wait for about four hours for the tide to go out. Talk about sitting ducks! I had a three-ton Bedford lorry and was lowered by a crane over the side of the boat into about four feet of water. Very unnerving, especially as you're not quite certain that it is four feet of water you're going into! It took about three hours to get all our vehicles on to the beach and we then formed a convoy and set off to get off the beach as quickly as possible.

After travelling only a few miles we had to all pull onto the verge as the place we had been told to go to was still held by the Germans. One of our convoy just in front of me pulled onto the verge and there was a loud bang as it ran over a mine. The driver was killed instantly and in that same instant the realities of war and what could very well happen to any of us became apparent. We could only bury him at the side of the road and put a wooden cross on his grave so that the Red Cross or someone could arrange for him to be buried properly later. After a short stop we were told to move on and after a few miles we were guided into a field and told to dig a slit trench to sleep in for our own safety. We had only just finished and were getting ready for our can of soup for supper when we were ordered to get back into our vehicles immediately and pull out. This was all getting beyond a joke! Apparently the Germans were only three hundred yards away on the other side of a slight rise in the ground.

Driving without lights, dog tired from lack of sleep, our despatch riders guided us back almost to Hermanville, where we had started out from. We pulled into a field which was to be our base for the next two weeks. There we had to start work immediately on repairing tanks and other vehicles. I had a crew of five on my Bedford truck and early next morning we had to go down to the café on Hermanville beach. One of the Sherman tanks had hit a mine and finished up only twenty yards from the café. We had to get a bogie and track plates off a damaged tank that had been dragged into the vehicle 'graveyard' that had already been formed just off the beach. Five hours' hard graft and the tank was back in action.

The next few days were busy, repairing damaged tanks and vehicles of all sorts but work slowed down alarmingly for a few days when the whole of our unit spent most of the time sitting on a long wooden pole over a cesspit! The water we had been drinking was found to be contaminated and we all had acute diarrhoea. One day as I walked past a farmyard with dead cows lying bloated on the ground with their legs in the air, I came to a Bofors gun site. Sitting there in the gun-seat was my younger brother! I hadn't seen him for three years and we had quite a long chat. Suddenly two

Messerschmitt fighter planes came roaring in low over us and before I could blink he was firing away like hell at them. I didn't see him again for over two years until we were both demobbed.

As the Germans retreated we set up a new brigade workshop. I was given the task of repairing one of our DD tanks that had run over a mine. I took my crew to it in a field and found that the bottom of the radiator had been badly damaged. I was told to get it repaired as quickly as possible as it was one of only four in the 13th/18th Hussars Regiment that was equipped with a seventeen-pounder gun and was desperately needed at the front. We worked like hell until dark getting the engine out under appalling conditions. Apart from anything else we had to get the armour plating off that had been bent in the blast. It was so urgent that we had intended to sleep under the truck but after we'd finished supper the Germans started shelling and hit an ammunition dump in the next field to us. Ammunition was exploding everywhere so we spent a pretty sleepless night in the ditch! The next day, worn out, we had to go back to the tank graveyard to remove another engine complete with a good radiator and then get it back to the field. It took another two days of hard work to get the job done.

Back at base I dug myself a slit trench near my vehicle and covered it with the armour plating off the old tank and then soil on top. I was soon very glad that I'd done it. As night began to fall the six of us sat in the back of our truck enjoying our supper of soup and biscuits. Then without warning we heard the sound of a plane diving and bombs falling and with cans of soup and biscuits flying everywhere we dived out of the truck and into our slit trenches. Seconds later the bombs exploded only twenty feet away and the side of our truck was peppered with shrapnel holes where we had been sitting only seconds before. Three of our unit were seriously injured.

The very next afternoon we saw an American Boston

bomber flying round and round our base in a circle, and then we saw the crew bale out. The plane flew in the same circle for, amazingly, almost twenty minutes and then it started to stall. Then the engines picked it up again and we all stood there watching as it dropped and climbed and dropped and climbed in a fixed circle getting lower and lower all the time. We were all worried sick where it would drop – there was nothing we could do about it. Then it came down in the next field in a ball of flame.

Two days later I was working on a tank with a fellow staff-sergeant when the time came to get back to the cook-house for dinner. As we walked across the field the Germans started shelling our base and so I dived to the left to my trench and he dived to the right to his place. I'm sorry to say he didn't make it and he was one of three of our unit that died that day. I remember thinking, 'There but for the Grace of God...' and somehow it didn't seem fair that I should survive and he should be killed. But it was then decided 'higher up' that we were too close to the front line for a base unit and so we were moved back. We were still only four miles from Caen but at least we were out of shelling range for the first time since we'd landed. Shortly afterwards we had the best meal since we'd landed as well. One of my crew, a lad from Liverpool, found a plot with carrots and potatoes growing and he made us a super dinner, to the envy of the other crews!

A Churchill tank Crocodile (a flame thrower) was knocked out in the middle of a field not far from Caen and orders came through that the tank and its trailer must not be allowed to fall into German hands at any cost. A battle went on for two weeks with the Germans trying to get to it, and our lads determined they wouldn't. After a five hundred bomber raid one night our lads were able to get it back, but first it had to be sprayed with disinfectant as the crew inside had been dead for that time.

At seventy-seven my memories of things perhaps aren't as

good as they used to be but my story does show the day-to-day difficulties that everyone encountered, and future generations will then perhaps realise what thousands of young lads went through. I'll never forget all my pals.

John Wall, Loughborough, Leicestershire

101 Squadron was a special squadron. Flying Lancasters, they carried the most secret wireless equipment and an extra crew member. In FS Hopes' crew I was that extra man.

Our job was to listen out to German fighter control and interfere with any instructions after identifying the language as German. With the aid of three powerful transmitters we were able to jam three frequencies within thirty seconds. The whole undertaking was known as AIR BORNE CIGAR, or ABC – that made it easy.

It appeared that whilst training to be a signaller (air) at Madley, near Hereford, I had let slip to my flight sergeant that, before joining the RAF, I had had half a dozen lessons in German. I finished the signallers course and was awarded my brevet and sergeant stripes in April. Four days later I found myself attached to No. 1 LFS (Lancaster Finishing School) at Hemswell. There I met three other newly promoted aircrew sergeants, all as mystified as I was. The next day the four of us assembled in a hut with a flight sergeant instructor. 'Through that door,' he said, 'is something top secret. If you go through you will commit yourself to going on operations. If you wish to withdraw now, you may, and will not be considered LMF.' Needless to say, none of us did. So the mysteries of ABC were revealed to us. I was the only one of the four to survive a tour of thirty operations.

There followed about ten hours flying to familiarise us with Lancasters. On 17 May I arrived at Ludford. On the 18th I was crewed. On the 19th and 20th I completed squadron training. 21 May was my birthday and on the 23rd my commission came through. I, at last, got my leave, during which I was fitted out with my officer's uniform.

By 30 May I was back at Ludford; and on the night of 1 or 2 June 1944, at the age of nineteen I went to war.

5 June 1944 found me a veteran: I had survived two bombing operations. The first was against Berneval-le-Grand and the second was on the night 4/5 June against a gun emplacement at Sangatte. This was part of the softening up and diversionary tactics prior to the great assault on the European mainland. Returning, we found it impossible to land at base. We landed at another 1 Group airfield... Faldingworth. This meant that preparations for operations 5/6 June took place away from our prying eyes.

Rumours flew thick and fast. Eventually, some sort of truth began to emerge. There was to be an abnormally high fuel load. But what of the bomb load? And I was on the battle order. Two nights running... Ah well!

At briefing, all was revealed. There were to be no bombs. The purpose of the trip was to carry us over enemy occupied territory in order to interfere with radio communications. Twenty-four crews from Ludford were to fly over an area Beachy Head to Dungeness, then across Northern France along the line of the Somme, a dog leg towards Paris, then back along the line of the Seine. We flew over this area many times during the night and into the early hours of 6 June. Apart from concentrated jamming, the intention was to give the Germans the impression that this was a gigantic bomber stream. We learned afterwards that the Luftwaffe had put most of its fighters among us, only to find, because of our action, it was impossible to give clear instructions to their crews. All was confusion. The result of this

was that the airborne troops, spearheading the main attack on Normandy, were able to get through with casualties far lower than had been expected.

After seven hours in the dim light of our equipment, listening to the chatter and to the wailing note of our jammers, we returned home and crawled into bed, still unaware of the importance of the day.

In the short space of time from 29 April to 6 June I was trained in the use of ABC, commissioned, crewed, been on leave and taken part in three operations; one of which was probably the greatest in the history of warfare. I was involved in a highly secret, sensitive operation requiring a knowledge of the enemy's language, yet nobody had tested my proficiency in German.

Ron Crafer, Swindon, Wiltshire

Day after day, night after night, we'd rehearsed our role for D-Day. On moonlit nights when every man, every vehicle, was silhouetted against the backdrop of the silvered sky: on Stygian nights of impenetrable darkness, when a vehicle three paces in front suddenly disappeared at five paces. Rehearsals were practised under all and every condition, sometimes in silence, when the only sound was the click of a bolt as a live round was rammed home. Yes, absolute realism was essential. Month after month we practised to the state of exhaustion so that every detail, every movement, every tactic could be done automatically, without thinking, in our sleep: in fact many rehearsals were done in our sleep, when exhaustion overwhelmed us. We were all impatient for the word 'Go!' We'd trained to the peak of perfection – we were ready. When we left, as it happened we passed by my wife's house, en route for embarkation. I kept my eyes front as we passed: I couldn't trust myself to look.

The night was pitch-black; rain slanted down hissing into the turbulent, foam flecked sea. The LCT with our 3 Division badge painted on its funnel wallowed its way through the sea. After several false alarms we were on our way to the Normandy beaches.

There was not a glimmer of light anywhere; it was impossible to see where the lowering sky ended and the sea began. Men whispered together – one wondered why, out here in the middle of the Channel? Perhaps because of the secrecy of the whole invasion we were reluctant to disclose our whereabouts by 'idle talk'! No smoking was a strict order to be obeyed, but it made a fag all the more desirable.

We were in the last boat but one in our echelon, on the extreme left flank of the convoy, destined for Sword Queen Red Beach, the furthest spot on the left of the whole invasion force. The skipper's aim was to put us down alongside the Orne canal east of Ouistreham. The boat behind us was the rescue launch: in front of us was an LCT loaded with lorries carrying fuel oil and all the other paraphernalia of modern warfare. We were loaded with composite loads of ammunition for direct supply to forward troops of 185 Bde on D-Night. It was comforting to know the rescue launch was so close in spite of the explicit order we were given before sailing from Portsmouth Hard: 'On no account will any craft stop to pick up survivors.'

We ploughed our way on through the night. Suddenly, without warning, all hell was let loose! The sound was as if some giant's hand had torn a large canvas sheet asunder, to be followed by a blinding flash of orange and white light as the LCT in front of us seemed to be lifted out of the water, throwing the vehicles and other equipment like children's toys into the air, before they cascaded down into the water. From a pitch-black night it had suddenly turned into an aurora borealis of light: a rich orange colour with the stark silhouettes of human Catherine Wheels hurled into the sky against the tremulous motion of the streams of light. The horrendous screams, torn from the shattered bodies, penetrated our eardrums, etching seared scars in our minds to

return in the silent nights of
future years. I shall never forget.
Black evil-smelling diesel oil
poured out over the sea – men
frantically calling out for help
from this turgid mass through
which we passed.

Just as our paralysed minds
and bodies were recovering from
the shock of the explosion,
another cataclysmic explosive
detonation came from our rear. The rescue launch disappeared skywards to rain down as a million disembowelled
parts a few seconds later.

Were we next? Against orders our skipper hove-to; a boat
was lowered. It rescued as many survivors as possible before
the boat was ordered to return. These battered, bemused,
shattered men: still covered in the thick clinging oil, which
had so polluted the area with its stench that men on our boat
were vomiting over the side. The poor devils, snatched from
the sea, had swallowed this obscene oily liquid: it was in
their lungs, their stomachs. Violent retches wracked their
bodies as they made vain attempts to free themselves of this
nauseous, loathsome liquid. They were covered in blankets
and made as comfortable as possible. We gave them what
succour we could: there was so little we could do.

The skipper gave the order to 'go ahead'. I looked over the
side. We were alone, so alone. I knew how the ancient
mariner must have felt, 'Alone, on a wide, wide sea!' From
the darkness ahead, miles ahead or so it seemed, appeared
flashes, rather like sheet lightning on a midsummer's night.
But we were alone, nakedly alone.

Out of the dim shadows a ghost-like shape appeared: fea-
tureless, unidentifiable: menacingly it approached. Were we
to be the next casualties? The memory of the two craft so
recently destroyed was too immediate, too vivid in our mem-

ories not to cause us to catch our breath. An apprehensive shiver ran through our bodies as the prow of the boat sliced through the water towards us. Was it going to ram us? Suddenly the grey shape veered to our rear and a calm voice came over the Tannoy. 'I say, you're way behind the convoy... Press on; we'll stay with you until you catch up.'

So it did. The Royal Navy destroyer escorted us like a sheepdog shepherding a stray back into the fold, just as I'd seen so often on our Cotswold farm.

What a relief! We didn't know we'd all been holding our breath until we released it together. Our landing on D+ seemed uneventful by comparison, or so we thought! I was soon to be disillusioned; but that's another story.

Story sent in by Tim East, New Costessey, Norwich,
on behalf of his father Major 'Tiger Tim' R. T. East,
172 Infantry Brigade

In 1944 I was a member of A Company, 9th Parachute Battalion of the 3rd Parachute Brigade, 6th Airborne Division. Our job was to silence the coastal battery of four guns at Merville about a mile inland and to the south-east of Ouistreham on the Normandy coast. The battalion was sealed off in a camp next to the airfield of Broadwell in Oxfordshire and on the evening of 5 June we took off at 11:15pm in thirty-two Dakotas of 512 Squadron. I well remember sitting on the floor of the aircraft loaded with fifty-six pounds of equipment and parachute. There were metal seats running down each side of the Dakota, but it was easier to sit on the floor and rest the parachute on the seat. More comfortable too!

I was to jump No. 1 from our stick of twenty men, so I was sitting close to the open door on the port side. Our arrival over the drop zone was to be 00:50am on 6 June at five hundred feet. I sat there thinking of Mum and Dad all the time. After all I was only twenty years old as were most of the lads in the battalion. As my home was in Sussex I also wondered if the noise of our planes passing overhead would wake them. What a stupid trivial thought but I found out later that it did!

The RAF dispatcher passed round the food – would you believe it a box of jam sandwiches! The condemned man's last meal it seemed. With five minutes to go we were standing and ready hooked up, each man checking the man in front to make sure his static line was fixed properly to the wire running down the roof of the aircraft. The atmosphere became electric.

'Stand to the door,' came the shout from the stick commander, which meant me! I moved to the open doorway, feet on the floor edge, hands gripping each side of the opening. For a second I looked down and all I could see in the moonlight was water. I then looked up to the red jump light above the door. When it turned green it was time to go. This then was the moment of truth – what our training and fitness was all about.

I remember that just as the green light came on there was an almighty bang outside the aircraft causing it to drop downwards and flinging me out of the door at the same instant, whether I wanted to go or not! My head hit something, probably the tail plane, knocking off my helmet. My chute opened and although dazed I was somehow conscious of floating in the darkness. I could still see masses of water below me but then seemingly within seconds I was on the ground and scrambling out of my harness.

I had a 2-inch mortar and bombs plus a Sten gun and so having no helmet I shoved on my red beret and there I was, ready now for war! All the fears and feelings I had felt in the aircraft had gone. I was positively raring to go! We had landed in the right place and so I made for the rendezvous point. I was one of the lucky ones – sadly only one hundred and fifty men out of the original six hundred and fifty arrived at the checkpoint. Quite a large number, burdened down with equipment and caught up in their parachutes,

had drowned in the water I had seen.
Apparently this was the River Dives,
which had been flooded by the
Germans.

The commanding officer decided
to advance – it was about one and a
half miles to the battery perimeter, a
journey full of bomb craters and dead
cattle from the attentions of the RAF.
We should have had seven Horsa

glider loads of heavy equipment but not one turned up in the
drop zone. Also three Horsas with sixty men of 9th Para,
were supposed to crash land inside the battery to support us
as we came in from the outside. We were still awaiting them!
I lay near the cattle fence, which was the outer perimeter of
the battery defences. My original job had been to be in a firm
point as reserve, but now as there were only one hundred
and fifty of us this was all changed. Major Parry, Officer
Commanding of A Company tapped me on the shoulder.
'You're with me, he said. 'No. 1 Gun.' At that moment two
of the gliders appeared over our heads. One broke away and
disappeared. The other seemed to be waiting for us to fire
star bombs from the 3-inch mortars, but we couldn't. This
was the equipment we had lost!

Then it happened. I shall never forget the sight as in the
moonlight he was hit by anti-aircraft fire from the battery.
Trailing white smoke the glider actually touched down inside
the battery but going too fast he pulled up, whistling over
our heads to crash only a few yards away. I don't know if
anyone survived because at that moment the wires of the
inner fence were blown and with shouts and cries and a few
curses as well we charged after Major Parry over the minefield, through the gap blown in the wire and straight for the
guns just as fast as we could. I found myself spending half
the time running up and down bomb craters also made by
the RAF in earlier raids and I expect my mates were having

the same problem! I saw Major Parry go down and several of my pals hit as they charged forward.

There was a machine gun pit which suddenly appeared in front of me almost without warning and two men scrambling out shouting 'paratrooper, paratrooper' and I remember thinking for a second that it was some of our men who were missing and had arrived late. I don't know why I thought that but it flashed through my mind and then I realised that they were Germans who had recognised us and were getting out quick!

They disappeared into the darkness and then I reached the massive casemate of No. 1 Gun. I dived in through the open rear doors and much to my relief I can tell you found some of our lads already there. Perhaps they could run up and down bomb craters quicker than me! We dropped grenades down the air vent, shot up the German soldiers we found in one room – no time for niceties – and came to the front of the casement to find the gun. It was much smaller than expected – 100mm instead of 150mm. We only had Gammon bombs (plastic explosive) to damage them. Major Parry, wounded, had by this time arrived and ordered the gun to be blown. We set up the explosive and then we were ordered outside and I curled up beside a wall. There was an enormous bang and smoke came curling out of the doorways. Following up we took just over twenty prisoners, some of them still in a state of undress having been asleep inside.

Now we had to get out. Not so easy as there were still minefields all around and already quite a few of our lads had been killed or wounded by them on the way in. Then someone had the idea of marching the prisoners in front! So that's what we did, with protests from them! But we were in no mood to listen and with a bit of prodding and a lot of luck we got outside with no more mines going off.

So we had done it! We then moved to our rendezvous point at a Calvary to the south of the battery. A count of fit men was taken and there were sixty-five of us on our feet.

The rest were either killed or wounded. The time was 05:30am on Tuesday 6 June 1944. Dawn was now upon us, the early morning mist rising from the fields. Not many hours before, only six hours in fact, six hundred and fifty men of 9th Para, had boarded their planes for France. Now we survivors marched off to further battles. We were sad at our lost pals but proud of what we had done.

Frederick G. Milward, Hastings, Sussex

I was a corporal in 44 Royal Marine Commando and when I was to later wander around the war graves area, my mind pondered the question of the twenty-four hour postponement of the intended D-Day. 'Who now lay dead ... may well have survived ... a quirk of fate that was perhaps to see myself a SURVIVOR?'

On the night of 4 June I was told to 'stand by' (I was a cox'n of LCM landing craft'). Rumour abounded. Some said, 'It's cancelled,' many were busy writing the 'final letters' home, some even 'in prayer' with the padre. But all in deep contemplation.

No official word was forthcoming as to the twenty-four hour postponement.

In the twilight of Monday 5 June 1944 we sailed – still no word of our destination. It wasn't till we were well across the Channel we were eventually told, 'You're going to NORMANDY.' Nearing the French coast, and, by now actually manning my landing craft... two words can only describe the sight and sound: Dante's Inferno

My orders? Keep in line, should you see any survivors in the water, don't stop and keep a sharp look out for underwater obstacles. Engines throbbing and each moment nearing our targeted beach. The gunfire of the huge battleships, the bombing, the explosions of little landing craft, caught in the underwater obstacles, even cries of 'help me' etc., from drowning personnel. All hell let loose!

Call it luck or was it my steering clear? No doubt credit to the training I received, for eventually I did touch down – albeit later than expected with a load of precious cargo of supplies. No sooner unloaded than a beachmaster told me to report back to get further supplies. This was to continue for many runs to the beaches of Courselles-sur-Mer (Juno Beach).

One occasion, I chanced to see lying nearby an obviously seriously wounded soldier, clinging to a broken hulk of a blown up landing craft; I warily went to him. It was now known that snipers were very active in a nearby church spire of the parish church of Bernière-sur-Mer. His ashen face said it all; blood oozing from a chest wound. I held his hand. 'Speak to me corporal. Am I going to be OK?' He asked.

'I can't,' I said, my own eyes misting over. Suddenly I said, 'We've got the Jerries running son.' He couldn't have been but twenty years old (I was twenty-five). He died minutes after. I ofttimes think of that lad; dying like that is not like one sees in a John Wayne film – nor even a *Rambo* film.

But there were amusing incidents. On 7 June, D-Plus One, still running my little landing craft to and from the Mulberry [harbour] I saw, having beached once more, a group of German prisoners being escorted. One looked at me, and said, 'F...... hell! They've got Errol Flynn with them.' He was very fluent in his use of English, I must say. I smiled and gave him our 'V' sign.

Another very notable experience was whilst engaged in supplying the beachhead. I got into difficulties and found my little craft in danger of drifting into possible minefield area etc. and broadside on, thus in danger of overturning, not only with our precious supplies, but, putting myself and my little crew of three marines into Davy Jones' Locker. Imagine my amazement when from nowhere came a small Royal Navy vessel and the very willing hands that pulled me inboard were two of my own hometown pals of peacetime days. Able seamen Boniface and stoker Jones, both two very great pals of mine. Can you imagine the odds against that occurring in the huge armada of shipping involved?

I never saw stoker Jones ever again and it was with a sad heart that I attended the funeral of my dear friend A. B. Boniface in November 1991.

Tom Roberts, Bebington, Cheshire

It was a wet morning one day in June 1944 when we drove out of our barracks in Aldershot. We made our way to what turned out to be Tilbury docks where our group boarded two American liberty ships. Artillery guns, AEC truck, three ton lorries, fifteen-cwt [hundredweight] wireless cars, Bren carriers, Jeeps, half-tracks – they all went up the ramps! The vehicles and equipment went in first – reversed up. Then the men to find spaces below deck! I was a sergeant in the Royal Artillery and allowed on deck.

When our time came to land the captain ran the ship into shallow water and lowered the ramp. Now I realised why the vehicles had been reversed into the ships hold. They were now ready to drive off head-first. The first vehicle down the ramp was a Bedford three-tonner, which promptly vanished in deep water! Apparently the ramp had been lowered on the edge of a bomb or mine crater. So the captain re-sited the ramp and ordered the next vehicle off. Sad to say no one was in a hurry to follow the fate of the Bedford! There were no John Waynes among us –we were butchers, carpenters, painters and rent collectors. Reluctant heroes you might say. 'I'll shoot the next bastard who refuses my orders,' the captain bellowed as he drew his revolver and fired into the sky. So with mixed feelings and prayers on our lips we drove down that awful ramp and onto the beach of Normandy. Our training was now about to be put to the test. 'Dig yourselves in,' we were told and my four cable-laying signallers and myself dug a trench about twelve-foot long and two-foot deep. Should be adequate. The German shells came over and we promptly went down a few more feet! More shells – more digging. By the following morning we had steps to get in and out. A plane circled our position. 'One of ours,' I said. There was a burst of machine gunfire as the pilot mistook us for the enemy and we all dived for cover. We were learning fast. But many didn't get the chance.

I shall forever remember those simple wooden crosses at the beaches. There were no names – only numbers. One NCO and twelve men of the KSLI. Four men of the Lanes Fusiliers. Two NCOs and six men of the Royal Marines. There were so many buried where they had fallen. Left behind of necessity by their advancing comrades. A sight that brought a particular lump to my throat was of an American glider, which had evidently lost its bearings as it shouldn't have been in our sector. It had got caught in overhead wires and nose-dived with terrific force into a grassy bank. All the crew were still inside including one man still sitting in a Jeep, his hands on the steering wheel ready to drive off should the landing have been successful. The force of the impact had shot the Jeep to the front of the glider, causing it to double up and trapping

the driver between the steering wheel and the folded back of the vehicle. The sad part of it was that on the side of the glider in big white letters was the message 'Home – via Berlin' and 'Don't worry Mom

– we'll be back'. I read those words over and over again and looked at the lifeless bodies inside; young men who had died without firing a shot.

In another location in what remained of a small cottage and orchard were the scattered remains of a fighter plane. The pilot's torso was in what was left of an apple tree and on the ground amongst the debris was a flying boot with part of a leg still inside. Everywhere I went there was carnage. A Sherman tank with a hole a little bigger than a cricket ball in the turret – evidence of where an armour-piercing shell fired from a German 88mm gun on a Tiger tank had found its mark, killing the crew. I still picture our battery commander, a major only twenty-three years of age, shot through his steel helmet by a sniper whilst standing in the turret of his tank directing fire into enemy positions. A small wooden cross at the roadside with his helmet and khaki scarf wrapped round it marking just how far he had advanced into Normandy before he made the supreme sacrifice.

The battle had in fact only just begun. We still had a long way to go, and throughout there was a constant prayer on our lips.

Harry 'Bombardier H' Hartill, Rhydyfelin, Pontypridd

When I joined the ATS in January 1940 I was not yet eighteen and totally fluent in German. I was assured then that full use would be made of my qualifications and skills (which included a Teaching Diploma) but it was not so. It took a long time to realise that a male 'closed shop' operated. We learned about gun-laying radar and then we were posted to Greenford, Middlesex where the first dozen or so girls to qualify were trained in actually repairing radar equipment. The standards and responsibility required were tremendously high.

Despite all this there was still considerable male chauvinism. Despite my qualifications and practical experience when I was posted to Swansea to the Royal Electrical and Mechanical Engineers, I was greeted by the major with the friendly words, 'They'll be sending us monkeys next.' What a thing to say! Then another officer actually made us remove our trade and profession badges with the words, 'You couldn't have actually earned them.' But we showed in our work and exam results that we were as well trained and qualified as the men and soon, I am happy to say, our badges were restored. But it may be interesting for people to know some of the attitudes that were adopted.

To be fair that wasn't always the case – we girls mixed with men from all sorts of backgrounds, including deprived homes and prisons, and they were great to us. They never used bad language in front of us and from them we experienced chivalry and companionship of an order, which would be quite impossible today. Anyway, back on to D-Day!

By May 1944 I was helping to perfect the servicing of the radar that would be used in the later stages of the battles in Normandy and I had recently been posted to Gopsall Hall near Twycross in Leicestershire. That would be about two weeks before D-Day. We had briefings on the new Westinghouse generators, which were worlds in advance of our diesel generators. Our old diesels were huge, required priming, and often needed six people on a rope round the starting handle in cold weather! Not much fun! But our main job was modifying the old Army WT17 backpack radio sets by adding Rhomboid aerials in order to extend their range to about two hundred and fifty miles.

After days of concentrated briefings and training we started the first complete practical tests, by coincidence on 6 June. Suddenly as we carried out the tests we heard clearly and distinctly the voices of British soldiers as if they were in the middle of a furious battle. We were hearing a lot of the background communications and appraisal from street fighting in the vicinity of Caen. But the full realisation only came when someone remarked that they were speaking en

clair with confidence and sureness. Significant parts of the British Forces battle communications in Normandy were there in our ears in Leicestershire and we were all transfixed with disbelief. The urgency and reality of the battle situation rang out so clearly it was as if we were there with the troops, and I have never forgotten those magical moments that were so unexpected and unique.

So much was encapsulated in mere words and sounds that spoke of the horrors of battle. We continued to listen and although we tried to work the atmosphere became more and more subdued as we all silently came to terms with the reality of how those words and sounds would be translated into deaths and wounded. In an effort to 'lift' things some of us wandered around and talked about 'after the war' because we were all sure it would be over soon now. But three of our girls in the ATS had husbands who were prisoners of war and cried with a mixture of relief and fear of what could yet happen. Personally I remember I could not even begin to visualise the return of my husband and three brothers so I understood how they felt. By lights out on D-Day there was total silence but the seeds had been sown for most of us looking forward to being human beings again.

Mary Drake, Norwich, Norfolk

I was with a small Royal Engineers works section attached to the Third Infantry Division. We were timed to land at Sword Beach at 8am, and as the light grew stronger we became aware of the immense scale of the operation – there were landing craft as far as the eye could see, and several naval support vessels, around frigate size were buzzing around.

Around 6am we were about two miles offshore and the game was obviously in progress. Just out of view to the east was the large port of Le Havre, but a number of German gun batteries were visibly blasting away at us from this direction. The first landings, which had been preceded by the para-troopers, were in progress on Sword and Juno beaches, but vicious small arms and artillery fire was coming from many of the bungalows and buildings above the beaches. The Navy were heavily involved and their smaller craft went quite close in and blasted the buildings involved – one could see tracer shells going clean through some of the buildings. A large battle cruiser, rumoured to be the Ramillies, stood further out firing 15-inch shells over our heads, and her attention was then concentrated on to the enemy batteries near Le Havre with telling effect.

The German airforce then reminded us that they were still in business as a squadron of bombers flew parallel to the beaches at low level and unloaded bombs. These were the first enemy planes we had seen but were not to be the last. But the RAF usually appeared to have monopoly in the air, and we had seen many of our fighters.

As the shelling from Le Havre reduced we prepared to land. Our landing craft grounded on a rather steep section of beach and the ramp was lowered. I had my engine running and drove off the ramp and thud! We had landed but in about two feet of water, and stumbled on for a few yards before the engine spluttered to a halt. We jumped out to inspect the problem but an RASC beach officer bawled out, 'Leave it, we'll tow you off, get out of the landing area,' and I then saw that a number of vehicles were in the same plight. Drowned, as we called it and awaiting tow, so we then contacted our officers near the sea wall and they had better luck with their vehicle, a four-wheel drive Jeep. The remainder of our unit had waded ashore and we were a complete technical unit of around fifteen officers, NCOs and sappers.

The truck has been towed clear, with a tracked vehicle, and I stripped off the waterproofing materials and dried off plugs, leads etc. It appeared the ramp had not properly beached due perhaps to catching one of the many obstructions kindly left by the enemy, and my truck had dropped almost 12 inches off the ramp and displaced the seals. I was thankful when it started and we followed our officers off the beach, and I saw a street sign marked Le Brèche d'Hermanville. As we moved cautiously through the village, my attention was drawn to a lady waving near a cottage gate and I stopped. She did not understand my poor French but clearly wanted me to go inside. I had no time for niceties, but her face was grave and inside I found a dead officer, shot through the head. He had headed the initial assault earlier that morning and had crawled into the cottage to die. She wanted me to arrange the brave man's burial and as we had a Pioneer Corps section attached to our group I therefore informed Captain Josey and this was done together with that of several other brave lads who had given all.

We were then encouraged to see a few groups of German prisoners being marched off under the supervision of British soldiers to compounds prepared for them. Apart from these and our own units now moving through the village in large numbers, as heavier transport and armoured vehicles were landed, we saw nobody. Civilians were 'keeping their heads down' and I saw no welcome committees, as we moved into a small farmyard to regroup and receive instructions. We were warned that a German counter-attack was likely, as our forward troops had not taken Caen, and were in fact about two miles away. On our west flank near the village of Douvres-la-Délivrande, a well-equipped German fortress guarded by a massive concrete wall, and armed with a full range of artillery and ammunition held out against all our attacks. They were to dominate the road to Caen for a few days, until a monitor, which I understand was the HMS

Warspite, standing just offshore, bombarded them continuously for almost two days with their maximum firepower of 15-inch shells. We were instructed to dig slit trenches for cover, and prepare to stay overnight, and we dug ourselves trenches in a mole-ridden paddock. In the adjoining field was our attached field company RE, about two hundred and fifty strong, also digging themselves in. Around 2pm we opened our ration packs, and I vaguely remember chocolate, beans and soup.

During the day we had seen several groups of British fighter planes, but few German planes since the morning raid, but we had a sharp reminder that they were still in business. Around 4pm a squadron of twin-engine bombers zoomed low across the fields, and as they unloaded and the string of explosions came nearer I screwed up in my trench, face down with helmet on the back of my head. The last bomb had exploded just through the hedge and I knew there would be casualties in the next field, but we were not permitted to get involved and were warned not to discuss casualties with anyone. One of our jobs would be to supervise road repairs near the Pegasus Bridge approaches, and this was a continuous job due to bomb, shell, and persistent mortar fire from German positions just beyond the tiny bridgehead. We were also to be involved with repair and improvement to the third lateral, which was a posh name for the narrow coast road linking Hermanville with Lion-sur-Mer. I was to be involved with a check on water supplies of which large concrete water towers were a feature, but most of them had the legs blown off or large shell holes through the reservoirs. Our discussions were sharply disturbed by the rhythmic explosions of mortar bombs as they exploded nearby. These became more intensive and nerve-racking, and continued for more than one hour, so we took to our dugouts.

The mortaring continued intermittently after dusk and seemed concentrated just south of our position and we prayed they were perhaps just out of range as we lay on our blankets unable to sleep.

So ended D-Day for 205 Works Section RE – a long nerve-racking day which had started after midnight, and we thanked God we had no casualties and looked forward to doing useful work on D-plus one.

Eric Saywell, Fiskerton, Nottinghamshire

In June 1940 I was Signal Platoon Sergeant in the 4th Battalion The Border Regiment and on the 10th we were all encircled by the German armour at Fécamp. Half the battalion got away to Le Havre, and half were taken prisoner, except me. I was walking down the N138 towards Saintes when I was taken in by Monsieur Huby's father and mother. They sent me to their son's place in Verneusses 'for a few days'. I stayed until I was repatriated in October 1944!

The village of Verneusses where I found shelter with the Huby family is to be found just south of the main N138 road between Bernay and Gacé. It had between two hundred and three hundred inhabitants. In 1944 there were five of us – the mother, Marie-Louise aged forty-five, Pierre the father aged thirty-nine, Yvette the daughter aged thirteen, Jean the son aged two years and myself. Monsieur Huby had a well-equipped workshop and was variously the village carpenter, joiner, undertaker, wheelwright, cartwright and sometime blacksmith. Usually there were three or four of us in the workshop.

In 1942 there was a faint glimmer of hope that an invasion would take place, to be reinforced during the spring and summer of 1943. But by 1944 the French were convinced that it was inevitable to happen at any time now. The Allied preparations for such could not be totally camouflaged, either in the aerial attacks on the Atlantic Wall, the marshalling yards, communications or the heavy bombardment of German cities.

The situation throughout the village was worrying, even thought I had been there four years. Several people knew my nationality, some were suspicious and apparently all the kids at school knew I was an Englishman! German troops had frequently occupied the village, and indeed in previous years had even used the workshop. But in 1944 they were hardly ever away and during July several were actually billeted in Monsieur Huby's house. There was, to say the least, a mounting tension and increasing nervousness!

On the night of 5 June 1944 I went to bed in a neighbour's house but later than usual. The old lady would have been asleep. It would have been about 11pm when I quietly climbed the stairs and stretched out in the soft feather bed. I propped my head up on an extra pillow in order to listen more clearly to a bombardment taking place. I guessed about thirty miles away towards the coast. They always seemed to last about twenty minutes. Then there would be the usual inky black silence broken occasionally by the barking of a dog, and then I would sink down into the bed and sleep. This night however was different.

The house shook slightly, the windows rattled, and even the panes of glass vibrated. It must be heavy stuff I thought. It might even be naval broadsides. Whatever it was, it was music in my ears! Long gone were the depressing days of September 1940 when I had counted seven hundred and fifty German bombers passing overhead on their way to London. Recently I had seen happier sights – one thousand five hundred Fortresses in broad daylight flying eastwards! Waves of one thousand had become almost a common sight. I gradually realised that the usual twenty minutes were up, and it was still going on. I became excited.

Midnight struck and still the windows rattled! It was well after 1am when things quietened down and I dropped off to sleep.

Although I had gone to bed later, I was still up at my usual time of 06:30am. I walked through the village, along the cemetery to the workshop. The misty sky was very low. The village was silent. There was nobody about. I was determined not to build up hope only to be disappointed, when the first news came through. Unexpectedly a fighter plane had banked low over the village. Turned a full circle and left in a northerly direction. This had never happened before. I felt that something might be going on. Can anyone imagine what the invasion meant to me and the Huby's? The culmination of those years of nagging stomach-turning worry. The possibility, however remote, of my returning to my family in Carlisle once again.

'What a night,' exclaimed Monsieur Huby, 'Do you think it could be the landing?' Not wishing to build up too much hope I simply said, 'Something special is going on,' and I told him about the plane I had just seen but had been unable to recognise. After breakfast I went to work with the others. It was now 7am; Monsieur Huby turned on the radio. Nothing. It was too early for the BBC news.

At the workshop René Beautier, the young hand, related that the Germans from the Tremblay Chateau, usually so  quiet, were assembled already for leaving. From the village came the news that the Germans in Villers-en-Ouche, with tears in their eyes, had left quickly in the direction of the coast. It was now quite obvious that something was happening, but what? Every half hour the by now overexcited men left the workshop to get the latest news. Still no mention of anything special. I tried to remain as calm as possible and got on with my job.

I was using the planing machine with deliberate slowness, alone in the workshop, trying to keep my mind on the job when it finally happened. The others had just gone once again to listen to the BBC. It was 11am plus a few seconds. Abruptly, a voice in the courtyard. It was Madame Huby.

'Jean ... quickly ... they have come ... they have landed!'

She was all excited. Who wouldn't be! What a precious moment. The culmination of four years of anxiety and waiting. Marie-Louise served us real coffee and as an extra celebration we drank the mature Calvados! We all shook hands and embraced. What a delectable moment.

'No more work today,' decreed Monsieur Huby! That about said it all!

PS Incidentally, Pierre Huby and I were awarded the Medal of Freedom by the Americans for saving fourteen aircrew who had been shot down, five of whom returned to duty via Spain and Gibraltar.

John D. Vallely, Carlisle, Cumbria

Many stories have been told of D-Day and many more photos published of the event. All portray strapping six-foot commando types rushing up beaches armed to the teeth, determined to dislodge an enemy deeply entrenched and equally determined to defend their position at all costs.

But was it really like that?

What about the many ordinary blokes, who make up the majority in all crowd scenes? After all there was a crowd! Hundreds of ordinary blokes all carrying out their orders to the best of their abilities. This is the story of one of them. A

Driver in 231 Brigade, 50th Northumbrian Division who, after four long years of very active service, had risen to the dizzy rank of corporal.

First on our barge was a Bofors gun, carriage and crew, then a Bren gun carrier and crew, two Sherman tanks and crews; finally our two Jeeps side by side nicely positioned to be first keels like any self respecting boat should and I felt sure the sound of all this slapping around would have been heard for miles, right across the Channel in fact and that Jerry would be well aware of our coming!

I'm a poor sailor at the best of times, but this period of waiting was made completely miserable not only by the movement but also the stench of diesel, which pervaded everything. I remember very little about that week's wait; most of the time I spent curled up over an anchor chain, which I had found in a little cubbyhole alongside the ramp, filling thoughtfully supplied vomit bags! I suspected it was all part of a grand overall plan. I was quite sure that if I lived to reach the other side, even had Jerry been as thick on the beach as Blackpool on a bank holiday, nothing, just nothing, would have stopped me getting ashore.

We were all so well equipped; the order of the day was 'battle order', which meant we carried our small-pack on our shoulders attached to our webbing equipment with Sten gun ammo pouches on either breast. On my right hip my water bottle, gasmask on my chest and gas cape on the back of my neck. Steel helmet and Sten gun at the ready, all as laid down in the Army Handbook. But as I had the mine detecting apparatus on my back, my small-kit had to be carried on my left hip, and because I was serving a field ambulance unit I couldn't carry my Sten gun! This had to be packed with my other gear, which would follow later.

The army realised we may well get our feet wet, so they issued us with waders. These were two tubes of gas cape material sealed together at one end to make trousers and on the end of each leg had been sealed a plate shaped piece of hard board, to make feet, not unlike snow shoes. They had tapes at the waist to hold them up. In my case these waders came right up over all my equipment, and tied up over my shoulders! It was thought Jerry would use gas, or even chemicals, so we were issued with a second gas mask, which also had to fit around the waist. To detect these attacks quickly, we were issued with shoulder detectors which needed fitting under the shoulder straps. By the time I had all this on I looked like a pregnant turtle stood on its tail with helmet tipped over my eyes caused by the gas-cape on the nape of my neck! The army hadn't finished yet! As I waddled to my position at the foot of the ramp, a long rubber tube was thrust into my hands. 'Blow that up and tie it across your chest,' I was ordered. 'It's a Mae West – you may need it.'

As I was doing this there was an almighty explosion and the barge shuddered to a halt. It had impaled itself on an underwater obstacle and detonated a mine. Still the army hadn't finished with its surprises even now! As the ramp went down the order rang out: 'All those wading ashore grab that rope and take it with you.' This rope apparently would unroll an enormous roll of coconut matting intended to make the undersea surface better for the following vehicles. I grabbed the rope and leapt in. We were further out than planned and I leapt into at least eight foot of water. Down I went – fortunately the Mae West brought me to the surface again just in time to see my helmet float gently away out to sea. Down I went again; this time the waders filled with water, the straps broke and they started to fall down my legs, making it impossible to use them. I surfaced again and started to struggle for the shore. Looking around, I realised, I would never make the shore unless I freed my legs. Just ahead, to my left, I could see the core of the coconut matting roll floating like a giant cotton reel.

I felt I could just about make it. I said to Charlie, a medic struggling alongside, 'Charlie I'm not going to make it. I

shall have to let go, and make for that.' 'I should,' he said, 'you're the only bloody fool pulling it!! I'm coming with you.' I let go and looked over my shoulder and was off as soon as the ramp went down. Our zero hour was H+11, which meant we were due to hit the beach eleven minutes after the first assault wave went in.

It must have been about 31 May; when we were loaded on, we were towed out into Southampton Sound, tied into large raft-like formations and covered with camouflage nets, then lay there, slapping, sliding, pitching and rolling waiting for the off. Barges don't have the matting billowing out up in the air like a darned great sail. No wonder I was making so little progress! I struggled to the reel and hung on for grim life. Soon Charlie joined me and I struggled to free my legs. Taking a moment's rest I looked up just in time to see that as we rose up with the big rollers coming in, on the same rise a floating mine was coming up with us, fortunately falling away again as the roller passed, leaving a gap of about three feet between us. I yelled to Charlie, 'Look at that, let's get the hell out of here.'

Fortunately just beyond us, another barge had just started discharging lorries. 'I'm making for that,' I shouted, 'and hope it'll tow me ashore.' 'Good idea,' said Charlie. 'I'm coming with you.' As we got nearer to the lorry it slowly started to sink, and by the time we had reached it, it had sunk! The driver had to scramble first onto the cab and then onto the canvas back covering his load. First he pulled Charlie on board and then between them they dragged me over the side, looking more like a stranded porpoise than an invader.

Meanwhile the barge off which we had leapt was still firmly fixed onto the underwater spiked girder and had been swept by the strong tide parallel with the beach so that the back end of it was now only about twenty foot or so from where we were stranded. A sailor stood there. I yelled to him to get a rope to pull us back on board and this he did. I walked to the front of the barge to see what was going on. 'Oh! Hello, Tubby,' was the greeting. 'We thought you'd been swept out to sea. Nice to see you. We got the first Jeep off and the sea promptly turned it over. You've lost your mine sweeper!' 'What a pity, what a pity,' I said. 'But we'll have to get this other Jeep off, we're stopping the others from going.' Just then the commander of the first tank came up and said, 'There's an urgent call for armour, we shall have to get by.' 'Right,' I said, 'If your lads will help, we could push the Jeep to one side and you might be able to squeeze through, and then, if you do would you let us fix our towrope to the back of your tank and tow it ashore for us?' 'Right,' he said and no sooner the word and the action. Anderson, the Jeep's driver, said, 'Look Tubby, you're already soaked through, why don't you take the Jeep. I'll scramble on the back of the tank and perhaps share some dry clothes with you later.' It seemed a sensible idea, so I agreed.

The tank squeezed by, up the ramp, and then down the other side at full throttle – the towrope tightened – the Jeep took off, the wheels hit the ramp once, up it bounced – flew to the top, the wheels just caught the top of the ramp, and there I was sailing through the air, hanging on for life once again! It hit the water with an almighty splash and off I rushed through the water like a champion surfer. All went well until the tank hit the beach, when on pulling clear of the water it churned something up from just below the sand which stood up above the surface, and caught the two front wheels of the Jeep stopping it dead in its tracks. The tank went on up the beach trailing my front bumper bar and radiator grill in tow, leaving me still sitting in about two feet of water!

The only thing to do in these circumstances is to keep the engine running to keep the water out of the system – you can't engage gear or water will get into the clutch – and wait for help. The beachmaster saw the problem and sent an armour-plated bulldozer which had just come ashore to push me the last few feet to dry land. I was then able to engage gear and drive to where Anderson was waiting to take over again.

I then gathered myself together and looked around for the path along which we were being directed. I was wet through and thoroughly dishevelled. I joined the infantry making my way inland. Just then a voice bawled, 'Down, get down.' I just did what everyone did and threw myself flat. Automatic fire from a nearby pillbox was raking the 'crown' of the beach. I gently peeped up over to see what to do next, just in time to see the same bulldozer which had pushed me ashore, slowly cover the pillbox over with sand, completely covering the slit out of which the automatic fire was coming.

We were all then able to make our way forward to our various rendezvous. By now not only was I soaked through, thoroughly dishevelled, but also covered with sand sticking all over my drenched uniform and equipment. I am quite sure that had Jerry seen me coming ashore looking the sight I did, he would have died laughing, and lost the war anyway!

So, when in future you see pictures of these fine specimens of manhood rushing around causing havoc to our enemies: spare a thought for the many, many supporting bods, who were also there doing their bit to the best of their ability – very, very few of them are born heroes.

Len 'Tubby' Lane, Margate, Kent

It was soon evident when we embarked with a number of civilian 'boffins', together with a variety of packing cases on HMS *Inman*, that this was not to be one of our usual convoy escort duties. Soon after we sailed from the UK the captain announced over the tannoy that we were to be stationed in the mid-Atlantic as part of a force of three ships, each acting independently, to measure and record prevailing weather conditions and data from the upper atmosphere to be radioed to the UK every six hours. Our initial amusement at watching the meteorologists coping with the sea conditions of the North Atlantic as they filled their observation balloons and operated their assortment of equipment soon wore off. Most sea trips are rather boring but usually have periods of excitement, especially on convoy duties when we at least had the satisfaction of protecting the convoy from enemy attack. But the endless steaming around in circles whilst the meteorologists carried out their functions was particularly tedious. It was only enlivened by the occasional sighting of an aircraft or ship, or the detection of a U-boat, which caused us to be closed up at 'action stations',

We were not, however, particularly happy at the necessity to break radio silence every six hours to transmit meteorological data to the UK as this could readily be interrupted by enemy listening posts on ship or shore and our position plotted by them with consequent enemy action against us. We were most apprehensive throughout our stay on station but were lucky enough not to have any unwelcome visitors. I have, however, often wondered what the enemy thought we were doing sailing around way out in the Atlantic for such a long time, ignoring the most basic rules of radio silence!

Eventually after some weeks of the same routine, the skipper announced that the invasion of Europe by Allied Forces had commenced and that the weather information we had been radioing had been of inestimable value to the meteorologists at SHAEF [Supreme Headquarters Allied Expeditionary Forces] back in the UK in forecasting the expected weather over the invasion beaches in the English Channel, and had been instrumental in the final decision of whether or not the invasion fleet was to sail. We were of course delighted to know that we had taken part in such a vital operation and all our disgruntled thoughts of the past weeks at sea were immediately changed for the better! Unfortunately I do not recollect the ship's crew receiving the ultimate accolade of 'splicing the mainbrace', which, in view of the dangers we'd faced for some weeks, was most disheartening!

By the very nature of their good seakeeping qualities ex-Royal Navy Flower Class Corvettes were used by the British as civilian weather ships following active service. Initially HMS *Marguerite*, HMS *Thyme* and HMS *Genista* were so employed, followed by ex-Castle Class frigates, HMS *Oakham Castle*, HMS *Amberley Castle*, HMS *Pevensey Castle* and HMS *Rushen Castle*. I am sure that the crews of these fine ships, who gave such good account of themselves with the escorting of North Atlantic convoys during World War II, will be pleased to know of their ships' extended lives, which prevented their being consigned to the scrapheap immediately following the cessation of hostilities.

Finally, may I say that our work wasn't John Wayne stuff, but it was hard work and very dangerous. I have read a few accounts of D-Day but no mention has ever been made of that assignment we undertook, which was so vital to the ultimate decision. I don't want any laurels for me or my shipmates but it is disappointing to read sometimes of the involvement of so many on D-Day and for there to be no recognition at all for those lads who acted as 'sitting ducks' to get essential information to England. Perhaps

everyone should remember something else. While General Eisenhower had to make the final decision – 'Lets go!' – about the invasions, it was the 'weatherman' Group Captain Stagg who put his reputation on the line by forecasting better weather was on the way. That did take courage and it was based on our reports.

Eric W. Airey, Sidcup, Kent

While in the WAAF, because of my art college training, I was assigned to the team who made models used in the planning of assault landings, commando raids, for the briefing of aircrews and for the use of resistance organisations. For Operation Overlord there were ninety-seven panels, each five feet by three feet in size.

The work was carried out by three teams of American and British model makers, each working eight hour shifts for twenty-four hours a day and with approximately twenty members to each team. A rigid wood and hardwood covered base was made and onto this boards of suitable thickness cut to the shape of selected contours traced from maps were mounted. The resulting terraced assembly was waterproofed and provided the control for the modelling of a basic landform with a mixture of paper pulp and Plaster of Paris affectionately known as 'jollop'. Jollop hardened very quickly, so whilst one lot was being used another was being 'bashed' by throwing it as hard as possible against the sides of the sinks until it reached the right consistency. It was a great release from any build up of tension caused by the precise nature of the work! Photographs were carefully studied through a stereoscope and more detailed

modelling of embankments, excavations, spoil tips, rivers and lakes and changes of levels not shown on the map were completed and the basic colouring applied, taking care to register the position of fields and other surface detail of a two dimensional nature.

Meanwhile, another group of model makers would be busy constructing houses, churches, factories, engineering works and other three dimensional installations and, on average, an ordinary three bedroomed dwelling house would be about one eighth of an inch square, but roof detail was an all important feature for recognition purposes from the air. Heights were established by measuring the shadows shown on the photograph, taking into consideration the time of year and the time of day at which they were taken and using what was called a 'shadow factor' to work out what the exact height was.

Small buildings were usually made out of linoleum and cut into shape with a sharp razor blade while holding the minute pieces with a pair of eyebrow tweezers. A slip of the tweezers could often result in one of these tiny buildings being flicked into oblivion in the dust and debris of the workshop and was usually accompanied by a frustrated bellow – or something even stronger – as twenty minutes or so of painstakingly detailed work was lost forever.

The painting of roads, rivers, tracks, railways, airfield runways and other relevant information was added and the buildings then transferred and stuck to the model. Hedges were applied with something like a fine cake icer filled with a coloured mix of alabaster and paint, and coloured sawdust of varying degrees of fineness were used for scrublands, woodlands and forest etc., and finally any military or other required annotations or symbols, were added. Throughout, the model was known only by a number and any names on maps that came into the section had them obliterated first to preserve the utmost secrecy.

The model making section was concerned with virtually every major operation in World War II and a fitting tribute to the section's skills and ingenuity was included in the book *The Eye of Intelligence* by Ursula Powys-Lybbe, when she referred to the 'realism and beauty' they portrayed, and it is sad that none of the original models can now be traced.

Secrecy was such that for some considerable time we had no idea what these particular models were for, but on the morning of 6 June 1944, as I sat with several colleagues at breakfast, the announcement was made over our crackly old radio set that the invasion of Normandy had begun.

Suddenly there was complete silence in the mess as we looked at one another, not only in disbelief but in comprehension.

'So that's what it's all been about,' said the quiet voice of reason, breaking the silence. But I wasn't the only one to shed the odd tear over breakfast that morning.

Mary Harrison, Radcliffe-on-Trent, Nottinghamshire

I was a navigator of a Stirling four-engined bomber on Squadron 149 engaged on 'special duties' – mainly dropping supplies to the Maquis, which required flying low-level, at about five hundred feet, above enemy-occupied territory at night.

We learned fairly early during the morning of 5 June 1944 that 'ops' were planned for that night. Then stories came from the armourers that the 'bomb' load we were to carry was extraordinarily light in weight and that they had been told that if any canister failed to release, they would be court-martialled! As the day wore on, we learned that the interior of our aircraft was being filled with two tons of 'window' – metallised strips of paper of varying lengths in bundles, each of which looked like an aircraft on the enemy's radar screens – and that we were to take with us two extra volunteer aircrew, who would help us throw it out!

At the navigators' pre-briefing that afternoon, we learned that the dropping point for our canisters was beside Caen in Normandy and that two other crews were detailed for the same dropping point. This was a great relief, as our usual trips entailed long flights into France and occasionally, Belgium. However, our route was to fly from Portland Bill, then to the west of the Channel Isles, turning east once we had passed south of Jersey.

At main briefing, we were told nothing about the purpose of the trip – nor did we guess, even though it was common knowledge that an invasion was planned! It seemed an unnecessarily long way to get to Caen, since Caen was only a dozen miles from the coast, but it was not for us to question why. From Portland Bill, our bomb-aimer was required to throw out of the front hatch two bundles of window every twenty seconds and our flight-engineer to throw one bundle of a different size down the flare chute every ten seconds. The two volunteers were required to carry supplies to them. We were to cross the Channel at one thousand feet and keep our height five hundred feet above the hills of Normandy, then gently dive when we came to the plain surrounding Caen so that we would drop the load from five hundred feet at an airspeed of one hundred and thirty knots. This would necessitate the use of flaps to slow us down. Unusually, I was required to drop the load on specified coordinates of my navigational radar. We always asked whether other aircraft were expected in the area, because they attract enemy fighters, and we were astonished to be told in a matter-of-fact voice, 'about one thousand'. But we still did not guess the purpose of the trip! Maybe our minds were on more practical matters.

When we arrived at the aircraft at 9pm in the gathering gloom, we were glad that we were all slim young men, because the interior was filled on both sides with boxes of window to the roof, leaving a corridor about a foot wide. I had difficulty dragging my bag of navigation equipment through. The hour before take-off was always the most worrying part of an op if all the instruments etc. were performing properly, because there was nothing to keep one's mind away from the trip ahead – but this night we had to appear nonchalant to our volunteer aircrew. We took off at 10:10pm and had no difficulty in keeping to track. Fortunately, over France there was intermittent cloud cover, because in the clearings we saw many flashes of small arms fire shooting at us. The load was dropped according to plan and there was some light flak as we turned starboard returning on the same track, arriving back at Methwold, Norfolk, at 3:30am.

After returning, we learned that we had been simulating a parachute drop, in order to draw German troops away from the shore just before the army was to land on the beaches. The window was intended to make our three aircraft appear on German radar to be an armada and the 'bomb-load' were fireworks, which appeared and sounded like small arms and parachutists. To our surprise, the other two aircraft did not return. We learned later that one pilot had miraculously managed to make a wheels-up landing and the whole crew had escaped uninjured, and were smuggled back across the front line a couple of weeks later.

Derek C. Biggs, DFC, Inverness

I was corporal crew commander of a Sherman tank in the 10th Canadian Armoured Regiment (Fort Garry Horse). We were attached to 3rd Canadian Division and landed on Nan Red Beach.

The secret of our tanks, known as DD (duplex drive), was that they could be converted into amphibious vehicles by a canvas screen providing buoyancy enough to support a 28-ton Sherman, fully armed with one 75mm cannon and two 300 Browning machine guns, one in the turret and one in the hull. The crew of five consisted of a driver and co-driver in the forward hull, gunner, loader/operator and crew commander in the turret.

The collapsible screen of heavy rubberized canvas was raised by inflating rubber air pillars by compressed air from a single cylinder, (barely enough air for two inflations). When fully raised, struts were locked into position by the crew commander kicking each one with foot or hand.

When the screen was inflated and the tank was afloat guns could only be seen from the air. About fifteen inches of screen was above the water, making it look like a shallow boat and thus hiding its true identity. No one would believe that such a flimsy looking craft could possibly be an armoured vehicle. DD meant that the tank not only had tracks but had two propellers, which could be lowered to engage in sprockets coupled to the rear track bogies to become a boat capable of about eight knots. When not required the propellers could be disengaged by the driver as the tracks made contact with the beach.

The DD tank was one of the best kept secrets of the war. We spent months training with these vehicles usually under cover of darkness and with Valentine tanks instead of Shermans. We were on the south coast of England near Calshot, across the water from Portsmouth, and used to swim the tanks to the Isle of Wight one night, hide them in the grounds of Osborne House and then swim them back the next night. The longest swim I had done was from an LCT (Landing Craft Tank) about seven miles from shore.

On 4 June, my troop embarked on LCT 1406, manned by the RN and under their orders while on board. I was the first of five tanks to embark, which meant that I would be the last tank to disembark. We spent the night of 4 June and all day 5 June on board in the harbour waiting for weather conditions to improve. We set sail during the night of 5 June and at daybreak were nearing the French coast.

Myself and crew were among the very few who slept or made a breakfast. Most of the crews were seasick but those who had eaten were in better shape than those who had not. I'm sure many thought it would be a blessed relief to be killed!

After having breakfast we checked over our tanks, released our chocks and inflated our screens ready for the instructions from the RN to disembark. The four crews in front of me all got into their respective tanks ready for disembarking. With screens up crew commanders were unable to see while in their tanks and with radio silence imposed were completely unaware of what was happening.

I ordered my driver and co-driver to get into their seats and to make ready. My gunner, loader and myself remained out of our tank, standing on the hull so that we could observe what was happening. From our position we had a clear view over our screen and over the front and sides of our LCT.

As we approached the coast of France we could see and hear the naval guns firing over us, rockets from rocket launchers mounted on some LCTs, fighter aircraft and heavy bombers overhead, going in to soften up the coastal defences and disrupt the support areas. I have never seen anything like it since and will remember it forever.

We were still several thousand yards off France when our LCT naval number one climbed on board each tank in turn to tell us that due to the rough seas they would take us as close to shore as possible and hopefully right in to make a dry landing.

On receiving this information the front two tanks remained ready for either situation, keeping their screens raised, but tanks three and four immediately dropped theirs, the crews remaining in their tanks awaiting instructions. As I was still out of my tank I could see that it was unlikely that we would make a dry landing so I too kept my screen raised. Our guns could not be used whilst on board the LCT, even with the screens down.

By this time we were under fire from the enemy shore defences and our LCT had been hit. The number one then ordered the tanks to disembark and the ramp was lowered. I could see we were about seven hundred to nine hundred yards from the shore. He (number one) ordered the tanks to disembark under his direction. The first tank went down the ramp, engaged propellers and swam clear, followed closely by the second tank. The third tank with screen down was ordered to the ramp and then into the water where it immediately sank from sight. The crew commander, who was also the troop commander, swam clear of his tank followed by his gunner and the loader operator. They inflated their escape devices and became buoyant. The driver and co-driver drowned in their seats.

In the meantime the commander of the fourth tank had realised a dry landing was out of the question so opened the valve on his partly-emptied air cylinder and started to raise his screen. The low air pressure and volume was just enough to finish raising the screen as the tank went off the ramp into the water. He was able to engage propellers and move clear. He came under fire from shore defences, his screen was holed and his tank sunk in shallow water. His crew evacuated, inflated their escape devices and survived by holding on to their tank's aerial. When the fourth tank was clear of the ramp it was my turn to disembark. As I proceeded down the ramp and into the water, the LCT received another hit, or struck a mine, and the crew abandoned ship from the stern.

We managed to swim our tank to the beach and though under shell and machine gun fire, we remained afloat until our tracks engaged and pulled us out of the sea. We were able to drop our screen and use our guns to defend ourselves and to support the infantry regiment with covering fire as we fought our way off the beaches and into Saint-Aubin-sur-Mer. We supported the infantry and some engineers by shooting up possible observation posts, machine gun nests and any enemy troops who appeared.

The beach became strewn with various vehicles that had struck mines or had been hit by cannon or mortar fire. There were also a number of dead and wounded soldiers lying where they had fallen. We got through the town by about midday although some snipers and other pockets of resistance were not cleared up for a couple of days.

I knew my immediate objective was the village of Tailleville so I proceeded in that general direction. I saw my squadron OC and informed him that I was the only tank from my troop still in action. He allocated me to another troop and we proceeded to Tailleville, a walled hamlet held by German soldiers. My own troop was reformed a few days later from reinforcements and I was promoted to troop sergeant. After more casualties to tanks, crews and infantry, we eventually routed the enemy from Tailleville and headed in the general direction of Caen but that was only taken after many days of hard fighting.

We carried on during D-Day until darkness when we formed a laager and waited for supplies. We had food, sleep, and when I removed my helmet I found that it had been gouged by a bullet. It could have happened at any time during the morning but with all the excitement I had not been aware of the near miss!

When we replenished our supplies during the night of 6 June I had only seven shells left for my 75mm cannon and the barrels of both machine guns had been so hot that they could no longer be removed and so both guns had to be replaced. The rifling in them had become so worn that I could see the tracer bullets leave the barrel in an ever-increasing spiral with absolutely no hope of hitting a target. Both guns were replaced D plus one.

Thus D-Day had ended, we were exhausted and had an

hour or two of sleep before being available for action again by daybreak. It was days before we realised what we had been through! D-Day was probably the most exciting day of my life although not the most frightening. I was too inexperienced at that time to know what to fear. From the moment we embarked on our LCT on 4 June I became oblivious to everything else. I had a carbuncle start to swell on my right elbow that day but was able to ignore it until D plus one when it became extremely painful. Every time we made tea my crew would make a poultice with the hot tealeaves. It came to a head and burst late on D plus three and my gunner pulled out the core with a pair of pliers before applying first aid. I still have the scar!

Harvey 'Willie' Williamson, Kingswinford, West Midlands

At 9:15pm on 5 June, the 8th Parachute Battalion was all packed up and raring to go. The load each one of us was carrying was horrific. What with different types of grenades, mortar bombs, rifle ammunition, rations and spare clothing, a pick or shovel or trenching tool etc., etc., we could barely walk with the load, let alone jump from an aeroplane! But we all fell in on parade and marched across the road to the airstrip on which was lined row upon row of Dakota aircraft.

I remember the officer in charge of our group of eighteen noted that one of the lads was carrying a canvas bucket of six Bren gun magazines in his hand and on being challenged admitted that he intended to jump with them in this manner! The officer snatched them from him with some rude remark and then he took the magazines out of the bucket and distributed them around the section, handing one to me. I objected, stating that I just had nowhere to carry it, but I wasn't allowed to get away with an excuse like that and I was told to 'find somewhere'! There's logic for you! In the outside breast pocket of my parachute smock I had a phosphorus smoke grenade and a tobacco tin full of cigarettes but I found the inside pocket was empty so I put the magazine in there which, as you will read later, proved to be rather fortunate. And so we enplaned and took off, safe in the assurance from our commanding officer that a lot of us were making a trip from which there was to be no return. Not a comforting thought! I remember the flight over very well; I was  number sixteen to jump. I can remember looking along the plane and wondering what the other chaps were thinking. There was a dim red light along the plane that apparently would not affect our eyesight when we jumped out into the darkness. A few of the lads were relaxing as though trying to sleep. Some were chatting. A couple I remember were reading war comics! Despite the situation there did not appear to be any stress in that plane at all and there certainly should have been! On the contrary, it was rather relaxed.

That is until we went over the French coast and then it was hell let loose. Everything seemed to be coming up at us. The sky seemed to be full of anti-aircraft shells exploding and tracer bullets coming up very slowly and then speeding upwards. The plane was being thrown all over the place. It was the nearest thing to hell I ever want to be, and there was only one way out of it and that was down into it! Eventually the green light came on over the door and the time had come to carry out the job for which we had been training for so long. Out we went into the darkness at 00:50am on D-Day, 6 June 1944.

The plan was for all of us to land in a dropping zone close to a village called Touffreville. We were then to move to a rendezvous point on the edge of the village by following red and blue Very lights being fired into the air by some of our lads who had dropped about an hour before us. We were then to form up and carry out our first task, which was to move through a small town call Troarn and, with the engineers, to blow up bridges on the River Dives to prevent German tanks crossing the river into our area.

After all the planning and briefing it was soon realised on landing that most of our battalion had been dropped over a very wide area and out of six hundred and seventy men, only one hundred and ten arrived at the rendezvous point to carry out the first tasks. I had been dropped eight miles from where I should have been! On leaving the plane I can only say I felt very lonely except that the sky was full of bullets coming upwards. Fortunately it wasn't long before my feet hit the ground with a thud. Almost as soon as my feet touched the ground I was to find that I had landed directly in front of the muzzle of a German Machine Gun and I received a burst of fire straight at me. I can remember being hit and spinning round with a sudden yell of shock and finishing up flat on my back. The gun continued firing bursts over me for quite a while and I was getting the 'flash' from the gun all the while as I was only a few yards in front of it. I lay there rather dazed for a while, expecting to be hit again at any moment. It was difficult but I was able to keep control although not really aware of how many wounds I had received. The only defence I had was three grenades in my waist belt but they were under my jump smock. That meant pulling a long zip down at the front to even start getting at one. My rifle was in a bag at the end of a rope about twenty-five yards away.

After a while the gun stopped firing and I was close enough to hear the Germans talking. I couldn't understand what they were saying, but they appeared to be very excited. When the firing resumed I realised I was not getting the flash from the gun and they were now firing in another direction. I then decided to get hold of a grenade, expecting to be shot at at any time. I managed to get the grenade out and pull the pin and then I threw it at the gun. It seemed a very long four seconds before it exploded! Then I was aware that I had hit the target – the gun had stopped firing and there was no reaction from the gun position.

I got to my feet and retrieved my rifle. That made me feel better! But I now felt lonely and isolated, still dazed and in pitch darkness and with still a lot of anti-aircraft guns and machine guns firing around me. I was aware that my left arm was now useless, but unable to check the extent of the damage. Whilst unpacking my rifle and collecting myself I became aware of a figure advancing towards me along the hedgerow and to my relief found it was another parachutist of the Royal Engineers. We moved along from this spot to the corner of the field we were in and after finding a wound in my upper arm where a bullet had passed right through my muscle my new pal applied a shell dressing to the wound. He then told me we were on the outskirts of the village of Ranville, which was about eight miles from where I should have been and that his rendezvous spot was too far away as well! It was then decided that as he had a Sten gun and I had a rifle that it would be better if we changed weapons. I could handle the Sten gun better with one arm. We also agreed that even though we were both miles from our rendezvous points, we should part company and try to find them. So he left and disappeared into the darkness and I moved away in the opposite direction, towards Ranville to try to find my way towards Troarn.

After moving a short distance I picked out the outline of a church in Ranville and became aware of German soldiers rushing about in a state of panic and my arm was now getting very painful. So I made my way by a circuitous route to the churchyard, narrowly avoiding the Germans in the process. The tower of the church is a separate building, and at the bottom of the tower are three doors. One is a toilet, the middle one leads by steps to the top of the tower and the other is a coal hovel. I chose the toilet in which to take refuge, so I went in and sat on an old box type seat! This proved to be a fortunate choice as I found out next morning that through the next door leading up to the top of the tower there was a German machine gun position manned by a number of German soldiers.

I hadn't been sat too long when I heard someone trying the door of the toilet and I was soon aware from the noises the person was making that he was in a lot of pain. So I opened the door and found a German soldier on the ground who had lost most of his right foot. So I dragged him in with me as best I could. By this time two things happened: it was beginning to get light and there was quite a battle going on around us. There was not a lot that I could do for my companion but I decided we could have a cigarette and so I undid my top left hand pocket and took out my tobacco tin full of Woodbines. When I did so I found that a bullet had hit me just below the button, gone straight through my tin of Woodbines and into the Bren gun magazine in my inside pocket and stopped there. Otherwise it would have gone straight through my heart. All my Woodbines were unsmokable but thankfully the German had cigarettes, which he produced and we smoked them instead!

Before long we found ourselves in the middle of a battle for Ranville. The top of the tower was blown off to destroy the machine gun position and before long the Paras had taken the village and I was soon on my way to a field dressing station, and two days later on my way back to Blighty to hospital. I guess I was one of the lucky ones thanks to that Bren gun magazine that I had grumbled about. I was back in Normandy within five weeks and fought right across Germany to the Baltic Sea.

Every day since then has been a bonus to me and I am, and have always been, so proud to have been a member of the Parachute Regiment. As a matter of interest, I still have the breast pocket cut out of the battle smock that I was wearing on D-Day, plus the tobacco tin with the hole through it! And I often wonder what happened to the German who shared his cigarettes with me because I hadn't any to share with him! I wonder what happened to him and where he is now?

John Hunter, Peterborough, Northamptonshire

I was a member of the Royal Observer Corps and after volunteering for operations I was put on a training course at Bournemouth. Life there was one mad rush. Lectures on discipline, first aid, survival etc. and, above all, aircraft recognition. We were expected to pass 99.5 per cent in that. British planes were known thoroughly, from Albacore to Whitleys, and German planes, from Arado Ar 230 to Messerschmitt 410s.

On passing the tests we had Seaborne flashes to add to our RAF Observer uniforms and RN brassards as petty officers. Quite a mixture. We were then secretly moved in RAF vans early one morning to Cowes, Isle of Wight, to board our respective ships.

Have you ever tried climbing up a rope ladder up the side of a heaving ship? I tried – carrying my kitbag and my hammock. The hammock fell into the sea (cheers from the ship's crew!). I reported on arrival on the deck to the gunnery officer who commented that I'd forgotten to salute the quarter deck. What a start! I was escorted to a spacious cabin where the regular POs slept – so my dripping hammock wasn't needed! This was the HMS *Monowai*, a pre-war New Zealand shipping company pleasure cruiser of 11,000 tons, but now heavily armed. My duties were to describe through loud hailers to the ship's crew every plane in the vicinity with their specific identification points.

On the Sunday we steamed out, only to return – operation cancelled because of inclement weather. The real thing was then on – we left Monday evening for France. We could hear

overhead a constant stream of our planes as they flew to bomb their targets. The route was marked clearly by a series of buoys of various colours as we zigzagged towards our destination. I was on the bridge – binoculars ready – next to the gunnery officer. Though we'd had strict orders not to look at the sea but constantly search the skies for any intruder, very early that morning, I thought  I saw a submarine on the starboard bow and pointed this out to the gunnery officer who said 'excellent'. 'All guns range so and so prepare to fire.' The ship's captain asked, 'What is it, guns?' On being told he said, 'Good show, Taff,' then looked carefully with his binoculars and shouted, 'Guns, Taff, haven't you seen a so and so (strong words these) paravane before?' (Drawn by minesweepers to clear mines.) That was a good start.

On the dawn of D-Day the French Canadian Commandos on board embarked on their landing craft which bobbed up and down in the very rough sea and many were seasick. I waved to one very young sergeant from Régiment de la Chaudière (who had many a chat with me previously and had asked me to say a prayer for him on his departure). Between watching carefully for any sneak raiders, I watched the landing craft approaching Courseulles-sur-Mer and saw my little sergeant and his company land safely only to be wiped out by the German machine gun from the sand dunes. What of my prayer?

Scarcely any planes to identify – though the black and white stripes made our planes easier to spot. I saw two of our Spitfires shot down by our own rocket gun ships as they swooped down from the low clouds. The shelling from the battleships behind us was terrific – Cherbourg to our right being a special target. The activity was intense – while we bobbed up and down at anchor – landing craft on both sides emptied men on beachhead Juno.

Sirens sounded on some ships and suddenly from the coast flying very low towards the ships came Spitfires. I shouted, 'Spitfires.' The gunnery officer disagreed. 'They're Messerschmitts. All guns prepare to fire.'

I shouted, 'You are not to fire Sir.'

'Pity help you Taff if you've made a mistake.' They roared overhead – with perspiration running down my face I smiled at him and he winked back. 'Good show, Taff.' They were Spitfires.

For twenty-eight hours I stayed on the bridge – not moving; watching – and being proud to be part of the spearhead of the invasion that liberated Europe. I like to think I deserved the gunnery officer's remark: 'You were worth your weight in four-inch shells.'

Let us with pride remember those very gallant men who fifty years ago gave their lives that we might live. 'Greater love hath no man than this, that a man lay down his life for his friends.'

Rene Jones, Llandysul, Ceredigion

I was in a company of engineers formed especially for the invasion at Blackwater in Essex. There were only four of this type of company in the army and we were called Inland Water Transportation Squadron. I was in 940 IWT, Royal Engineers. Our job was to deal with the landing of special tanks on the initial assault and in our company we had lightermen from Liverpool and London especially – men who understood and were used to working on small craft. I was eighteen at the time. In the company we had a wide range of boats and equipment. There were PBRs (Power Barge Ramp), Rhino ferries, large USA rafts with two large engines with propellers that could be winched

up when going in to beach in shallow water, and other items as well.

The USA rafts were used to support LST ships three miles off shore in the early stages of the assault. We went back and forward through the smoke screens unloading Funny tanks, field guns etc., and to help us we had various tug boats to clear away damaged landing craft and other obstructions as quickly and as best they could. I was once the 'ramp sapper' on a Rhino ferry, which was loaded completely with jerry-cans of petrol – dozens and dozens of them. As we came in we were hit and the petrol cans blew up. There was a hell of a roar and fire and explosion, and we had to just grab our issue life belts and jump into the sea and manage as best we could to get away.

There was the added danger of landing craft ploughing back and forth through the smoke screens, which gave a dense smoke cover, but I managed to float inshore safely where I eventually got onto the beach. It had been my first or second trip and when I landed it was still only about 7am on D-Day and daylight was still breaking! There was very little smoke on the beach at that stage, but as it got lighter the beaches became covered in black smelly oil. The smell was always there for many weeks afterwards: the smell held in the texturing of your uniform. The only gear we had was what we stood up in – 'battle order' was the name and it was very appropriate. When we had time for a break on the beach later we were told to dig into the ground – two to a hole. I remember on D-Day night that snipers left behind gave us trouble from houses on the beachfront and an infantry regiment with flamethrowers mounted on Bren carriers was called up to clear them out. That included the cellars and some tunnels that connected some of the houses, which had been dug by the Germans.

I remember seeing the German signs 'Achtung – Minen', and also, which perhaps many people don't know about, our own signs 'Dust Means Death'. That was an important one. Lorries travelling at speed could easily make dust clouds, and I remember one lorry doing exactly that being subject very quickly to German .808 shellfire. I also remember having very sore gums with having to eat hard tack biscuits for too many weeks! It was ages before we got any bread and some men when going out to ships at anchor would gladly swap a German steel helmet for a nice slice of decent bread!

I still have many more thoughts and memories even after all these years and I often sit and think of various comrades. When you are a member of such a unit, formed and trained for a special job such as the invasion, your comrades mean such a lot to you. I was the unit's youngest sapper when it all happened and I still have a few mementoes of what was undoubtedly the most historical part of my life.

Richard Fisher, Keswick, Cumbria

My bomber Squadron was the 552nd B-26 Marauder Medium Bomber Unit of the US 9th Air Force in the UK. I was aged twenty-two and we flew to England from Homestead Air Base in South Florida, our departure point from the USA.

It was to be a remarkable journey, especially for an inexperienced crew, with a real roundabout route with England the final destination. The route was designed to fit the range limitations of the B-26 and involved an engine failure, a forced landing, horrific storms over the Caribbean, skimming across the Amazon delta, searching for Ascension Island in the wide open spaces of the South Atlantic and then two nights in primitive Africa. Finally, up through a cloudy pass in the Atlas Mountains and to marvellous Marrakesh in

Morocco, where to my delight I fixed up a date with a charming French girl! Then on up the Atlantic, on the lookout for German fighters from France, and finally a very nervous night-time landing at Land's End.

After two combat missions as co-pilot in another B-26 I was told I was now ready to fly my own plane in combat. And so to bed on 5 June. At 3:30 the next morning (which turned out to be D-Day) I was woken and told that I was to fly on that morning's mission. So, full of high excitement I reported to the briefing room where our colonel told us that General Omar Bradley had selected our group, because of its fine record, to be the last to strike the Germans just before our troops landed on the beach. What's more, as best I can recall, we were to bomb an artillery position somewhat behind the beach fortifications and then dive down for a low level attack on shoreline gun turrets just before the Allied landings were to begin. So that was to be my FIRST mission as pilot with my own crew!

All this was enough to shake my confidence even before take-off. But to add to the problem I was then told I was to fly in the 'Tail End Charlie' position. That meant that in all the groups of planes that were flying on that mission I was not only in the LAST group, but I was in fact the LAST plane in the LAST group – in short there was no one behind me to cover me! Well, tremendous excitement is an emotion that is hard to explain. Our mission was important. Our lives were very much at risk. Who could foresee the outcome? I knew that for me it would be the hardest job I had ever undertaken – and it was! I decided that the only solution was absolute dedication to the controls of my aircraft. I remember mostly the sweat and the muscle aches, which came from that concentration and trying to keep in position. It was probably that supreme concentration that temporarily put aside my fears. At first we flew through German fighters but these were soon driven away by our fighter escort. Then came the flak and the machine gun fire, which downed several B-26s, but I came through unscathed. Just getting to the target, that

was an unforgettable experience. Below us were thousands of Allied ships in the Channel. We looked down on them in utter amazement. Their deadly ordeal was ahead.

Then the bombing attack itself. Lou Hengst, our navigator/bombardier, had his moment of glory when he let our bombs go right on time and on target. Then somehow we survived the low level attack after which we pulled up and headed back to our base at Great Dunmow in Essex with enormous relief. We chortled in our joy!

On the ground I have to admit that I walked with perhaps a touch of macho pride to the debriefing tent where I poured out my story of the raid! I was then offered my 'mission whisky' – a small shot of liquor for the nerves! It was by now about 9am and, knees shaking a bit with nerves and excitement, I walked back to my hut for a rest. But we couldn't – we talked and talked and talked with other crews about the events of that momentous morning. Later that afternoon we took off on a second D-Day raid – but it was such an anticlimax after what we had been through early that historic morning.

Colonel John Cutler, US Air Force (Retired),
Florida, USA and London, England

For months we had waited for the day; months of rehearsing, wet landings, etc. to make sure that at least once, we would have practised a landing something like we were to experience on this day, the most important day of our army life. Weeks of waiting in transit camps, each little move a little nearer the real thing. The transit camp system meant a week or two in one area, then a move to another area, perhaps to confuse the enemy. It certainly confused us! A vast network of camps covered the whole of southern England. The ones concerning us spread around Portsmouth, Southampton and Winchester. During this time, we had our first experience of strict censorship. All leave being stopped and mail closely checked. We eventually came to a stop in a camp designated C6, about six miles north of Southampton, and by the sight and sound of things, this was no exercise.

Briefing now took place. This was quite interesting and an imaginative way of putting us in the picture of our activities in the not too distant future. A sand model of the area we were going to land in had been constructed right down to the smallest detail, including the way we were to exit from the beach. All place names of course had been replaced by false names. About a fortnight before D-Day we had all been issued with French currency, especially printed for the occasion. We were of course confined to our camps at this time and woe betide anyone trying to escape!

On the morning of 2 June we marched out of camp on to a little used side road and loaded onto trucks not belonging to our own unit and then started a slow crawl in the direction of Southampton. Every lamppost had a sign on it exhorting us to keep silent, and speak to no one. Such signs as, 'Walls have ears', 'It is forbidden to speak to civilians'. No singing was permitted, no slogans must be written on trucks, no indication, in fact, must be given to show that anything other than an exercise was taking place. Considering that most of the roads in the south of England were chock-a-block with military transport of one kind or another, of all different nationalities, it was patently obvious that something serious was afoot!

Eventually we embarked on a Landing Ship Tank, at about 7pm the same day. Like many of the exercises we had been on these last few months, this was to be no pleasure cruise. We were even more crowded than we had been on some of the past exercises. For instance, the accommodation on a LST was for a maximum of one hundred and fifty with a bunk bed each. We had three hundred and forty men on board in addition to the crew! That night men slept anywhere they could. The bunk beds were soon filled, some with two to a bunk, sleeping head to foot, some on their vehicles, or in any odd corner they could lay down, rolled in a blanket. Morning was a welcome relief. Though we did not know it then we had three more nights in front of us like this. We hadn't taken long to load up on this first night, and soon after completion we set sail only to anchor in the Solent until the night of 5 June.

On this last evening, 5 June, we weighed anchor and set sail. We were called to a final briefing. This time it was head surgeon of the 34th Surgical Unit, Major Strang, and his anaesthetist Captain Gilbert. Any doubts we may have had about whether or not this was the real thing were now dispelled, as maps of France were issued to the RASC drivers. A message of good luck was read out from General Montgomery to us. Shortly after this he was promoted Field Marshall.

The sight, as we passed the eastern end of the Solent, was something I shall never forget. Ships of all kinds, large and small, old and new, anything that could sail appeared to be there. There must have been hundreds, far too many to count, either moving into position, or anchored to await their place in the queue. We, being a slow craft, had to set sail before many of the faster ships, some, now designated 'Landing Ships Infantry', had once been cross Channel ferries, IOM boats, merchant men, etc., and of course, custom built infantry landing craft. By now it was getting dark and, as we had been told reveille was at 5am it was time to get a bit of shut-eye, although I don't think many of us expected to sleep very well. Stomach trouble had broken out, and there was a constant stream of men heading for the hards!

Trying to sleep in these conditions, which included wearing a Mae West, was to say the least, difficult. However, I did eventually fall asleep, and was surprised to be awakened by one of my colleagues, instead of the sound of gunfire, which I had expected. We had a hurried breakfast, in shifts of course, for it was not possible to feed all these mouths at one sitting. In any case we had to be prepared in case of enemy action. Though at this time there was no indication of us being anywhere near the coast of France. What an unusual state of affairs – so near the coast of Hitler's Europe and not a sound from the Germans. I had slept with the vision of being strafed by the German air force, or maybe a torpedo attack from the German navy. But was not sorry to find it all so peaceful, yet it was an uncomfortable feeling, expecting so much, and finding it so quiet. We could see LSTs all over the Channel, in every direction, and occasional flights of RAF fighter aircraft to protect us from the German air force.

It's a peculiar feeling having left England behind, for me. This was the first time I had ever been abroad. I could only wonder would I ever be returning. We sat on top of the transport vehicles, seeing who would be the first to spot the French coast. The weather was dull and cold for the time of year, and a stiff breeze was blowing. Visibility was good though, and before long a smudge on the horizon gradually took shape, and as we drew nearer, the distant sound of gunfire could be heard, nearer still, and we could see the flashes of gunfire.

By now ships were getting more and more crowded as we joined the rest of the invasion fleet, which had anchored about four miles from the coast of Normandy. The landing ships, mostly with empty davits, had already unloaded their human cargo and certainly many would not see their landing craft again, as they lay wrecked on the beach. Around us all sorts of ships were at anchor, ships of all sorts of shapes, and sizes. Close by the battleship HMS *Rodney* was pouring salvo after salvo of shells into the enemy positions. At midday it was time to transfer to the Rhino, for the next stage of our journey into the unknown.

A Rhino is a sort of very large raft, made of many steel tanks linked together and large enough to hold about thirty vehicles, and some sort of outboard motor to give it headway. This was exceedingly difficult. It was hard enough in very calm conditions, but in the heavy swell it was a miracle we ever got the vehicles transferred successfully. I was glad I wasn't a driver. Somehow the job was completed. Then the RASC driver who had charge of the raft had the very difficult task of manipulating the raft to the beach, about four miles away. The motor only made headway at about two knots and the pilot had all on to even get its head in the right direction. We were on the raft (Rhino) about six hours, though actually we had been meant to land four hours after the initial assault. Had everything gone according to plan, it would have indeed been a miracle. We regularly swept the beach with binoculars, which we could now see quite clearly. It was strewn with many wrecked landing craft and damaged transport.

At about 5:30pm on this historical day, 6 June 1944, our Rhino, No. 34, finally headed for the beach, abreast of three others, all containing millions of pounds worth of vehicles and equipment, required for the invasion and of course, the men of the army and air force. The trucks, ambulances, tanks, etc., had been manoeuvred into position according to the requirements of the beach control and in our case, the first vehicle to land was an RAF recovery crane. The Rhino grounded less than ten yards from the shore. The crane descended the ramp, but sinking into soft sand, stuck tight completely blocking the exit. On the beach itself, several bulldozers were in operation to help keep the beach clear and one of these came to pick us off the raft enabling us to land with our feet dry. While all this was happening, a German aircraft dropped two bombs through the clouds. If we were the target, I'm glad to say he missed! No damage was done. Ack-ack fire was terrific, all hell was let loose, but he managed to escape. Major Strang, who was the leader of our party, took the lead, to get us away from the beach. The seven others who formed our group very

carefully followed in Major Strang's footsteps. The time was just before 7pm. It had been a long day, though it still had a way to go.

Our destination was a farmhouse, about half a mile inland in the village of Greye-sur-Mer. This was surrounded by a high wall and several orchards. After having taken a wrong turning and arriving in the outskirts of Courseulles, we eventually arrived at our destination at 7:30pm. This mile or so walk from the beach brought to me the realisation that the war was now a real part of our lives. There were shell holes all over the place, houses on fire, and buildings damaged. A wounded soldier, with his head bandaged walking aimlessly, looking, no doubt, for a first aid post. We couldn't help him. A dead military policeman, hit as he ran from the beach, head partly buried in the sand, arm stuck up in the air, a sight I shall never forget. Another dead soldier, a Canadian signaller on the side of a sand dune, still with his radio on his back. On our left we passed a hurriedly dug grave of a Canadian sergeant. In later days this grave was removed to a hurried cemetery, in a corner of a field further inland.

Having at last arrived at our destination the farm, we joined all the other groups, most of whom had arrived before us. The reason for arriving in small groups, of course, is to spread out any casualties we may receive. Together now, we set about establishing the field dressing station. Most of those who landed before us had been working on the beaches, attending to casualties and after treatment, putting them onto any craft they could find that was returning to England. Four of our own troops had been returned this way, fortunately none seriously wounded. One of the officers, wounded early on, had continued to work until he could go on no longer. He later received the Croix de Guerre. One of our troops was evacuated with, of all things, appendicitis!

Our first task was to dump our packs, with all the rest of the gear we had brought with us, then make ourselves something to eat and drink, using our twenty-four-hour emergency packs. We had been issued with two each. It had been some time since we had drunk anything. We had strict instructions not to drink local water. We had only a short time for this. Then our first task was to set up a reception area, in a commandeered Sunday school, bordering on to the farmyard. From there, depending on the nature of their wounds the casualties would be sent to either a ward tent, resuscitation, or the operating theatre, set up in a barn. Some walking wounded even returned to the beaches, and a boat trip back to Blighty!

One minute we seemed to be getting ready, then events overtook us and we were in the thick of it. I found myself in reception assisting Captain Cormack. Time flew. I have very little recollection of the next few hours. Darkness overtook us; the patients requiring attention, came in a never-ending stream. Some, though by all means not all, required a change of dressing, some required injections, many were stretcher cases. The main task being to sort them out and dispatch them to the next stage of their journey back home, a company of the Pioneer Corps acting as stretcher bearers. The whole unit, operating as a casualty receiving station, consisted of no.'s 1 and 2 Field Dressing Stations, 33 and 34 Surgical Units, and 33 Blood Transfusion Unit. The two surgical units worked together as a team in the barn used as an operating theatre. And by 9 June, having worked continuously round the clock since arrival, we had clocked up over ninety major operations.

The field transfusion unit worked with the resuscitation unit, who were under canvas as were the wards. Everyone worked like ants for three days, with little sleep. Some didn't get their heads down at all in that time, others a little better organised, adopted a sixteen hours on, eight hours off schedule. I was one of these. During your eight hours off, we had to make ourselves a bivouac, working in pairs. We must dig down twelve to eighteen inches, making a hole four feet by six feet, with a way in and a cover over our heads in case of rain.

Ernie Robbo and I managed to find ourselves a sheet of corrugated iron, together with two groundsheets and a few empty ration boxes, so we made ourselves a presentable residence, which lasted us our stay there! In fact, our entrance was so small that on the subsequent CO's inspection, the orderly sergeant (a big man) couldn't get in. Which was as well, for we had been taking tins of self-heating Horlicks out of ward's stores for our own use, leaving the evidence of empty cans! Many others had been doing the same thing, and some got caught and were awarded three days confined to barracks, hardly a punishment under the circumstances!

Of course death did overtake some of the more seriously wounded, which was inevitable, but our rate of recovery, we were given to understand, was in the region of ninety-eight per cent, thanks to the use of penicillin, just coming into use for the first time on such a large scale and the use of sulpha-nilamide. In these first three days we returned to England over seven hundred injured men.

Leslie Sharrocks, Rochdale, Greater Manchester

I was a member of a fifteen-inch gun crew on the battle-ship HMS *Warspite*. When the captain told us over the tannoy there was a complete stillness throughout the ship. The only thing to be heard was the continued thud of the ship's engines and the wash of the sea over the bows as we ploughed our way to the place of operations.

D-Day arrives and at approximately 05:00 hours the first Allied shells begin falling on the French coast. I didn't know a great deal of what was going on since my action station was between decks, but I did know that our fifteen-inch shells were being fired at an alarming rate.

We had been closed up at action stations for almost twenty-four hours and had very little to eat, in fact all we had eaten was a couple of sandwiches and our action ration, which consisted of two barley sweets, two packets of chewing gum and six malted milk tablets. Needless to say, hunger was very prominent, so when the order to 'stand down' came through at approximately 17:00 hours our thoughts travelled, as indeed did our bodies, to the mess deck for a good meal. Not all of the guns crews were able to relax and those manning AA guns had to remain closed up ready for emergency. We had our first view of the enemy coast and never before had such a conglomeration of ships, from battleships down to small assault craft been seen in any one operation. By this time of course the infantry had established a beachhead but even so the coming and going of tank and troop landing craft was still on a large scale. We didn't have much idea as to the extent of casualties suffered by the assault troops but we had picked up several chaps whose craft had been literally blown out of the water. We did see one or two dead bodies and these poor devils had paid the full price of war.

Now came the most awe-inspiring sight I have ever seen or for that matter am ever likely to see. This spectacle must have been a definite boost to the morale of our lads on the beaches – not that their morale was low, far from it I would say. No doubt the enemy felt otherwise! The approach of the Airborne Forces was the cause of all this excitement. The sky was literally black with aircraft – it reminded me of a flock of starlings, the only difference was that the planes were continuous whereas the birds are only momentary. We never saw the actual dropping of the paratroopers because the dropping zone was further inland. Of all the thousands of aircraft taking part in this operation we saw only one shot down and this particular plane was a Halifax and I think the pilot deserves a word of special mention. The glider he was towing had just been released and no sooner was this done the Halifax received a direct hit from flak and it was obvious that he would crash. It appeared as if nothing in this world could prevent him from crashing on the assault troops, but whether it was by a miracle or sheer gallantry on the part of the pilot, he somehow managed to keep the plane in the air until he was well away from the landing forces. So it was then that yet more men paid the full price of war.

That night we only saw one enemy plane and this came swooping in very low along our port side and all our AA guns opened up and for a moment all hell was let loose. I think our gunners were too excited because they never as much as touched him! No further incident occurred and I was intent on watching the coast. I have seen some very good firework displays but never anything to equal this. The sky was ablaze with light and purely artificial – with tracer crossfire forming a steel curtain around our troops.

Next day we were called upon by the Americans at their beachhead along the Cherbourg Peninsula to dislodge a formation of enemy tanks. We proceeded with all haste to help the tanks and received this message from the American commander: 'Good shooting,' so it was evident that the enemy tanks no longer existed.

D-Day plus two. We go back to Portsmouth to re-ammo ship. We get shore leave for one night and we are asked how things went 'over the other side'. The daily newspapers carried headlines of the *Warspite's* exploits – what do you know, we were in the news!

Arthur Hopcraft, Brackley, Northamptonshire

I was an officer with 536 Company RASC when our company commander informed me that he was sending me on a course to the Lake District. He said that for various reasons he could not tell me about the course, it would be explained to me when I arrived there.

I was amazed when I learned what it was all about. The object was to work on the lorries to cover all parts of the engines to make them watertight so that they would work under water. A pipe had to be fixed to the carburettor and raised high enough to get above any possible water level. The same with the exhaust pipe. Lorries were worked on and then driven through the side of the lake with the water just above the bonnet. The reason for all this was that there was the possibility that we would be invading France. As the ships would not be able to get near enough to the beach, the lorries had to be waterproofed. We were warned not to talk about this of course. Our vehicles were parked up in a huge area and when we had finished working on the waterproofing we had a large area dug out, filled with water, in order to test the vehicles. I warned my lads that if a vehicle did not get through the water without breaking down it would not be towed out! They would have to jump in and push and pull it out. Another officer, Jimmy Salter, commanding another platoon, had been involved with me in this whole operation. Anyway, one vehicle did get stuck and Jimmy and I, both in our denims, were the first to dive in. The lads did the same and then it was towed out, amidst much laughter! Jimmy and I then walked back to the major's office.

The major grinned and said, 'Come on chaps, have a drink with us,' and poured us each a Scotch. That was how our platoons worked – officers, NCOs and men – all together, a big happy family.

It was not until we arrived on the Welsh coast at Aberdovey that we discovered that we were to have a change of vehicles. Thirty-three amphibious DUKWs. We had to start learning all over again! What a difference they were from our usual lorries. We had been practising on the coast for a couple of days when my sergeant said to me, 'I'm a bit worried about our lads, sir – they're saying that they chose to join the Army, not the Navy!' I replied, 'Get them on parade Ambrose and I'll have a word with them.'

'NOW, look here you chaps, you're not in the Navy, the Americans invented the wonderful DUKW and you're lucky to be driving them. You're still in the RASC but you have vehicles, which can go where ordinary lorries and ships couldn't. Now then, any of you who wish to complain, take one pace forward, but remember, if more than one of you takes a pace forward that would be mutiny and you all know what that could mean to you!' Not one movement. 'Right,' I said, 'Dismiss and off you go.' They all raised their arms, laughed and dashed off.

The platoon now consisted of thirty-three DUKWs and ninety-nine men.

On 5 June we drove to Southampton where the American navy had some large ships lined up and waiting. We backed onto the ships – so that we would be able to drive off, which was essential. We spent a thoroughly miserable night on a very rough sea and landed on the beach of Normandy on 6 June 1944.

To my surprise and the delight of my chaps they named the whole event after me – D-Day!

Colonel Reeves of headquarters, who was responsible for the development of the Duplex Drive tanks, was given a lift ashore to enable him to obtain first-hand pictures of them in action. Later I received a communiqué from Colonel Reeves enclosing pictures he had taken of us on the road at Southampton and on the ship.

What a day on the beach – who could possibly forget 'D-Day'?

Douglas Day, Greenford, Middlesex

I was in the 8th Battalion, Sherwood Foresters and it was during the fighting in Norway in 1940 that I was taken prisoner. After three years in Germany I was moved to Poland where I worked with the old blacksmith who was called Janeck. He was Polish and a Communist. I used to work the bellows for him sometimes and as he worked he would very quietly whistle the Russian anthem, give a knowing wink and smile and curse all things German! Occasionally he would supply me with sandwiches as food was scarce and Red Cross supplies could not get through because of the bad winter. This had happened every winter I was a Prisoner of War, with the roads and railways snowbound, and up to thirty degrees of frost. In fact in the winter of 1940–41 temperatures reached minus forty degrees – the worst winter for over one hundred years. In 1944 talk of the invasion grew. Then one beautiful June morning I was working away in the joiner's shop when Janeck came and asked if I could lend a hand in his workshop. I followed him and as I entered he suddenly grabbed me and pushed me into a corner. 'British and American troops have landed in North France this morning,' he said in German, putting his finger over his mouth as he whispered to me. I must have jumped a yard off the floor! The news we had been waiting for for over four years had at last arrived. For the rest of the day I could scarcely contain my joy and delight and also my apprehension about how things would turn out. Then the others who were working in the fields came back at the end of the day – they already knew! There must have been a hidden wireless somewhere among the Polish workers. They were considered by the Germans to be 'sub-human' – 'Untermensch' was their word – and not allowed radio sets. There were severe penalties if caught and indeed the Germans were in the same position if caught listening to the BBC.

Can you imagine our chatter and delight that night? Out came half a bottle of schnapps we had been saving for just such an occasion, together with what tins of food we had saved for a rainy day. But of course the guard had still not received the news at that time so we had to celebrate very quietly! Of course, in the middle of our 'silent' celebrations we were all very apprehensive about whether the invasion would be a success. We knew the dangers our troops would be facing and that there would almost certainly be many casualties, and amidst our own delight we all, I know, were thinking of our lads in France and hoping they would come through it all right. We all honestly thought the war would be over in a very short time – at least September or October and certainly before Christmas, but of course this was not to be. It was another eleven months before I met the Americans on the banks of the river Elbe after an eight hundred mile march through the bitter winter of 1945. That march was through horrific scenes of refugees freezing to death, and old men,

 women and children dying horribly in so many different ways and of different causes. That march was a story in itself. Although many years have passed my memories have not dimmed one iota nor will they ever. Even after all the years I still go into Nottingham, walk through the streets, look in the shops and call in somewhere for a meal. And then I remember the days when I was far away from home and my loved ones, lonely, cold and very often very hungry, and I just used to dream of such things and of home.

The Polish blacksmith who first gave me the news was aged about fifty-five to sixty and I don't know what finally happened to him. He had fought against the Germans in 1914 with the Russian army and then fought with the new Polish army against Russia in 1921 when the new Polish state was established by the Treaty of Versailles. His two sons had been taken by the Germans to Germany for forced labour and whether they survived or not I don't know. I like to think they did and that they were reunited with their father because he was a good man, but probably it didn't happen. The Poles were detested by the Germans and were subjected to degradation at the slightest excuse.

But I know personally that many good deeds were done by them for the British Prisoners of War at great risk to themselves, and I know many others will forever be grateful to them.

John K. Gilbert, West Bridgford, Nottingham

To go back to Normandy had become an obsession over the many years, for the impact of those beachhead days had seared a scar across the surface of memory, a scar which divided for always that which went before and that which followed.

The ramp drops slowly to give exit for the cargo of cars, caravans and holidaymakers. They file ashore in orderly fashion to the directions of the officer-in-charge. He does not shout or scream, nor do they curse their day of birth. There is no carnage to greet them, there is no reluctance to move forward and their path ashore is not marked by tapes of white. Water does not engulf them for their landing is dry and their faces reflect the pleasures they anticipate. They will return, of that there is no doubt, and there is no fear among them. When they move on there is nought to show where they have been.

A blue and red sign by the roadside carries the symbol of men from the sky and this canal bridge is named Pegasus. Words carved into a block of stone standing on the enemy bank tell of those who died for this bridge. Boys fish and girls play, and Pegasus, with wings spread in static flight, is not a part of today. The road along the home bank of the River Orne is tarmac now. Dust no longer means death, but now there is no dust for the surface is tarmac as it rises to meet the road that crosses the second bridge that fell to Pegasus yesterday. At its junction there is no small plot of fresh turned earth with a helmet askew on a makeshift cross of sticks. The ground is not hallowed and there is no reminder of the inevitability, which for this paratrooper came sooner than its time.

These are the River Orne and the Caen Canal, but the carcasses of gliders, which gutted themselves to disgorge their human load after a silent descent, are not here, for they lie by another Orne and another canal, both of which will not be seen again. Boys fish for their pleasure and they catch only fish. No bloated corpses with the tide, no crosses to make, no ground to hallow, and there is no fear.

The river and the canal seem broader now, and speedboats tow surf riders along their lengths, while campers settle near the water's edge. The young French family take supper before retiring to their tent. The night is still after the heat of the day and the water laps gently against the bank. The dusk does not bring a fury from the sky and sleep comes easy for there is no nightmare of violence around them. The morning will dawn and they will again enjoy the day for they will be refreshed. For them, night and day will not be one in anger. There is no fear and the gentle lapping of the water was not heard yesterday.

The ditch is spanned by a bridge from another life and Bailey panels rust. Grass overgrows decking and the quarry is the site of oil tanks. Was this the place that was cursed and swore at as pontoons slowly bridged that other Caen canal?

'Forward panel party!' 'Transoms here!' 'Get the pin in and bloody well move!' And above all, the noise of hell on earth.

Now, the water is empty and the night still, but this bridge over this ditch has known the sweat, and the hands of fresh men. It has trembled, as they trembled, and now the panels rust and are red.

Graye-sur-Mer, Reviers, Amblie, Saint-Aubin-d'Arquenay, Ouistreham, Ranville, name after name are yesterday's and today. The village of Reviers is quiet save for the column of children who are led in orderly fashion by their teachers for a trip into the country. Their chatter is occasionally broken by laughter and the large building standing in its own ground, which they leave behind, is not a hospital for wounded, but a holiday home for underprivileged children. A woman stops and speaks of her work there as a nurse during her beachhead days, then she returns the waves of the children before going about her business of today. The sound of other children singing is carried across from the open windows and they are happy in this Normandy, for no man will bleed or die in this place that is also their temporary home. An occasional car or farm vehicle negotiates the crossroads and two old men, sitting on the form in front of the cafe, puff contentedly at their pipes.

The graves of this military cemetery are tended by men who knew war and the comradeship of war. It shows in their work. The rows of white stones stand out in sharp irreverence against the green of the lawns, their numbers inspiring awe, yet by that very fact placing their full meaning beyond the bounds of normal comprehension. The flowers between them, and the information inscribed on stone are the only individualising characteristics. From the endless ranks of khaki to a plot, a row and a number in that row. Their names are as distant as the years except for those who knew and loved them including those who saw them die. Memorial panels bear the names of those who found no grave, and all these are the visual receipts of a price paid.

Alan Cairns. Row G. No. 14. This is not where we laid him! The hedge beneath which he fell stands innocently in the sun, its leaves tremble and rustle in the breeze. The gate, the field, and the village of Amblie along the road, are now quiet today. The field bears its corn and the gate is locked. Beneath the hedge the grass is not red nor the vision bloody. Is this the spot which was the shallow grave of a blanket-wrapped Cairnsey? There is no cross, and corn grows golden where the eyes of men as young as he secretly shed their tears.

In this place there is a stone. Alan Cairns, like me, serving then in 234 Field Co., Royal Engineers. Aged twenty-three. The shock of his dying, our first, is as the shock of yesterday. What reason gave him this lawned plot while I stand and give respect in the only way I know? What would he have made of the years between? Would he have felt such an involuntary sacrifice worthwhile?

He died, as did all here, in the belief that the children he was never to father would live better lives because of they who had to give that which was most precious. It was not a spoken or even conscious belief, but it was a meaning, a reason that made the lunacy acceptable. Their dying was not done voluntarily and there was no glory in their dying. They did not part willingly with life, for death was the lot of the other fellow, and death does not come any easier to the young.

My daughter, aged eight, calls me to go. Alan would have loved her as he would have his own. He was like that. He would have been happy to know he was remembered by a pal who had journeyed, a lifetime away, along a path that for him had ended on that day in June, 1944. We shall return home to continue the life he and they left for us. It was not for them to enjoy the peace they had helped to win – it was for us to give their loss some meaning – it was for our children to enjoy what they made possible.

God bless you Alan. A stone tells those who care to look that you are twenty-three, and we have been together again for a little while in this place that is Normandy. I have trod again the beach you trod and seen the things you saw. They were not pretty then, when fear walked with us. Gone are the barbed wire, the mines and the stench. Here and there stands a gun, a blockhouse, a memento from the past, and everywhere are the memorials. People finger and gaze without emotion at the weapons of war implanted to stop you, the dead, and we, who lived. The iron, the concrete, the bullet-scarred houses mean nothing now. They revive the memories of we who knew, but they are not now of the time that saw you die. That was another world in another age.

Museums, films, may perpetuate the happening in documentation and illuminate the glory that was supposed to be, but death for the living is a myth, while for you, the dead, it is an experience.

It is your names, not the stones, that are real for us who knew. Thank you for our children and for our children's children. They will never comprehend the price you paid, nor would you expect them to. These names on stone are youths brought prematurely to manhood and who died involuntarily before their time. Pals, buddies, husbands, sweethearts, brothers and sons. Only we who saw them die can know of the love they had for life, and the fear we shared of death. We enjoyed a comradeship that only war seems to bring and they died with that comradeship in their hearts.

Life is richer than it may have been because of them and it is their unconscious gift to us all. Have we used the years given to us and which were lost to them? Have we justified the hopes that are every name upon a stone? Would he, and he, and he, be able to say: 'I am proud to have known the living?'

We have years yet to come, pray to God that we use them, for these years, past and future, constitute a lifetime that should have been theirs, a lifetime ago.

Richard 'Jacko' Jackson, Bramhall, Stockport

The training was over – no more manoeuvres sending the skipper white haired with anxiety. This was the real thing. We loaded up with five tanks of the Green Howards at the hards at Portsmouth. As is pretty well known D-Day was cancelled for twenty-four hours due to inclement weather, so we had some pretty miserable squaddies on board I can tell you! They were feeling a bit sick even at anchor. We eventually sailed with our craft LCT 1079, twelve little tank landing craft in our group, setting off for who knows what.

That night there was a strong feeling aboard that we were going to do this damned invasion all on our own for all that we could see! But as the dawn broke gradually came the most incredible sight. Everywhere you looked there were landing craft and ships of all descriptions including just astern of us HMS *Warspite*, which made me feel a hell of a lot braver than I had been until then!

Gradually the French coast came into view and at about 6:30am the skipper told me to hoist the battle ensign and pipe all hands to battle stations. This I did, feeling quite a bit proud of myself as I did it I can tell you. I still have the pipe and a remnant of the ensign to this day.

With the ensign flying we headed on towards our objective, Gold Beach, and as we passed under a posh cruiser, the *Belfast* no less, she let go a broadside which scared the hell out of every one of us! I don't think anyone had to dash for clean underpants but it must have been a close run thing!

As we came in nearer we could now see and hear the rocket and gun landing craft letting fly. Things were really hotting up now. Then we saw our planned landing point on the beach and if anyone had looked on the bridge all they would have seen were two steel pimples – the skipper's and my steel helmets. We were not afraid of course – just being very careful. But as a matter of course nothing ever goes to plan and this was no exception. As we headed for our planned arrival point we realised that there was nowhere to land – amazing but true. We just had to manoeuvre and change course until we did find a space, which fortunately for us was still in roughly the right area. That fact in itself perhaps will give people today some idea of the number of craft and men that were there – all heading pell-mell for the same beaches.

Suddenly we hit the beach with a crash, there was an almighty explosion on the port bow and two winchmen shot out of their little cubby holes with eyes popping and mouths wide open and looking up at the bridge, as if to say, 'What the bloody hell did you do that for!' The skipper, who sported a natty ginger beard, suddenly changed from being 'wavy navy' to 'Royal Navy' and told them both to get back into the winch house. 'There's good chaps.' Or words to that effect.

We dropped the ramp and the first tank managed to get ashore, although submerged to a depth of about four or five feet, and amazingly, bearing in mind the noise, shells and God knows what else, we managed to get all the troops, tanks and equipment ashore in pretty good order. While all this was going on remember that other landing craft were also charging in and generally having a rough time of it. Two on our starboard bow blew up in short order before they hit the beach, bodies being thrown in all directions.

Just after the two landing craft were hit a report came in that our engine room was flooding. I went belting down and found the stoker with his feet on the control panel with about two and a half feet of water sloshing around him. I also saw a chunk of iron rail sticking up through the deck! One of Rommel's little gadgets had worked only too well on our craft! However, the stoker assured me he was confident he could keep the engines going so I returned to the bridge to report.

Having done so I looked about and could see army men in the water and on the beaches, all heavily loaded and wearing battle green. Some of those in the water were struggling and some of their mates on shore were trying to throw heaving lines to them but to be honest they hadn't a clue. So we joined in and managed to pull five or six chaps out of the surf, which was very heavy at the time, but there were others we weren't able to help in time and it was heartbreaking to see some of them drowning in front of your eyes. I think that, more than anything else, upset me and my shipmates.

Eventually the tide went out leaving us high and dry, and we were able to get ashore and assess the damage. The port bow had a hole in it about seven feet by three feet, and was turned back like a sardine can. As mentioned before, the engine room had a tetrahedron up through the deck and we were lying on a hump on the beach, which had buckled the craft amidships.

Some distance away I could see a body lying just out of the surf. Walking over I saw it was a young marine commando aged about twenty. I looked down at him and I remember thinking, I wonder what your mother will say and feel when she gets that telegram in a couple of days' time.

A few of us explored the gun emplacements, which our ships had been plastering; we found that they had not done all that much damage but the commandos had gone up to the embrasures with flame throwers and the ammunition inside the gun emplacements had exploded.

All we could find were three or four charred boots. The walls were lined with steel plate and it looked like a colander where the shrapnel had pierced it. But the emplacement itself was completely intact. These guns were not taken without loss as the five British bodies outside testified. By this time German prisoners were arriving on the beach and it seemed about one in four were Russians, which seemed very odd to us at the time. The RN beach parties were also there and were busy welding up the holes we had sustained while making the landing.

We were ordered to anchor for the night and to proceed to Portland at first light. None of us had had much sleep for forty-eight hours, and me less than most, being the only one that could read the signals. So guess who had the midnight watch. Yes, muggins was on watch for four long hours. While on watch and listening to the rumble of gunfire off the beaches, I was staring at three tanks burning just on the shoreline and should mention that I was stood on the iron ladder leading down to the mess deck with my arms leaning over the hatchway. The next thing I knew was Jimmy shouting, 'Bunts, wake up. Get up on deck immediately!!' Well, my brain registered this but my legs were as dead as doornails, I could not, repeat, could not move. What with him hollering at me and an almighty effort on my part I somehow got up on deck.

Of course this meant I was in a lot of trouble. Asleep on

watch, off the enemy coast. I was put in front of the CO next morning and I gave him the blarney about having no sleep for two days, which he knew was the truth because he hadn't had much sleep either. Anyway, I got a fortnight's No. 11 [punishment of stoppage of leave], which didn't matter much because we were on duty non-stop anyway.

Now the skipper had a nice little Wren back in Portland and when we finally set sail, instead of going through the swept Channel, he went diagonally across the Channel to Portland. Quicker you see, but bloody dangerous, but we made it. I had managed to get my head down for a couple of hours when there was the dreaded cry, 'Bunts. On the bridge at the double.'

When I got up there, there was a big red lamp about two feet across, flashing away like mad. It read STOP OR I FIRE upon which I made the fastest recognition signal in the annals of the British Navy! The ship flashing was the harbour guard ship and although it was only a big trawler she had a four-inch gun trained smack on us.

Well, that is more or less the tale of D-Day as I remember it. We were sent on leave for two days while repairs were carried out and, while visiting an old aunt who lived in Bang's Road, a woman stopped me in the street and asked me what I was doing walking around Banbury while her son was across the Channel fighting Germans. Well, to say I was stuck for words and nonplussed was putting it mildly. It was not a pleasant feeling, being handed the verbal white feather. I think I managed to convince her I had done my little bit, but as they say folk is funny.

Ray 'Lofty' G. Fletcher, Banbury, Oxfordshire

I was in the King's Regiment No. 5 Beach Group. Everything in our training was geared up to the landing on the Normandy beaches and although talk of the invasion was a daily occurrence in training, it was almost unknown outside the beach groups. The long and indeed arduous days of training came to an end when we moved south to Havant, near Portsmouth. It was like a tented city as troops moved in from all over the countryside for the final briefing and kitting out. Each man was given two twenty-four-hour food packs, two bandoliers of ammunition, hand grenades, a complete change of clothing, a jerkin and lifebelt, and a blanket wrapped in a groundsheet. We also received two hundred 'liberation money' French francs, a can of self-heating cocoa and a can of self-heating soup, both of which turned out to be excellent and satisfying.

We were all keyed up and ready to go on 4 June but the weather changed and the whole show was delayed for twenty-four hours which was a real anticlimax after such a massive mental build-up. Next day we returned to the landing craft at Newhaven and moved out into the Channel into the assembly area. As we started the journey it was a fantastic sight – everywhere you looked you could see ships of every shape and size, an armada that had to be seen to be believed. It was very comforting I can tell you to realise that we had such magnificent support, but that didn't help with the weather! It was still rough and most of the troops on board were seasick. In fact if truth be known, some of them were in a hell of a state.

When we got within shelling distance of the French coast it seemed as if all hell had broken loose. Landing craft on either side of ours had been hit and were on fire or already sinking. Our ramps were dropped when we came close to the beach and we charged out through the water as best we could. The waves were very rough and the water was still shoulder high. There was one consolation – as we hit the water our minds were so concentrated on getting ashore safely that the seasickness disappeared!

Actually, as we stepped onto the beach, despite all our fears, was a marvellous feeling. As we made our way forward there seemed to be mines and mined obstructions everywhere, and many landing craft and tanks on fire. There were dead and wounded everywhere on the beach, both on the sand itself and in the water, and at the water's edge. It was painful but we had to press on – the medics would see to those that could be helped. Indeed as the Germans were pushed back from the beach, the Beach Group Organisation took over and the whole system amazingly started to work exactly as had been planned in our training. All that in spite of continued heavy shelling and gunfire.

At about 5:30pm our company managed to reach the first road from the beach after heavy fighting. I was operating a controlled-radio set but was unable to make any contact with one of our platoons. As the company commander was worried about the missing platoon the Sergeant Major took over the radio and sent me off to try to locate them. Making my way along the road I heard a salvo of shells over my head and then an enormous explosion. The next thing was the excruciating pain of shrapnel in my back and right forearm. The worst part was that the missing platoon turned out to be all right and in position. The only problem was that their radio had gone on the blink!

I was badly wounded in my back and forearms and destined to spend all night lying on a stretcher in a dugout in the sand. That in itself was quite traumatic as I was on my own

and could only use one hand to try and keep away the sand which covered me each time the guns fired. Lying on my back, unable to sleep, I had at least the privilege of seeing the second wave of paratroopers coming in that night. The parachutes mixed in with the searchlights and all interlaced with tracer bullets created a fantastic sight, never to be forgotten.

At about 7am next morning all the stretchers were lifted on to a DUKW and we were taken along the beach, and then out to the ships lying offshore and finally back to Blighty. They called D-Day the 'longest day'. It was certainly the longest day of my life!

James McCall, Wigan, Lancashire

The date, 3 June 1944. The time, 21:00 hours. I was in Royal Navy Intelligence at Normandy. I had embarked onto a U Class submarine to patrol the coast of Normandy and to go ashore in a rubber dinghy. The weather was terrible, gusting winds and squally showers, the seas running at about four to six feet high. My job was to monitor any troop movement on the coast and report. We were not to engage the enemy in any way. There was not much to report, just a few military vehicles at dawn on 4 June. We returned to base on the south coast. Troops were already loaded into landing craft – hundreds of them.

On the evening of 4 June, 20:30 hours, I was again ordered back to the Normandy coast. On the way out we passed landing craft of all sizes, crammed with troops and heavy armour. These poor lads had been on board for three or four days owing to cancellations with bad weather. You could almost read their minds, some just huddled up with their own thoughts, tension written on their faces, perhaps saying a silent prayer not knowing what to expect at the other side. Most of these young men had never fought before and this thought must have been going through their minds. A lot of these lads never returned. Thousands were to die on that first day, 6 June.

We stayed off the Normandy coast all night but early morning, 6 June, as the slight mist lifted we saw the Channel crammed full of ships and landing craft of all sizes. I transferred onto a command destroyer to coordinate the landing on Gold Beach of the 50th Infantry

Division. Suddenly at 05:00 hours all hell broke loose with every warship of the Allies opening up a barrage of shelling such as has never been known. The RAF went over with bombers and troop carriers. They, in turn, towing gliders full of paratroopers, each plane with the distinctive white strips on wings and fuselage for easy identification.

Immediately the guns opened, the first wave of assault ships headed for the beaches. My job was then to see all the landing craft arrived at their allotted area of beach. Any broken down or damaged we immediately towed out of the way so as not to cause congestion but, sorry to say, even then mistakes were made. I saw one landing craft stop too short of the beach, unfortunately still in deep water. Several of the men were drowned by having their packs on. Again we saw a tank disappear after having been landed in too deep water.

Sadly on these occasions you felt inadequate at not being able to help and to myself they were very upsetting to watch. The RAF glider lads unfortunately had their own troubles with many a glider crashing, killing most on board, but even so this was the best secret of the war as the Germans were totally surprised, possibly due to an earlier decoy attack further up the coast. It did not take them long to recover, however, and then some fierce fighting went on. This was the turning point of the war. We held the skies and seas and now a foothold on French soil, but we paid a high price in men, ships and aircraft. Breakwaters were then formed with 'caissons' – floating boxes of concrete. These were sunk and formed a Mulberry harbour. This speeded up landing of vehicles and heavy armour. At the time we had approximately five thousand ships and two hundred and fifty thousand men, but to a man they gave their all. There were many acts of bravery; some will never be known. It amazed me that they had the strength to run onto the beach after being cramped up for days in such appalling weather, but they did it with such courage and devotion to the job in hand it made this the proudest moment of my life, to have served with these men, and to all that survived I know that this was one day in their lives never to be forgotten – D-Day.

I give thanks to the Lord that I survived but my thoughts will always be with those men that did not return, those lads I knew and also the thousands I never knew but was so proud to be a part of.

Walter R. Marshall, Cleethorpes, North East Lincolnshire

The assault landing craft bobbed up and down on the choppy sea; on board were men of the Ox and Bucks Light Infantry, part of the 3rd Division.

The beachhead was now in view. Smoke and flame could be seen all along the wide front. Shells continued to pound the positions ahead, the screaming noise as they passed over our heads was horrific as I am sure they were only passing a few feet above us. I understand that it was guns from our battleships out at sea. I remember seeing the Ramillies when we passed through on our way in.

We were getting close now. I still recall the intense noise, the cold sweat on my skin. I was not aware of any fear, perhaps a tinge of excitement, a strange feeling that I was not there! Everything was in a confused mixture. I do remember checking my kit for no reason at all for I had done it a dozen times before. I tried the magazine on my Bren gun to make sure it was secure in position and that the safety catch was on.

There was a sudden lurch of the craft as it struck the

sandy beach. The ramp was down and the lads in front of me were taking to the water. I heard the commands 'move, move'. I walked off the edge of the ramp into the water. I could smell the seawater as it ebbed around my waist. I held the Bren gun above my head and slowly moved forward.

Not far away, to my left, I saw a body, face down in the water. His still inflated Mae West was keeping him afloat. The air was filled with a pungent smell of burning oil tinged with what I assumed to be cordite.

Through the heavy smoke I ran, oblivious of the load I carried and heard the sound of heavy machine gun fire. I scrambled up the slippery dune, saw an abandoned tank perched on the top, its engine still running. To my right was a large house and through a hole in the roof an enemy machine gun was spraying the beach behind me. I slipped over the top of the dune as more machine guns began to open up. In front of us I saw a couple of our lads fall. I then went to ground, took up a firing position, and opened up covering as wide an area as was possible. My number two came alongside changing the magazines. We must have fired six before I realised the barrel was now getting quite hot. It was a great relief to see tanks passing through at great pace. I think they were the Polish Brigade. Things got a little easier as we pushed inland. I suppose we must have penetrated a couple of miles when the order came to dig in. Our point of position was a hedgerow somewhere near the Caen road.

The platoon officer came round, said all was going well, but be prepared for possible counter-attacks. He collected the little brown cards that were issued back in England. They were a simple card that were already printed out, saying you were OK and you would write soon. All one had to do was address it home, put your name and army number in the space provided, and sign it. The officer promised it would be on its way home that night. I remember feeling good about that.

I did return on the 6 June 1985, as did so many others. During my visit I met up with a Canadian, a tall figure, aged now, with the need of a walking stick. It inspired this poem, dedicated to all who took part in the greatest invasion of all time.

He stands beside the water's edge,
Stooped with age yet alert,
Deep in thought he sees once more,
The race across the hostile shore.

Dawn awakes with thundering sound,
Of firing guns, and all around,
The cries of beings duty done,
Fall to the ground, one by one.

Friend and foe on blooded sand,
Find peace at last, on foreign land,
Stillness shrouds their final quest,
No more in battle, they lie at rest.

Now the thinker in faltering gate,
Moves once more over the sands of hate,
Looks for comrades, who perished there,
They did not falter, they did not dare.

The lonely beach is empty now,
Save for the figure on the dune,
Standing in silhouette against a ghostly moon,
His tear-washed eyes mournfully,
Scan the horizon to eternity.

Have I in ignorance, made intrusion,
Upon this sacred past illusion,
Or can it be that I was led,
To see a ghostly spirit, of the D-day dead.

Arthur Saunders, Alfreton, Derbyshire

It was approaching midnight on the 5 June 1944 and the engines of my Dakota were droning away, awaiting take-off. For days we had been confined to camp, together with the Airborne Battalion, spending hour after hour at briefing, studying large models of the French coastline and the countryside beyond. We had memorised every house, road, telegraph pole, tree – even the cows in the fields! My task was to drop a number of paratroopers alongside a gun emplacement, which needed putting out of action. Their faces were blackened and they presented a frightening sight.

We took off in Vic's of three and both to my port and starboard sides were Dakotas only a few yards away. All lights and intercommunications were extinguished very soon after take-off and everything had to be carried out visually. Suddenly, we entered cloud and completely lost sight of the formatting aircraft. After what seemed an eternity, we were out of cloud and there in perfect formation were the two other aircraft to port and starboard. In the darkness around could now be identified many other aircraft heading slowly towards the Channel and the Allied Fleet could be seen in the haze below; a sight never to be forgotten. Ships of all shapes and sizes, many with barrage balloons at the end of steel cables stretching up towards us from the Channel below. I put the Dakota in a controlled descent, pulling the throttle back gently. At the dropping height, the signal to jump was given. When the last of the paras had left the aircraft, I pushed the throttle fully forward, climbing all the while, and turned for home. Just as we crossed the French coast all hell broke loose. Gunfire came from all directions, tracer bullets, anti-aircraft fire resulting in puffs of smoke and flashes from what seemed like the whole of the British and American fleets. It seemed that we were being used for target practice! To my starboard side I saw another Dakota diving in order to avoid the fire and he was dangerously low, risking entanglement in the barrage

balloon cables. A burst of smoke, close to my port wing, caused a cascade of glass to fall in the cockpit, through a smashed side window. Even the repeated firing of our Very Pistols Recognition Signal made no difference and I therefore made a tight turn of 180 degrees heading back to the comparative safety of mainland France. After climbing to over six thousand feet, I once again tried to cross the coast, heading north, but had to return once again! The barrage from the fleet was extremely formidable.

Continuing my climb in the now freezing cockpit, I headed east along the French coast and soon Le Havre loomed up underneath unlit, but still recognisable in the distance. There was only spasmodic fire from the ground and no sign of any night fighters. Any puffs of smoke were well off target. Crossing the coast was now easy, not a ship or aircraft in sight. It was still early morning of D-Day and, soon after debriefing, we were fast asleep. D-Day must have been one of the shortest days of my life!

During the next two weeks we engaged in numerous missions to France, including flying SAS personnel to deserted airfields in France close to the German lines. Their missions were completely secret as far as we were concerned. All we ever saw of them was during the offloading in France. Even then, their faces were covered with scarves. This was to ensure that, if we were ever taken prisoner, recognition was impossible. They were presumably engaged in all kinds of 'devious' activities.

One day I landed at a strip in a cornfield near Bayeux. The farmer was a very agreeable fellow and took me along to his farmhouse to meet the family and drink wine. He presented me with a large box of Camembert cheese, which I then transported back to the UK and gave to a doctor friend in Oxford. He immediately designated it to the dustbin saying, 'It is too smelly, and therefore absolutely unfit for human consumption; typical of the food eaten by the French.' Now I realise that the cheese was in its prime and the gift should have been appreciated and enjoyed!

J. Courtney P. Thomas, Falmouth, Cornwall

I volunteered to join the Royal Navy and was 'called up' in 1943 at the age of seventeen.

After training, in February 1944 I joined the light cruiser HMS *Scylla* as an Ordinary Seaman Radar Operator (O/S RP3). The ship had just completed a major refit in Chatham dockyard and she was equipped with the latest radar detection system and we were an entirely new crew. We were told by the captain that the ship would be playing a major role in the coming 'Second Front', eventually becoming the flagship for Rear Admiral Philip Vian, already a war hero for his exploits commanding HMS *Cossack*. He captured the German prisoner ship *Altmark* in the Norwegian campaign.

After sea trials at Scapa Flow in the Orkneys we returned to our home port of Portsmouth and 'second front fever' was high. The dockyard was crammed with landing craft, large and small, being made ready for the great invasion. Portsmouth city itself was packed with Allied soldiers and airmen. Pubs and cinemas were doing a roaring trade!

We were constantly putting to sea, patrolling the English Channel, taking part in exercises with other ships in mock invasions and night exercises.

On 4 June, Portsmouth dockyard was alive with military vehicles of every description. Tanks, armoured cars, trucks and many thousands of troops were boarding landing craft and going to sea. When we set sail, landing craft were everywhere, filled with soldiers, their faces blackened ready for combat. We anchored with the rest of the great armada off the Isle of Wight and then learned that the invasion was postponed for twenty-four hours because of rough weather.

The evening of 5 June came, but the seas were still very rough. But, the invasion was on despite the rough seas. We were taking part at dawn the next day, 6 June, in the D-Day landings, three weeks after my eighteenth birthday.

The invasion began at 5:30am. Our target was the town of Ouistreham. Our instructions were to bombard the town with our main guns, to soften up the German garrison. On our way across, we all had to make a will. The captain spoke to us over the address system telling us that they didn't know what to expect from the German defences and 'that by this time tomorrow we could all be in Kingdom Come'. I was on watch in the RADAR/PLOT room, directly under the bridge. Our job was to search for enemy surface craft and aircraft.

When we arrived off Normandy the bombardment began. It was like all hell had been let loose. Ships of all the Allied navies, large and small, were shelling the coast. The noise was incredible. The sky was full of aircraft towing gliders filled with paratroopers that would be landing in enemy

occupied territory. As we fired salvo after salvo our ship vibrated to the extent that everything had to be battened down. The air was filled with cordite fumes. Orders were barked down voice pipes from the bridge as we went about our task like clockwork.

As the day wore on we were allowed to return to the mess

deck, two men at a time, for a drink of cocoa and a sandwich. While I was in the mess deck I heard a violent explosion. All the men not on watch were ordered to the port side. A ship had been sunk and survivors were in the water. We threw a scrambling net over the side and our ship stopped to allow them to climb aboard. The men were covered in oil, some wounded, others obviously stunned. We reached down to haul them aboard and the deck was a mixture of water, oil and blood.

A German plane appeared over our stern, dropping a bomb that just missed us. That evening the whole coastline seemed to be on fire, church steeples were outlined against the flames. Later that night I went down to the mess deck; it was packed with Dutch and Norwegian sailors, survivors we had collected during the battle that day. But on 23 June at 11:30pm our turn came! We hit a mine, which broke the ship's back and we had to be towed back to Chatham.

Wilfred Foulds, Rossendale, Lancashire

I was a nurse at Westminster Hospital, London and shortly before D-Day a batch of us were moved to Basingstoke to the Park Prewett Hospital. There was tremendous activity on the evening prior to D-Day at the nearby airfields and we saw numerous large planes towing gliders (obviously laden with paratroopers) during that evening, and in the very early hours of the morning of 6 June. Of course we didn't know exactly what it all was, but all this intense activity prepared us in advance for the news that was eventually announced.

There had been a great deal of prior planning about patients coming to us from the battle zone. The wounded were brought back across the Channel by the Royal Navy and placed on trains that had been adapted for transporting casualties. The patients were then taken to Park Prewett and other hospitals as quickly as possible. We actually received our first batch of wounded on D-Day itself. Many of them

were commandos and they were suffering from all kinds of injuries. Temporary first aid had clearly already been rendered but the next stage of treatment fell to us and the awaiting medical and surgical teams. Patients arrived in many cases with their clothing still wet – sea water – and very often with the sand still on it, and many were still so shocked that they did not even then realise the injuries from which they were suffering.

But what was so outstanding and will always live in my memory was their behaviour; their utmost concern for companions and trying to make light of their own injuries. They tried in every possible way to be of as little a burden as possible; trying to get off stretchers to help themselves and always, always so grateful for anything that was done for them. Very often further injuries were discovered after they had been carefully undressed and more fully examined.

In the days that followed the casualty flow continued but the patients were never again in the wet condition that we saw on that first day. It was a day I am sure that all of us who were providing medical and nursing care will never forget. Over the years we had been treating air raid casualties – and there had been many – but this was the first time we had seen troops straight from the battle zone. And yet in all their pain their thoughts were of gratitude to the Royal Navy for getting them back home, and to the Royal Army Medical Corps for the work they had done until they arrived at the hospital.

We had many different nationalities to treat. Men from the Commonwealth, men who had escaped from their country and made their way to the UK and who were so proud to be helping to set Europe free. Poles, Czechoslovaks, French and many, many more. It was our privilege to now be able to help them and to be part of the plan for bringing freedom back to what until then had for five years been Occupied Europe.

Among our patients were also some German soldiers. The younger ones were still very arrogant and, despite everything, still very pro-Hitler, but the older ones seemed to be relieved to be safe and being looked after.

The feeling of being able to be even a small cog in such a big wheel was one of hope, and thankfulness that things had gone so well and that at last an end was in sight. I stayed at Park Prewett Hospital for several months and then returned to Westminster Hospital. Even then I still came across casualties I had attended to on D-Day at Park Prewett because that was the initial admission and sorting centre. Casualties were treated and then transferred to specialist hospitals such as orthopaedic, burns, plastic surgery etc., although at Park Prewett there was an initial plastic surgery unit for facial injuries and first-stage face, jaw and above-shoulder-level damage.

I get so distressed when I remember those young men coming to our hospital in so much pain, and then see books and articles written often by people who were not even born then, denigrating the actions of those who did the most courageous acts so that we might all enjoy the free life we can live today.

Winifrid Tuck, SRN, Horley, Surrey

I was in the Royal Signals, attached to 147 (Essex Yeomanry) Field Regiment RA. At 04:30 hours on 6 June the loud hailers on HMS *Nith* called all hands to stand to. As it gradually became light the sight that met our eyes was almost beyond description. Ships, ships and more ships. The lighter it became the more ships came into view, all sailing in the same direction, south. Overhead we could hear aircraft above the cloud. There seemed to be a continuous stream of them.

Suddenly there came the most appalling, devastating and mind bending crash of gunfire as several battleships quite close to us opened up with salvo after salvo of their main armaments. Broadsides of shells that weighed almost half a ton each went screaming off to land God only knew where, but we hoped would land squarely on the German coastal guns. What we did not know at the time was that the airborne boys were at that very moment dealing with the coastal guns.

We boarded our LCM at 06:15 hours but from our lowly position we were unable to see what progress was being made by the R-boats carrying the assault infantry and Beach Signals party. According to the time schedule our regimental run-in shoot should be about to start; also the 'hedgehogs' (low trajectory rocket launchers), which were designed to cut a swathe up the beach to destroy any mines or obstacles in the path of the infantry. Sure enough, almost dead on time the 'swoosh' of the rockets and staccato cracks of the twenty-five pounders on the LCTs started up. Soon we could see the beach defences. Lots of steel RSJs and bits of pipe welded together to form lethal-to-boats obstacles. The nasty ones were a post with an 88mm shell strapped to the top and a detonator plate pointing seaward. All kinds of other diabolical nasties that Jerry had thought up were waiting for the unwary.

From about one hundred yards out we could see the odd body lying about on the sand above waterline and a brewed-up tank just short of the sand dunes. The brigadier yelled to us, 'Don't stop to help casualties, get clear of the beach.' The RASC cox was looking for a clear way in between the obstacles but then stalled his engine (Scripps modified Ford V-8), which steadfastly refused to restart. By this time the LCM had drifted broadside onto the tide and as I looked over the side I could see an 88mm post-mounted shell about to brush the side. I leant back as far as I could against the Bren carrier and the shell exploded almost under my feet. The decking upon which we stood was about a foot above the actual outer skin of the LCM, but the detonation made my feet smart through the felt-soled assault boots! The in-rush of water into the lower compartment made the starting of the engine an impossibility and the brigadier called to the cox to lower the ramp. We had drifted bow-on to the beach again and could see the shit flying ashore. As senior officer, the brigadier sat on the end of the ramp and lowered himself into the water. At his mid-chest his feet touched the bottom and he yelled, 'All right Phayre, get the party ashore.' The colonel went next and being a shortish, plump officer he was only just in his depth. Even in such a dire predicament we all giggled at the figure he cut with his steel helmet knocked over his eyes. We all followed off the LCM, which had by this time settled by the stern and was a total loss taking the Bren carrier and motorcycle with her.

Finally we reached the edge of the water. The weight of our water-sodden clothing and gear was incredible and we were literally forced to our knees for the first few stumbling yards. The beach was fairly well pitted by craters from what we afterwards assumed to be mortar bombs, but we didn't stop to look. I told my pals Cpl Stan Lees and Sgt Bill Dick to follow me and then made a dash for the dunes, from which reasonable shelter we watched the CO strolling up the beach too buggered to even trot! After several back-tracks to avoid mined areas and being advised by infantry boys to keep our heads down at certain places, we finally joined up with the rest of the section. It was splendid to see the other members of the Signal Section all together again. What with being in separate camps before leaving England and travelling on different craft some of us hadn't met up for the best part of a month.

It was impossible at our level to know how the attack was going or if we were likely to be driven back into the sea. We did glean some information from the requests for fire. Most of these were given un-coded to save time since the recipients of the shells were the enemy. We could pinpoint where the shells were falling and so tell roughly where the front troops were located. The enemy must have got over the initial surprise of the landing because he was starting to throw stuff back at us in the shape of shells, probably 88mm, and multiple barrelled mortar bombs. These were particularly frightening since they screamed as they approached, but as someone remarked, 'The noise won't hurt you'.

Soon came the order to move forward. This was mainly to make room for more units to come off the beaches. By midday we found ourselves almost halfway between Arromanches and Bayeux. On the way up we had passed quite a number of dead German troops and a few khaki clad figures huddled by the roadsides. The occasional trickle of prisoners with their hands clasped on their heads came slogging back towards the beach, bound for POW cages in England.

A continuous rumble of tracked vehicles, mainly tanks, was kept up as more and more units were unloaded from landing craft. The amount of room in the bridgehead was limited and until the periphery could be pushed out, living was going to be pretty crowded. The armour of 8th Armoured Brigade, our parent unit, was almost the first ashore and had been in the thick of the advance all day. The Duplex Drive Sherman tanks of 13/18 Hussars were designed to 'swim' in from a couple of miles out, but since the sea had been rough, they had been brought right up to the beach by the landing craft pretty well at the same time as the assault infantry. This could have been why our trip up the beach had been so easy compared to other landings. Later we were to learn that the Americans at Omaha Beach had launched their DD tanks three miles out and had lost over seventy-five per cent of them. The Americans had also spurned the use of other British 'Funnies' of General Hobart. Among the Funnies was the Flail. This was a Churchill tank with a boom out in front upon which was a spindle furnished with lengths of very heavy chain. The spindle was driven from the tank engine and revolved at fairly high speed so that the chains thrashed the ground ahead of the tank, thereby exploding any mines in its path. The brigadier had led us up the beach in the path left by a flail. No doubt many lives were saved by the use of this marvellous device.

Another of General Hobart's brainchildren was called a 'fascine'. Here an enormous bundle of logs was carried on a couple of arms above the front of the Churchill. On encoun-

tering an anti-tank ditch, the bundle of logs was dropped into the ditch and the tank proceeded on its way across the ditch followed by as many more AFVs as necessary. Also there was the AVRE. This was a Churchill with an enormous mortar, about the size of a household dustbin, mounted forward of the turret. This was able to throw a huge charge against a pillbox or strongpoint, which usually disappeared in a cloud of dust. Another diabolical (for the enemy) device was the 'Crocodile'. This was a flamethrower capable of projecting a terrible jet of flame over a hundred yards. The chemicals were carried in a trailer, which was towed behind the tank and pumped to the nozzle mounted on the turret.

Such were the devices offered to the Americans. The only one that they chose was the least effective. The Duplex Drive tank. The result was the bloody slaughter on Omaha Beach. The troops were unable to move off the beach until almost dark and then at terrible cost.

When the RHQ moved forward we bypassed Bayeux and occupied a position south of a junction which we came to know as Jerusalem Crossroads. As we drove past, we could see scout cars that had been knocked out in the immediate vicinity of the crossroads. Also a couple of Sherman tanks had been brewed up close by. There had quite obviously been a terrific scrap for the area. It was fairly open country and the siting of anti-tank guns was easy. Further south the roads plunged into 'bocage' type countryside, which proved to be a tankman's nightmare.

Since we were pretty well up with the leaders of the advance, the OC considered it worthwhile laying lines out to the batteries. Shortly after our arrival the line parties from 8th Armoured Brigade and 50 Division brought in lines from their respective HQ. It was a pretty hazardous business to lay lines along the main roads since the number of tracked vehicles travelling south was enormous and since the weather had become rather more warm, the dust was increasing and reducing visibility to a few yards. The wireless links were kept open for fire orders and where possible the lines were used for administrative traffic.

Several times lines went 'dis' and the line parties were pretty stretched to keep them working. Jack Halford asked me to go out with him to clear a fault on the line to 50 Div. starting at our end, the divisional line party starting from the other end. As we suspected a break was located near Jerusalem Crossroads. I held on to the end of the cable from our HQ while Jack searched around for the other side of the break. It is possible for a vehicle to pull the end of a cable for many yards and it took Jack a few minutes to locate our cable. I bared the end of the cable and connected it to the DV, (Don 5 field telephone), shoved in the earth pin and called the exchange at our HQ. Straight away the exchange operator answered and I told him the position. At the same instant a battery of medium guns about fifty yards to my rear fired in unison. The fright I received left me shivering with terror and when Jack Halford returned with the other end of the line I was unable to speak for several minutes. As soon as Jack had spliced the line together the exchanges at both ends answered our call. Before we returned to RHQ we looked at a tank silhouetted against the sky. As we walked around to the front we could see by the light of Jack's hand-lamp two figures seated in the driver and gunner's seats through the open hatch doors. When we looked closer we could see that the figures were burnt corpses. No features or clothes, just an awful shape. Jack reached through the hatch and pushed one of them gently with his crook stick. It oscillated back and forth in a nodding fashion as though it was made of rubber. The mediums went off again and gave us another dreadful fright. I was very glad to get on the back of Jack's BSA and return to RHQ.

We finally settled in the inevitable orchard at a place we knew as Point 103. We were on the top of an almost imperceptible hill and had extended the slit trenches left by the infantry, as we were likely to be resident for a couple of days. The cooks had brewed up and a hot meal of some sort was being served. Visiting us from one of the batteries was their BSM (Battery Sergeant Major) whom the RSM had invited to have some food before he returned to his battery. Most of us were sitting in our slit trenches eating as the BSM walked across the orchard to join the RSM at the latter's Jeep. We all ducked when we heard incoming 'Moaning Minnies' approaching. After the explosions we looked up and saw that the BSM had gone. The blast had stripped all the foliage from one of the apple trees and had replaced it with shreds of khaki cloth. The BSM had literally been blown to pieces and later we had the doubtful pleasure of disentangling intestines from the branches of the tree. The rest of the bits were shovelled into a sack and buried. I wonder what the War Graves Commission made of it when they disinterred the remains.

Later we were told that an armoured counter-attack was coming in opposite our position. The gun positions were told to have AP (armour piercing) ammunition ready for use as well as HE. We were all well below ground level. All that is except the on-duty people who were mostly in light armour and fairly safe from shrapnel. One of the off-duty operators, namely RD 'Bob' Bruce, got out of his slit trench and stood relieving himself against the rear wheel of a three ton truck. When a mortar bomb burst on the other side of the truck, a piece of shrapnel pierced the water jerrycan on the near side storage rack, crossed the back of the vehicle, pierced the oil container on the off side and entered Bruce's buttock. We took him to the RAP (regimental aid post) and handed him over to Bombardier Spurling, the MO's orderly. Bruce returned to the section nine months later with the piece of shrapnel on his watch chain. They had not removed it straight away by surgery, but had let it work its way to a point near the alimentary canal and at the opportune time had fished it out via his rectum!

The Naval FOB had gone forward to see whether he could see any concentration worthy of his big guns. He was in our full view when he got out of his halftrack and stood looking forward with his binoculars. We saw the bomb explode very close to him and when the dust cleared we could see that he had been hit. I shouted Cpl Halford to come with me and together we ran out to bring him in. As we approached we could see him on his knees grubbing about on the grass. He stood up when he saw us coming. Jack wrapped a length of spunyarn around the stump of his left arm and used his pliers to wind up the improvised tourniquet, blood flying everywhere. When we finally got the FOB over to the doctor, who had barely finished attending to Bruce, the incredibly brave chap said to Jack Halford, 'Corporal, will you take my watch off the hand you will find in my trousers pocket?' Jack Halford died several years ago.

Douglas 'Pete' C. Morris, Caerwys, Clwyd

I served in the Royal Engineers. We were briefed to get inland as fast as possible and get a Bailey bridge over a waterway. No locations or names were given. The officer

commanding asked, 'Any questions?' No response. My mind went back to four years earlier when we, as conscript recruits issued with 1914 equipment and old Springfield rifles and five rounds of ammunition, sat as we did that day listening to the Training Battalion Intelligence Officer lecturing on the German army. He spoke at length of its superior weapons, the use of dive-bombing as artillery, and the famed Blitzkreig attack. A flutter of apprehension ran through the assembly. To end the address came the invitation, 'Any questions on the German army?' A lone voice from the back. 'Yes sir. How do you join it?'!

After the initial postponement for twenty-four hours, we were taken by road transport to Newhaven on 5 June, and at 18:00 hours boarded an LCI (Landing Craft, Infantry). Thirty minutes later we pulled out, a solitary Wren witnessing our departure from the quay. The LCI is not built with sea-going comfort in mind! It is in fact a flat-bottomed pitiless engine of war! Quickly responding to a fairly heavy sea, it began a continuous programme of rearing and plunging, which it kept up for the following fourteen hours. Below deck were arranged three tier bunks now occupied by stricken personnel, and from which hung discarded assault equipment soiled with cascades of vomit. The fetid atmosphere, a malodorous cocktail of retching and diesel oil, induced a nausea as overpowering as the seasickness itself. Presently I fell into a merciful, if fitful, sleep.

An hour or so after first light some of us, now fully equipped, were up on deck to see for the first time the great armada of assault craft and attacking battle cruisers around us. The French coast now appeared in view, draped in fire and smoke. Had the first assault gone in? How strongly were the beaches defended? These questions thrust themselves into our minds, to be resolved as the moment of landing approached. Whatever lay ahead I would not be sorry to see the back of that LCI.

The craft rammed the beach at about 8:45am lowering the port and starboard ramps into about four and a half feet of water. I went into the sea, chest high, Sten gun and mine detector held above the water. With mortar bombs exploding some fifty yards to the left I made my way up the beach and in that traverse of about forty feet I was struck by the sight of the corpse of a British soldier lying atop the eight-foot floodbank, face up, with hands across the chest as though in peace on that foreign shore. Enemy artillery was ranging onto the beach as we began the advance inland in deployed order. The advance, halted at times by enemy fire, took us near Colleville. It was here that the flank of the 3rd Division, under whose command we came, was being secured. A number of British infantry lay dead in the locality.

Fifty yards past the church at Bénouville and round a slight bend we came within sight of a building from the roof of which flew the French tricolour. This proved to be our objective – the mairie (town hall) of Bénouville. Two hundred yards to the east of the mairie the bridge, captured by the airborne troops in the early hours, crossed the Caen Canal. We now came under small arms fire and being in an exposed position, we doubled forward towards the mairie. This brought us into close contact with the 6th Airborne Division. I recall one of their number asking what we were doing 'up here'. Greeting us from a slit trench he was obviously surprised by our early arrival!

We dug in at Bénouville and sustained casualties – one man killed, three wounded and a fifth man to die from his wounds. The company had also taken a number of prisoners. They were marched back to the beach under escort

– presumably bound for the UK. By Landing Craft Infantry we hoped!

Very late at night, possibly in the early hours of D plus one, an enemy soldier, fully armed, was found hiding in a thicket. He surrendered his weapons and ammunition and appeared to be very scared. Someone gave the poor sod a cigarette – he was surely the last of the Bénouville defenders.

So ended D-Day. That night I slept in the courtyard fronting the mairie and woke at daybreak. A nearby garden boasted a water pump by the side of which lay the body of an Airborne Division soldier. He was lying half sprawled from a stretcher. His right arm was forward as if reaching for water. How long he had lain there, how much he had suffered I shall never know. Now it was too late. We had to go on regardless. So we refreshed ourselves and breakfasted on the 'compo' ration that each man carried, and then began the bridging operation over the waterway we had heard about at the briefing – the Caen Canal.

Bob Heath, Orpington, Kent

In 1944 I found myself at Elgin in Scotland, the depot of the Seaforth Highlanders, and during the next few months received battle-training (with the Black Watch), infantry signals and despatch rider training, at the end of which I went on leave to get married. The invasion of Europe was imminent and England was virtually an armed camp with everyone ready to go. What happened next is described below.

Being musical myself, when I look back to 1944, almost fifty years as I write, I think of Vera Lynn, Anne Shelton, Glen Miller, The Squadronaires and so on, but the other side of the coin, the serious side, was the impending invasion of Europe, the greatest military operation the world has ever seen.

I had just got married after several months of training with the Seaforth Highlanders and the Black Watch and was all ready for the job in hand. After returning from passionate leave (marriage) I duly reported to the embarkation camp in Newhaven only to find General Montgomery, together with all the Allied Armies had already left for France. They had gone without me!

After debating with myself whether they could manage without my valuable services, I found myself post-haste put on an American LCI (Infantry Landing Craft) together with various other soldiers for an overnight trip over the water. I had never seen a shot fired in anger up to this time, but during the next few months this part of my education was to be rectified quite definitely.

I found a bunk downstairs (below decks) and was soon in a deep and satisfying sleep. I was not at all seasick and never have been. When I awoke next morning, below decks were awash with vomit etc. from the unfortunate personnel who had not slept! The sky was blue and the sun was shining and we were off to the beaches at Arromanches in Normandy. The beachhead code-named 'Gold' had been formed and my division, the 15th Scottish, was involved in very heavy fighting towards the Caen area.

I felt quite exhilarated seeing the busy scene, which confronted me when I looked out from our boat. There were some fair sized ships which had been bombed and lay down in the water. There was also a line of old ships, which had been deliberately sunk by the navy to form a breakwater for the famous Mulberry harbour, which had been towed across in pieces and was then being assembled off the beach. Everything was bustle and activity, but very calm and orderly. Vast piles of stores, ammunition, munitions and tanks and guns were being unloaded and piled up on the sand dunes, and personnel were filing ashore calmly and quickly. Barrage balloons were up aloft and small boats manned by Marine Commandos and Royal Engineers were swanning about all over the place, together with Ducks (amphibious army vehicles) which were taking loads from the boats arriving and driving out of the water right up onto the beach before discharging their cargoes.

We went ashore and soon I saw my first French civilian. He was an earnest young man with the usual beret and small beard. 'Bonjour, Monsieur,' I called out in my best French. 'Good Morning, Sir' he answered in perfect English. I fell into conversation with him. 'Why do your fighter planes shoot up our little children in their school playgrounds?' he asked. I had to explain that from the air they would appear to the pilots to be German soldiers swanning about and so they were strafed by the trigger-happy airmen.

We were put in a transit camp and then I went with a party of other Seaforth Highlanders to join the 7th Battalion, which had just been severely mauled at Caen and had lost many men. We were the first reinforcements and I joined the Battalion Headquarters, which was in an apple orchard.

We were soon involved in the heavy fighting in Normandy and the colonel was killed early on and a new CO took over. He was Lieut Col Peter Hunt who after the war went on to become chief of the defence staff at Whitehall and was knighted.

Life became a mixture of walking, digging slit trenches, standing-to at dawn, hiding behind hedgerows and in ditches, and dodging shellfire, bullets, mortar bombs and snipers. We were facing the elite of the German army, the SS Panzer Divisions. It was not uncommon for a huge Tiger tank to come round a corner and start shooting us up or 'Moaning Minnies' (mortars that emitted a shrieking wail when they were fired) to come raining down on us. The most effective weapon that the Germans had in Normandy apart from the Tiger tank was the 88mm gun which caused absolute havoc amongst our tanks as their armour-piercing shells could go through the front of our Sherman and Churchill tanks like a hot knife through butter.

The difficult terrain of the bocage country we were in was no use for tank fighting as it consisted of small fields and orchards and high hedges, and the armour could not get moving, so we footsloggers had the grim task of flushing out the enemy.

I won't bore the reader with blow-by-blow descriptions of the many battles fought in Normandy, but one in particular, for a key position, remains with me. The plan was for Three Division to attack two large hills and hold them to enable the British to control the surrounding countryside and then for General Montgomery to 'unleash his armour' as he fondly put it. Our particular objective was 'Hill 309' and our task was to get right to the top and then stay there. Easier said than done! First of all the RAF bombed the summit and then we began the slow advance up the hill, supported by tanks of the Independent Guards Armoured Brigade. It was fighting all the way with huge casualties on both sides. The Germans threw everything they had at us but eventually after a few days we reached the top of the hill. The Germans then trained their artillery on us and kept up a ceaseless bombardment on our position and it was a question of keeping one's head down to survive. I very often had to go out on patrol or laying telephone lines to observation posts etc. It was a living hell and our numbers were severely depleted, but all things come to an end and after some days the armour got moving and started their historic advance which was to take them through France, Belgium and into Holland.

After the battle for Hill 309 I sat under an apple tree in an orchard and wrote a poem. It is the only poem I have ever written and it makes one wonder why soldiers write poetry after battles. Mine was written on the back of a signals pad and I have it to this day.

During the Normandy campaign the German 10th Army was encircled at Falaise and I witnessed the most terrible carnage I shall ever see in my life. The RAF had been busy and the roads and fields were choked with corpses, bombed-out vehicles and tanks, horses, carts and dead cattle bloated in the fields. The stench of death was everywhere.

After Normandy my division, the 15th Scottish, took part in many more battles and was the only division to do the hat-trick, i.e. assault crossings of the three major river obstacles, the Seine, the Rhine and finally the Elbe. Then the war was over and we were sent to occupy the town of Kiel on the Baltic.

I consider myself very, very fortunate to have survived and come through to the end when so many of my brave comrades did not. My adventures during the campaign would fill a thick book had I kept a diary. But then, I was too busy to do that!

After the war I settled in Norfolk and one day in the 1970s I was in a pub in a small country place called Southery, in the Fen country. A lorry driver was talking to the publican behind the bar and I overheard his conversation. 'I was in the battle for Hill 309 in Normandy,' he said, 'and I have never met anyone who survived that battle.'

'You're looking at one,' I said.

Allan Warburton, Spalding, Lincolnshire

I was a twenty-year-old parachutist, qualified as a signaller RA, a member of the 53rd Airlanding Light Regiment RA – the 75mm Field Gliderborne Regiment of the Sixth Airborne Division.

Our forward observation section was to consist of twelve parties of three men, one officer and two signallers to each party. One party to each parachute and airlanding regiment, plus a party to each of the three brigades headquarters companies.

I was scheduled to parachute in with the 1st Canadian Para Battalion, Lt Ted Ayrton being my commanding officer and Ken Lamzed my fellow signaller. Ken and I had joined the army together and had been together on initial training and courses and shared the same barrack rooms. We were the best of pals. However we were now split up. Gunner Webster became Ken's fellow signaller and I was moved to another group. Frank McGinley was to be my fellow signaller.

We attended a briefing and were told that the invasion would be into Normandy. The division's task was to capture the Caen Canal and River Orne bridges, capture and hold the ground to the east of the bridges, blowing up all bridges on the River Dives, from Troarn to the coast. We were to go in with Third Parachute Brigade whose tasks were – 9th Para Battalion – to capture and destroy the heavily guarded gun emplacements at Merville. The 8th Para Battalion's job was to blow up bridges at Troarn and Bure, and hold the extreme east perimeter. 1st Canadians Para Battalion's task was to blow bridges at Varaville, and hold the high ground at Le Mesnil. All battalions to be accompanied by sections of 3rd Para Brigade's squadron of Royal Engineers. We in 3rd Para Brigade HQ company were to get to a farm house, a short distance from Le Mesnil crossroads. We would be dropped on the same dropping zone as 8th Parachute Battalion, which was the farthest inland of all the divisions' dropping zones.

We carried a field dressing in our battledress trousers and were issued with a pair of buttons to sew onto our trousers which when removed and one button placed on top of the other, improvised as a compass! We were also given a small hacksaw blade to insert in your trouser seam. This was accompanied with a silk map of the area, so one could find a way back to divisional lines if captured or lost.

To carry our equipment from aircraft to ground we used specially designed kitbags. The kitbag was strapped to your right leg, a rope of twenty feet in length was tied to the bag, and secured to your webbing. When your parachute opened, you pulled a quick release pin and lowered the bag, so that it landed a split second before yourself. This method had worked well during several practice jumps.

I was to carry the radio transmitter, a No. 62 set. They were heavy and awkward to carry, but had a range of several miles, which would be needed to reach the seaborne regiments, as they got established beyond the beachheads. My fellow signaller Frank McGinley would carry the two accumulators needed to power a 62 set. Each kitbag weighed about sixty pounds.

On the morning of 5 June we were given a final briefing, told to pack our parachuting kitbags and small packs. The small packs were to carry all the personal kit we would need. Later on, our big packs would follow on by sea. A small pack carried mess tins, knife, fork and spoon, washing and shaving gear, spare pair of socks and two twenty-four-hour man ration packs. These contained a block of oatmeal (for porridge) meat cubes, bar of chocolate, powdered milk and tea blocks, and toilet paper! We checked our Sten guns, filled our pouches with ammunition, fitted camouflage netting to our steel helmets, and wrote letters home etc. (which would be censored and posted after the invasion had started). We were told to sleep in the afternoon. In my case I was much too excited – or scared – to carry that order out.

We formed up in our 'sticks', drew and fitted our parachutes. I think it was about 10pm or so (double British summertime was in operation during the war), so it was still daylight. We enplaned and took off around 11pm. We were packed like sardines, looking like Michelin Men. Most of us jumping with kitbags, parachute on your back, Sten gun tucked under the harness, airborne smocks bulging with chocolate, sweets etc. Webbing pouches holding ammunition, Mills bombs, etc. Entrenching tool and small pack.

To start with everyone was smiling. We sang all the paratrooper songs we knew, plenty of wisecracking etc. Looking around the dimly lit fuselage, I thought, if this lot were Germans and invading England, I would die of fright! With faces blackened, camouflage netting on helmets, airborne smocks and scarves, not to mention, rifles, Sten guns etc.

As we neared the French coast, we stood up and checked that each other's static lines were properly hooked to the overheard strong point and not caught up under equipment. The aircraft was bucking and swaying, avoiding flak and turbulence. I could see tracer bullets and exploding shells through the open doorway. It was very difficult to stand. The red light came on and we shuffled down the fuselage, green light on, time to get out as soon as possible. Captain Harrington was first to jump followed by Frank McGinley and then me. Captain Harrington got out quite quickly, he carried no kitbag. Frank struggled out with his load then it was my turn. I'm only a little chap and had great difficulty getting through the door, but eventually I made it. Up in the air went my right leg and away went my kitbag, wrenched from my leg and away into space.

I found I was oscillating badly when my chute opened, rigging lines twisted as well. Remembering the drill, I kicked like mad and pulled down hard on my front lift webs. I think I was reasonably in control, when splash, I'd landed in water! It was pitch black, I was flat on my back, being dragged by my canopy in water a foot or so deep. Struggling to release my parachute harness, and trying to keep my head above water, I lost my Sten gun.

After freeing myself of the parachute I searched in vain for my gun. Getting accustomed to the light I waded to dry land.

Lots of trees, so I realised I was nowhere near the dropping zone allocated to 3rd Parachute Brigade HQ Company. I had no radio, no gun, no small pack, soaked to the skin, no idea which way I should go, but I did have eight Sten gun magazines in my pouches!

After a while I heard someone approaching. What a relief when I heard a whispered 'Punch'. I quickly replied with 'Judy' (that was our code sign). My comrade was an officer, who's still unknown to me. He carried a Sten gun, as well as a sidearm, which all officers carried. He kindly gave me his gun when I told him of my predicament.

Being a mere gunner, I was more than pleased to let him decide which direction to go. Eventually we met a few paras, some who were heading for my destination of Le Mesnil. I think Lady Luck was on my side that night, as not only was I given a Sten gun but I also stumbled into a small pack, which turned out to have belonged to an airborne sapper. Goodness knows how it got there, or what had befallen its rightful owner. When I opened it a few hours later, I was pleased to find it contained the ration packs besides the usual everyday needs.

Dawn was breaking when I reached the farmhouse, which was to be 3rd Parachute Brigade HQ. Only a handful of soldiers had arrived. Brigadier Hill was missing so Colonel Pearson of 8th Para Battalion was standing in for him. The brigadier was wounded in a bombing raid. He turned up later on D-Day refusing hospital treatment. There was no sign of my two companions. I was appointed No. 2 on a Bren gun and positioned on a vantage point in view of the road into the farmhouse. Chaps were coming in all morning. I thought I was the only survivor of our FOO section, then much to my relief in walked Captain Harrington and some time later Gunner Frank McGinley arrived, having walked for hours carrying the two heavy accumulators. He wasn't in the best of temper when I told him I had lost the radio!

We dug our slit trenches on ground allotted to us, only a short way away from the farmhouse. This was to be our home for the next few weeks and as the shelling and mortar bombs increased, we dug deeper and deeper. On 7 June our FOO party came into its own. Captain Harrington and either Frank or myself went forward to observation posts and relayed targets to the artillery regiments as they got established on the beachheads and beyond. I'm not certain, but I think we were the only surviving party in 3rd Parachute Brigade. My friend Ken Lamzed, Gunner Webster and Lt. Ayrton were dropped miles off target. Ken was badly wounded and taken prisoner. Lt Ayrton and Gunner Webster were also POWs.

Captain Harrington MC died in the eighties. Have heard nothing of Frank McGinley or Blondie Webster, but am in touch with Ted Ayrton and Ken Lamzed.

David 'Dai' King, Ross-on-Wye, Herefordshire

D-Day was the most guarded secret of the war – and yet to Londoners it was the most open secret in the world. Where else could all those military vehicles be going, day and night? For weeks, long convoys of troops, tank carriers and lorries moved along London's arterial roads all heading in one direction – London docks.

As an army driver in OFP of the 11th Armoured Division, I recall that first week in June 1944 so well. There were flags and bunting all the way with cheering crowds yelling, 'Good luck, boys!' and giving us cups of tea to help us along. Yes, even then we had plenty of sugar! Once at the docks we were sealed off from the outside world. No letters, no phoning, for we had now been officially told our destination was France. Work consisted of waterproofing vehicles and checking equipment. Once aboard we rendezvoused with a naval escort and put our vomiting bags to good use! Luckily our landing was dry. I clearly remember driving across the beach between white ribbons – the sign that it had been cleared of land mines. The few houses were just ruins. British

bombers had gone in before us. The Germans had retreated and the fighting was going on way ahead of us. But British troops and vehicles were everywhere. We headed a few miles inland to a deserted farmhouse. Our first task was to unload the camouflage nets and remove sticky waterproofing from our hot engines, and then to dig in. That first night we were ordered to sleep under our lorries but I found a stretcher and had a comfortable night's sleep in the back of mine, the sound of gunfire in the distance. The most memorable thing about that first day in France was the smell: the stench of death. Not human flesh, but cattle. Scores of them all lying on their sides – pot bellied and dead. The sun didn't help much.

It wasn't until we reached Bayeux that we actually saw any French people. As far as the fighting went, on our front reaching out towards Caen, there was stalemate for some weeks while the Americans battled for Cherbourg. We made up for it later when we covered four hundred miles in six days in September to be the first troops in Antwerp.

The organisation and planning of the D-Day operation was brilliant – absolutely nothing was forgotten. Aboard ship every man received a printed message from the Supreme Commander, General Eisenhower wishing 'good luck on the great crusade'. On landing each man was given a pre-printed field postcard on which to write home. It consisted of sentences such as 'I am well' or 'I have been wounded', which could be struck out. We all had tin rations plus a portable Tommy cooker with tiny solid fuel tablets. I can still recall the delicious steak and kidney puddings. It was several weeks, though, before we had bread and so biscuits were the order of the day supplemented by the compulsory daily vitamin pill.

Special praise too for the Army Laundry Ablution Units. Dirty shirts and underwear were just exchanged for clean ones and if they fitted you were lucky! Every day was an uncertain one, but the comradeship and spirit has never been equalled. We were the British Liberation Army and we *knew* we were going to win.

John Frost, New Barnet, Hertfordshire

I began writing down my wartime experiences shortly after being released from the Royal Marines in March 1946 and some of these eventually appeared in *Marine Commando: Sicily and Salerno, 1943 with 41 Royal Marines Commando* published by Robert Hale. I am 'Unit Historian' of the veterans of 41 Royal Marines Commando 1942–46 and have written a history of 41, which I hope will be published by the Royal Marines Historical Society.

On D-Day, 6 June 1944, I was CC/X 100977 Marine Raymond Mitchell, a despatch rider with 41 Royal Marines Commando and landed with them on Sword Beach, the unit's first objective being the capture of two enemy positions at Lion-sur-Mer, codenamed 'The Château' and 'The Strongpoint'.

Prior to the landing we had been kept incommunicado in a 'concentration camp' on Southampton Common, which we knew affectionately as 'Stalag C 19', and to which we had been returned from a boarding point on the River Hamble on 4 June with the news that the invasion had been postponed. We awoke on 5 June to learn that it was 'ON!' After lunch were taken by TCVs (Troop Carrying Vehicles) to Warsash, on the Hamble, to board five LCI(S)s (Landing Craft Infantry, Small) which pulled out into the Solent to anchor while the rest of the armada destined to sail from that part of the coast assembled. At 21:15 hours, in the gathering dusk, the LCIs moved into their allotted position as the untold number of vessels moved off, destination France.

The crossing was uneventful and it was in semi-darkness that we were called out of the three small 'holds' of the vessels to breakfast and prepare for the landing. At that time the sea was extremely choppy and many of our number were soon suffering the miseries of seasickness. As the early morning was rather chilly I decided to eat my tin of self-heating soup, I recall that it was tomato, but the meal stayed down no longer than the time it had taken to prepare and eat! Flashes of gunfire could now be seen coming from the dark shapes of ships at sea and from the indistinct smudge that was France. Disappointingly for us, we were soon dragged away from this enthralling spectacle by being ordered below to 'get rigged'.

And there we stayed for the next half hour or more, as conditions outside became more and more noisy and disturbed. The thunder of widespread gunfire and the scream of incoming shells came down to us clearly, but we could only guess what was happening. The inshore waters, we could feel, were basically calmer, but they were becoming more and more disturbed as our craft rocked and bucked in response to nearby explosions.

After what seemed an eternity, the voice of authority came down to us, 'Right lads, we're almost in! – On deck! – Quick!' We tumbled out into a medley of sights, sounds and smells, of a beach strewn with burning tanks and other vehicles, exploding shells and bodies on the sand and floating in the sea. There was time only for a fleeting glimpse before getting on with the next (unnecessary) order of, 'Move it, lads! Get ashore.'

For me, as DR, this meant grabbing my seventy-five pound parascooter and starting to push it along the narrow port side deck and, as I did so, the vessel was rocked by the explosion of a shell striking, or narrowly missing, the starboard side. On reaching the bows we found that the port ramp led uselessly down into deep water, pointing in the general direction of England, so we had to queue up to use the starboard one. This, lying askew to both our craft and the beach, was swaying, bucking and bouncing under the combined effects of explosions and our craft wallowing in the tidal swell. To have attempted the standard 'drill' of humping the motorbike onto my shoulder and doubling down the ramp could have had no other results than one very wet marine and a useless piece of machinery. By the time my turn came to make it ashore, I had decided what to do. Cradling the bike in my arms, I sat down at the top of the ramp and, using the infant's technique of descending a staircase with a teddy bear in its arms, progressed by legs and bottom until I could drop off into shallower water and carry my charge safely ashore.

Then it was a case of 'follow my leader' as the troop doubled forward to take temporary shelter from exploding missiles and small arms fire in a huge bomb or shell crater a score of metres from the water's edge. I dropped my bike and rolled in. As I lay catching my breath, a Churchill tank trundled to a halt only a few yards away, between us and where we had caught momentary glimpses of field grey uniforms. The hatch opened and a crew member, limp and bleeding, was pulled out of the turret and laid gently on the sand.

With the troop collected together, the officer led us, at the double, along the beach to the right. Burdened with the par-ascooter, I soon dropped behind, and in only a few minutes my muscles just couldn't bear the weight any more. I dropped the bike to the sand and tried to push it, but the small wheels sank down to the hubs in the soft sand and I was simply gouging a furrow. After some time desperately alternating between carrying and trying to push the bike, I was lathered in sweat and had come to the realisation that, if I stayed with the bike I would lose the troop. I was then on the seaward side of a Churchill tank, probably knocked out as two or three of the crew were crouching beside it. 'Here, mate!' I gasped, 'Want a motorbike?' And, without waiting for any reply, abandoned the thing and ran towards a gap in the hedge at the back of the beach through which the rest of the troop had disappeared some minutes earlier.

Relieved of the burden of the parascooter, I was able to take in a little more of the chaos all about me. The landing had been planned to enable the landing craft to avoid as many beach obstacles as possible and the narrow strip of dry sand was crowded and littered with burning tanks and other vehicles, with bodies scattered here and there. The air was filled with the smells of smoke and of cordite, explosions and the shriek of incoming shells. One salvo was clearly going to land very close to me so I dived for the only cover close to hand – the body of a dead soldier – I'm sure he would have understood. The water's edge was a similar picture of burning vessels and amongst the wreckage bobbing about in the waves were more bodies, still being kept afloat by their lifejackets.

I reached the gap in the hedge and was amazed to pass some 'army types' actually digging slit trenches in the sand. The first tenet of any landing (and D-Day was my third, the others being Sicily and Salerno) was 'get off the beach', so I did just that, and moved into a completely different world. The hustle and bustle on the beach had given way to a quiet roadway, draped with the wires from shattered telegraph poles, fronting a row of tall, half-timbered houses. I soon came upon a solitary wounded soldier sitting at the roadside with his back against a wall and asked if I could do anything for him. 'Just give us a fag, mate,' he said, 'Then catch up with your pals.'

I came upon two other stragglers of our troop and we caught up with the tail end of the others on the outskirts of Lion-sur-Mer, then doubled along a pavement of the small town, making little sound in our rubber-soled boots, while the white faces of inhabitants peered at us from their windows. With the fighting troops of the commando going about their business some distance ahead, we of HQ were

halted somewhere in the town and flopped onto the pavement to catch our breath. My little group had come to rest on the forecourt of a small newspaper shop and the door was open for business! One of our number, having had his matches soaked in the landing and knowing that I spoke a little French, persuaded me to go in and buy some for him – which I did, and probably spent the very first 'invasion money' of the whole Allied landings!

We waited there for quite some time. Commando headquarters was operating nearby, with the noises of exploding mortar bombs not so very far away, and some civilians began moving about in the streets. On two occasions I was called forward to translate for agitated French ladies and found that they were reporting the presence of wounded soldiers in their homes. I went, accompanied by a sick berth attendant with the first lady and found the man fully clothed on her bed, oozing blood from a pretty bad shoulder wound onto her white sheets. The SBA put a field dressing on the wound and we left him where he was, with some of our rations, as his main concern was that he had lost the small pack containing his food.

Mortar fire was now being directed onto our part of town and the open streets were no place to be in such circumstances, so the CO moved his headquarters into the grounds of a nearby church and we all set about digging slit trenches. As despatch rider, I had to be near the signals officer's radio set, and the fact that I had no transport was overcome by someone finding a push bike for me. For the rest of the morning, I delivered a few signals in between flurries of bombs and digging.

Early in the afternoon I was sent off on the push bike back to the beach where we had landed, to find the first batch of the unit's transport, about six Jeeps, which were due to come ashore from a tank landing craft. For about a mile my ride was quiet, apart from desultory explosions, then I came upon a military policeman, resplendent in white belt, anklets and gauntlet gloves, directing traffic at a road junction and found that the whole beach area had been completely transformed.

The hedge I had slipped through that morning had been bulldozed out of existence and what had been a secluded and empty coastal road was now completely open to the beach and thronged by an unending stream of vehicles all (except me) going in one direction – towards the MP. The beach too had changed out of all recognition. There was still some desultory shelling but, apart from sunken wrecks, the infantry landing craft had gone and the shoreline was lined with tank landing craft, nosed into the beach, disgorging vehicles of all descriptions, or pulling off to return to Britain for more. Royal Engineers were at work with bulldozers, clearing the beach and constructing more roadways of Somerfeld tracking across the soft sand.

I had been given the number of the LCT to look out for, but didn't need it. Hardly had I made my way to a vantage point to watch what was going on, than I saw the ramp of one of the craft which has just beached splash down and Jeeps appeared carrying our 41 Commando number '93'! The waterproofed vehicles splashed through the shallows. I collected them on the track and had soon unloaded a 'real' motorcycle from one of them – one of the small 'Famous James' 125cc two-stroke machines, which were to take over from the RC parascooters of the initial landing. The engine burst into life at the first kick, but my triumphant first squeeze of its pathetic bulb horn produced no more than a squirt of water! Leading my little convoy along the track, I had to persuade the MP that this little lot was the exception.

All the rest of the unending stream of military traffic was being directed inland, towards Caen, but 41's vehicles were destined for Lion-sur-Mer, further along the coast. In the Normandy landings the role of commandos was different from usual as such lightly armed units would have been of little use against the strong Atlantic Wall. The plan therefore was for the tanks and guns of infantry divisions to 'punch holes' in the German coast defences, then concentrate everything on pushing inland, leaving the commandos to deal with all enemy resistance left behind.

On regaining the church, I was to find that Commando HQ was getting ready to move, so the Jeeps' arrival was fortuitous. All day long the Commando had been without any artillery support because all attached army and navy signals personnel in the initial landing had either become casualties or had had their sets destroyed. Therefore, when a strong German counter-attack, with artillery support, developed on one of our advanced troops, the CO decided to regroup in a stronger position. HQ moved to an orchard area about half a mile from Lion and the digging of slit trenches was resumed. Fortunately, one of the Jeeps I had brought up from the beach was a radio link with the navy, so a destroyer 'shoot' on the German positions was called for and our sector eventually quietened down.

It was dusk when the noise of many aero engines came to us and, across a sky made golden by the setting sun, we saw streams of aircraft crossing between us and the Channel, each one towing a glider. The 6th Air Landing Brigade was on its way to reinforce the 6th Airborne Division and No. 1 Special Service Brigade who were holding the bridgehead on the other side of the River Orne only a few miles away. We heard the crackle of German anti-aircraft fire greeting their arrival. As the tug aircraft re-passed us, heading home after having done their job, some nearby wag commented, 'Just think, those bloody pilots will be sinking a pint in their local in about half an hour's time.' Shortly after the RAF's departure, German night bombers started putting in attacks on the supply ships of the invasion force lying off shore, but we were able to spend a relatively quiet night in our holes in the soil of France.

The Commando, which landed with a unit strength of twenty-seven officers and four hundred and ten other ranks, suffered about thirty per cent casualties on D-Day: four officers and twenty-two other ranks killed; thirty-one other ranks missing, believed wounded; and four officers and seventy-two other ranks wounded.

My own saddest memory of that day is that my friend 'Geordie' Swindale was killed. A photograph of him, taken in Sicily appears in *Marine Commando,* and I have dedicated *Marine Commando Despatch Rider,* my account of my time with 41 Commando in north-west Europe, to his memory; he is buried in Bayeux British Military Cemetery.

Raymond 'Mitch' Mitchell, Newcastle, Tyne and Wear

My war story is all home front, with a very special memory of D-Day. During the London Blitzkrieg we Londoners spent our nights in underground shelters and by day I worked underground too. I was a secretary at the BBC and at the outbreak of war, the Corporation took over London's underground theatres and it was at the old Criterion (now rebuilt) in Piccadilly that the BBC broadcast programmes of messages to British forces in every theatre of war. When D-Day was getting closer, it was decreed that all messages from the folks at home to their fighting men must stop and I was transferred to a new network – the British Expeditionary Forces. Our chief was John Snagge, Head of OBs, (Outside Broadcasts) and in this department, former producers, announcers and actors became war correspondents and trained for the grand slam into Europe. The late Franklin Engelmann, known as 'Jingles' because of his German-sounding surname, was one of the BBC's war

correspondents. His former job had been to compere a homely radio show called 'Down Your Way'. David Niven, another war reporter, looked like the handsome film star playing an officer's part, except that this time it was for real.

Rehearsals for the forth-coming programme were mostly on discs from the studio; try-outs of the forces' favourites, jazz or 'dreamy' syncopation to serve as a familiar background for the armies. No reference to family or home was allowed, as any sentiment might impede victory!

For months the men in the office at Broadcasting House had not seen their wives or homes either and during the long wait for D-Day they slept in sleeping bags on the floor. Most of them lived as far out as Buckinghamshire and I was the only one of the staff who could get back easily to my London home.

The day of 5 June 1944 and the night, stand out in my memory because all the officers decided that they wanted to spend just one night at home. Surely after so many nights on the hard floor, D-Day would not break merely because they had decided to go home? They gave themselves a night's leave. I, as secretary, was given everyone's telephone number and instructions to ring them instantly if the vital message came through.

'You'll be working normal office hours,' Franklin Engelmann said to me, 'And the first in. As you live in London that shouldn't be difficult. Remember, ring us all in turn if anything happens. Repeat the message carefully, exactly as you heard it.'

On 6 June 1944, I arrived at the BBC in a 'nothing very much is going to happen' mood! In those days we received news from Reuters news agency, putting on headphones to type reports directly onto the typewriter. Shortly after I arrived I was surprised to receive a signal that a message was coming through. That was unusual, so early. Settling the headphones comfortably on my head, I heard what must have been the most understated delivery in history: 'A landing has been made in France.'

I just about managed not to leap into the air with excitement and telephoned every telephone number that I had been given, repeating those seven words that changed the world, resisting the temptation to shout to the heaven, 'This is it!'

Captain Engelmann answered briefly, as did the others. 'Be with you in half-an-hour.' And so they were, but soon the office emptied. They were off and 'over there', broadcasting the battle and later – victory.

During that eventful day, (don't laugh) I even found time to telephone my mother, who proudly phoned the neighbours in the street. 'Peggy was first to break the news of D-Day to the BBC', was her special message.

In that long war, many had their 'finest hour' but being the first with the D-Day news was mine.

Peggy 'Trotty True' Trott, Finchley, London

I was a naval wireman on a Landing Craft, Tank or LCT. At last the signal to sail was received and it was off we go to join the biggest fleet the world has ever seen. The organisation of the convoys was a masterpiece of planning. Try to imagine, if you can, five thousand cars equipped with only one miserable candle for lighting, approaching the spaghetti junction outside of Birmingham, on a dark and rainy night with no street lighting at all, and all them then heading off down the M5 in the general direction of Bristol with the road heaving up and down in five to six foot waves with the steering of each car slightly defective. Maybe that isn't the most vivid description of the scene on the night of D-Day but it may give you an idea of conditions. We owed much to the fleet of trawlers etc., which buoyed the course and our escorts who acted as sheepdogs, carefully shepherding us to our correct destination.

Dawn eventually arrived and it was only then that one could appreciate the size of the operation. As the skies gradually lightened, the vista gradually unfolded, and it was of ships and more ships, of a multitude of shapes and sizes extending to and far beyond the horizon, all tossing and rolling in a grey and far from friendly sea. By this time we were all closed up to action stations, all trying our best to put a brave face on things. It wasn't so bad for our crew as we had been in similar situations before, in the Med, but the sheer size of this operation was awe-inspiring.

Just before we sailed our skipper had called us together and had explained our part in the great design of things, which was basically, to sail to about two miles off the beach, launch our DD (floating) tanks then hang around until the beachhead was secured, then it was just a case of back to the UK to start the ferrying operation. All nice and simple and not involving a great deal of danger. The only proviso was that should the waves be over a certain height, it was then up to the skippers whether they launched the tanks or took them in onto the beach. The whole idea of the floating tank was to provide heavy support to the first wave of commandos and of course to have a demoralising effect on the defending troops. Can you imagine standing on say Brighton seafront early in the morning when a squadron of tanks suddenly appear out of the sea and proceed to pound the promenade to pieces? There was a quick exchange of signals in our flotilla and it was decided that it was too dangerous to launch them in such atrocious conditions and so it was a case of full speed ahead onto the beach, ditch them off and get the hell out of it as quickly as possible!

In this life there always seems to be a great difference between theory and practice and this was no different to any other time. Off went the flotilla leader in cautious haste closely followed by our craft. Goodness knows how but the leader managed to avoid the many obstacles on the beach and dropped his door. We followed close behind and our bow was just passing his stern when something happened which caused his stern to slew round and our bow took a nasty knock. I must explain at this point that the ramp door was held up by two dogs, one either side, which were arms made out of at least one-inch steel plate and which slipped under a couple of pieces of steel rod which were welded to the door to form supporting pins. These dogs were released by a wheel and worm gear right forward on the bows in full view of the enemy, quite a 'nice' arrangement if you hadn't to undo them and on this occasion, were released prior to going into our final run onto the beach.

By this time we were under quite a lot of fire from the defence forces who at last seemed to realise that it was our intention to invade. The order 'down door' was given, the brakes on the door winches were released and what happened – not a ruddy thing! One of the crew nipped up top, looked at the side of the door and discovered that in the collision one of the dogs had been bent around the door and was holding it up. Things were really hotting up by this time and Jerry was starting to throw all sorts of nice things like mortars, shells, and one particular heavy machine gun situated in a church tower was giving us hell. Our first lieutenant, a midshipman, dashed aft to get something to release the door and came back with a crow bar about twelve inches long and asked for volunteers to go up onto the exposed bows to try to straighten the offending dog. No one volunteered as it was immediately apparent that the only thing that would bend would be the crow bar.

A hurried consultation was held with the officer in charge of the Canadians and it was decided that the only solution to the problem was to bring the first tank forward and to let it gradually climb up the door until its weight forced the door down. At this stage I must tell you that we had a small battery operated 'comforts' radio up forward with us and amidst all this chaos the calm voice of the radio announcer said something to the effect that 'we wish to announce that the second front has begun and the invasion forces are making steady progress in the landings'. Which caused us a little sardonic laughter. The tank was called forward and was manoeuvred in position on the girders and gradually began to climb the door. At first there was no response as the angle of the tank to the deck gradually increased, then, as the tank attained a dangerously high angle there was a screeching of metal and door and tank crashed down.

How the tank ever remained on the door I'll never know and how the crew survived the terrible bone jarring jolt is beyond me, but they did and carefully made their way onto the beach clear of the door. They collapsed the canvas screen and then carried out the best bit of shooting I have ever witnessed. They fired a number of rounds in quick succession and, as it seemed, in slow motion, the church tower split apart and the machine gun and its crew fell to the ground, to the great relief of the rest of us. The tanks were eventually landed quite safely and it was a case of up door, up kedge anchor and away to hell out of it. We were very fortunate that we sustained no casualties but others in our flotilla were not so lucky. Recently I have been able to contact an officer who was on board one of our flotilla who weren't so lucky. They sustained two killed and a few injured and had to abandon ship while it was on the beach, not a ploy which I would recommend!

Wave after wave of small landing craft made their way to the beach under ever increasing fire. Overhead salvos of shells were whistling from the 'big boys', and higher up still were waves of bombers and flights of gliders being towed to their appointed positions. One incident among many that sticks in my mind was of a patrolling fighter which was coming in low to attack enemy positions on the beach.

Unfortunately, as he came low down on the beach an LCR landing craft released a battery of rockets and the fighter simply disappeared. He had been inundated with God knows how many four-inch rockets and the only thing you can say is, he wouldn't know what hit him and wouldn't have suffered very much. There was also the bomber, which had been badly hit and was heading straight for a group of landing craft. If he had carried on, on the same course, he would probably have made a 'belly flapper' landing in the sea, but as there was a chance of hitting the craft he quite deliberately nose-dived into the sea. I know there was some survivors picked up but whether the whole crew survived I shall never know.

As darkness fell we were ordered back to the Solent. We had been without sleep for about forty-eight hours and, against all security regulations, as there was a pub just a few yards from the hard on which we landed, the skipper allowed us to nip ashore and have a well deserved pint. It was a strange situation when we walked into the pub, dressed in scruffy overalls and, I suspect, in need of a good scrubbing. The locals had guessed where we had come from and pints miraculously appeared. Needless to say they were very eager to learn how things were going 'on the other side', but to their credit they never pushed for information apart from asking if we were OK and we didn't volunteer information as 'careless talk costs lives' as the wartime slogan went.

We were still ferrying vehicles and troops when the big storm struck. The anchor cable parted and despite our efforts it was then only a matter of time before the combined force of the wind and sea took its toll and we began to drift helplessly towards the shore. We were by this time quite close in and a second major tragedy happened; the main engine sand traps became choked and we were then without any means of propulsion. We drifted inshore and unfortunately ran against one of the roadways leading from the Mulberry harbour and against the floating barges, which supported the floating road, sinking them one by one. We tried to contain the damage by attempting to tie up to the barges but the conditions were too severe and at last we managed to get a tug to come to our assistance. By this time there was an American officer standing on what remained of the roadway pointing a rifle at our bridge threatening to shoot us if we didn't get the hell out of it, because as you can well understand it was the life-line for supplies to their comrades on the beachhead. The small tug managed to get a line to us but again, with our weight plus the wind and tide, all that happened was he was pulled shorewards and ran aground. Literally we had caused more damage to the cause than all of Hitler's battalions and had he known, we may have been awarded the Iron Cross!

It was a scene of absolute devastation as hundreds of small craft were scattered across the beaches in various states of battered immobility. Apart from our engines being out of action the mess deck was flooded, which meant that all the clothing we had was what we stood up in, which was, in most cases underclothes, a boilersuit, a rolled up balaclava for head gear and a soaking wet duffle coat. We were unable to use the auxiliary engine to generate electricity as we were well and truly beached. Our only saving grace was the old coal burning galley stove, which allowed us to at least have a warm drink. The problems that this storm engendered were so great that the Americans had more important things to do than look after a bunch of 'Limeys', with which we agreed, so again we were thrown on our own resources. We became experts at beach combing. One case we picked up contained some olive green tins, which only bore a code marking and we thought we were onto something good. Out came the can spanner and with eager anticipation the first tin was prised open. There to our delight was revealed something we had all been longing for, a survival kit which consisted of fishing line, hooks, lures etc.!

After living like the proverbial Gypsies for about a week the buzz went around that if we found our way to the coastal road, we could get a lift to an American CB camp and there we would no doubt be able to obtain some food of some sort. Having no idea in which direction the camp lay we decided to wait by the roadside until someone came past and like magic a Jeep containing four American MPs arrived out of the blue. We must have looked a real bunch of desperadoes, unshaven, dirty and wearing the obligatory navy blue overalls and rolled up balaclava. As they leaped out of the Jeep with firearms at the ready, they said, 'Who the hell are you guys?' We explained who we were and that all we wanted were directions to the CB camp to enable us to collect some food.

The sergeant in charge adopted a most considerate attitude and picked up his radio and arranged for a lorry to pick us up. The Yanks certainly know how to treat their comrades in distress. We waited by the roadside and sure enough up drives this lorry and we all piled in the back and off we steamed at a rate of knots. We thought it a bit strange as the driver was belting along frantically blowing his horn and traffic magically parted for us. This was red carpet treatment of the first order! Suddenly he made a tyre squealing turn through a gate and there we were, not in the Aladdin's cave of the CB camp but in a detention centre!

The attitude immediately changed and we were confronted by a squad of the biggest coloured MPs I've ever met wielding their night sticks (batons) in a most unsociable manner. We were wheeled in front of an officer who demanded our identity papers. When we told him they were under about five feet of water in our flooded mess deck and the only identity we had was our identity discs he wasn't the least impressed. We eventually managed to persuade him who we were and as a compromise he said he would contact our skipper who would have to come and identify us. In the meantime we would have to remain as their 'guests' and we were marched off to a large barbed wire compound.

This was a side of war that I had never appreciated, as in this compound were the sweepings of the aftermath of battle. All sorts and descriptions of men, both civilian and servicemen, who had been unable to prove their identity or who were considered of suspicious character. For instance, there were two American servicemen who they had picked up in a farmyard who had been having a whale of a time riding the farmer's cart horses trying to emulate a wild west rodeo. Others were there awaiting trial for looting and various other crimes, which don't bear repeating. We spent several hours in that situation and believe me we were glad when the skipper eventually came to bale us out. Even the laws of the jungle didn't pertain in that hellhole!

James 'Wires' Routledge, Whitley Bay, Tyne and Wear

I was a nurse during the Second World War at a very big hospital in Birmingham with over one thousand beds. The life was tough, with long hours and very little pay and of course during those years we dealt with air raid casualties.

However, with the invasion of Normandy we received a message from the War Office to clear certain wards and take severely wounded troops from the invasion. It was a horrific experience I shall never forget until I die. I am now eighty-two years old.

At that time we had no antibiotics and all dressings had to be hand packed into drums for sterilisation – no such thing as disposables in those days! Wards had to be prepared and all lockers and beds had to be washed with disinfectant to minimise the risk of spreading infection. We worked in

teams and had to be available to be on duty at any time, day or night, as the need arose.

It was a pitch-black night when the first convoy arrived. Some had been flown to us in batches of fifteen, laying on bare metal stretchers. Others arrived by train. They had come straight from the fighting lines and some were still in their uniforms, having been evacuated after initial treatment at base hospitals. Among our first batch were five Polish boys who had been doing forced labour work for the Germans. They had managed to escape and get behind the Allied lines and were in a terrible condition. They were nearly starving, some badly wounded, but even so it showed on their faces that they were so glad to be out and with us in the United Kingdom.

Others were from the invasion forces – some with limbs blown off and others with burns and body wounds. Our younger doctors had been called up into the services or sent to other hospitals, and so our hospital was left with the older medical staff. But later we were joined by French Jewish doctors who had escaped from France and had been forced to leave their families behind. They were truly wonderful.

Then suddenly there came information from the War Office that the new drug penicillin was to be released to us. It was the very first antibiotic. It came in small ampules with each ampule containing four doses of thirty thousand units per injection. It was then in pure form, costing in those days £80 per ampule, which was an enormous sum of money! It was so expensive that with it came explicit instructions from the War Office that it was only to be used for wounded troops. The supply was not only expensive but very limited. The effect however was miraculous. Countless lives were saved that otherwise would almost certainly have been lost. No one had been totally certain of the outcome of its use as it was the first time it had been used, but it was so successful that one could see the results almost daily.

They were wonderful lads, and so young. And they were such good fun once they began to get better. I remember one group asking if they could take me out to a supper in the city. 'Only if you get permission from your wives!' I told them. Not only did their wives agree but they sent them money to pay for the meal! That was life in those days!

But the money wasn't needed as it turned out. When the restaurant manager saw that they were wounded soldiers and that I was a nurse he insisted that we have the meal 'on him'! It was a wonderful evening and one I shall always remember, just as I remember those young lads who came to us from the beaches of Normandy.

Lillian E. Mills, Scarborough, North Yorkshire

At that time I was serving in the Royal Navy as an able seaman torpedoman aboard an American built destroyer, HMS *Blackwood*. At morning light on 6 June the Channel was alive with activity. Ships everywhere. Squadrons of planes. It was a most wonderful sight but I remember thinking, 'I wouldn't like to be on the receiving end of that lot!' Our job was to patrol the Channel to protect the invasion fleet from any attacks by U-boats or E-boats. I think the sheer numbers of ships and the demonstration of Allied sea power must have persuaded the Germans not to interfere too much so far as seaborne attacks were concerned!

We resupplied at Weymouth on 12 June, and then at about 7pm that evening, without any warning, an enormous explosion occurred at the forward end of the ship. We were a few miles north of Cherbourg at the time. When it happened I was on watch on the quarterdeck looking after the depth charge armaments. Was it a mine or a torpedo? At the same time the forward magazine must also have exploded. In an instant all the forward half of the ship was blown away. All the officers, petty officers and crew were killed instantly. Their mess decks had just disappeared.

We on the quarterdeck and the lads in the mess below us were lucky. Where I was in particular, I couldn't have chosen a more sheltered position if I had been forewarned. Some eighty or ninety men must have died in those few seconds, and about forty survived, many of them badly injured. I was one of the lucky ones. I wasn't even scratched.

I remember our watch officer, Doug Reid, a young man of twenty-six years of age. His job was to visit each position on the ship during his watch to see that everything was all right. At about 6:45pm that evening he visited my position on the depth charges. I remember he chatted about his wife at home who was having their first baby. He seemed thrilled about the prospect. 'She's getting as big as a Sherman tank,' he remarked. He left about ten minutes later and said he was going to his mess deck where he would be having a cup of cocoa if any panics occurred. Five minutes later the explosion happened. He must have been killed instantly. If he had only stayed with me another five minutes he would still be alive. The rest of the ship was being kept afloat only by the watertight bulkheads. We did what we could for the injured on our part of the boat, but as we clung on to what was left of our ship, another ship in our group steamed past at full speed and called us on the loud hailer that they had made contact with a U-boat and would come back later to pick us up. So there were U-boats out there after all. We were proof of it! But we never did see that ship again and it certainly never came back for us!

Nothing happened now for about two hours, which seemed an eternity. Then at about 9pm we saw approaching at full speed two RAF Air Sea Rescue launches clearly aiming to pick us up. We got all the injured first into one launch. The rest of us, about thirty men, then boarded the other one. The RAF lads were great; they had drinks and blankets ready for us the instant we got on board and at about midnight, still shocked, we were put ashore on the jetty at Weymouth, the very place we had so recently left. Would you believe it, even at that

time of night we were met by a group of Salvation Army ladies who plied us with tea and sandwiches. I will forever be grateful to those lovely ladies who did so much for us, and I am sure every one of my shipmates who survived would say the same.

Where do you think we went then? By army wagon to Portland Prison at the end of Portland Bill! Actually they treated us well. We had a bath, a hot meal and, most important of all, a change of clothing. We were then given bunks – two to a cell! Not locked in of course – it was all that part of the prison that had been taken over as a casualty-receiving establishment. Not surprisingly perhaps no one slept a wink that night. All we could do was talk of what had happened and of the friends and shipmates we had lost.

A couple of days later we were given fourteen days' 'survivors leave'. I went home to Wigan, met a girl called Margaret at a dance and on 29 August 1945 we married. We raised six children and now have eleven grandchildren, and had it not been for that fateful day when so many young lives were lost I would not have gone home on leave and met the lovely girl that I married. My children and grandchildren would never have been born. The tragedy is that the same event that led to a wonderful life for me also saw the death of so many fine young men who were my shipmates, and always I will especially remember Doug Reid who never saw the baby he was so thrilled about. If only, if only, he had stayed and talked for just a few more minutes.

Duncan Gleave, Wigan, Lancashire

I was in the RAF Volunteer Reserve and after training as a pilot I was posted to Kenley in Surrey. In August 1941 I took off in a Spitfire in a 'beehive' of about two hundred and fifty Spitfires and Hurricanes to escort bombers to bomb Le Trait in France. Over France I was attacked by three BF109s at thirty thousand feet and hit, and was initially unable to get out of the plane. I only managed it at three hundred feet, which is very scary I can tell you, and landed safely in a French field. I asked some French peasants where the coast was, hoping stupidly to find a boat back to England! They simply pointed to the German troops who were already approaching! It might be the influence of cowboy films but when someone points a gun at you, you put your hands up – I did! And so I was captured on 7 August 1941.

There were some surprises. At Dulag Luft camp near Frankfurt am Main I was offered a cigarette from a pristine packet of Players! But I'd forgotten they must have captured millions at Dunkirk. At camp Oflag X-C near Lübeck we had no Red Cross parcels and the day's ration was five slices of bread, ersatz margarine for one slice, and a bowl of thin soup at midday. We were so hungry that two of us caught a cat one day and killed it, cooked it and ate it without any conscience.

At Stalag Luft III, near Sagan where I was later moved, we did get Red Cross parcels and life was a lot better, and we had also set up our own secret radio. We were able to hear the news from the BBC and so on the morning of 6 June 1944 we got the news of the landings in Normandy. The Germans didn't! We daren't celebrate openly because that would reveal the existence of our radio, but word of what had happened flashed around the camp from hut to hut. Many of the men

had been prisoners for three or four years and the sense of elation and joy had to be seen to be believed. That was perhaps concentrated by the fact that we had to keep the news a secret so there was no dancing around the camp! Rather it was intense whispered conversations between prisoners, but the relief and pleasure could readily be seen. After years of captivity there was light at the end of the tunnel.

Nevertheless, as members of the Armed Forces our hearts and thoughts went out to those fighting in Normandy – we all knew from experience what they would be going through.

The German attitude at this time was quite different. Even before they got news of the invasion their attitude was one of resigned apathy. Afterwards I think they knew what the end was going to be, months before it came. For me D-Day is a day I shall never forget, a day when hope came back to men who had endured years of misery and deprivation. To those who survived the assault on Normandy I say now a personal thank you on behalf of all prisoners of war. To the relatives of those who died I can only express my regrets and ask them to remember that their loved ones died for the most noble of causes and that everyone should be proud of all those who made it possible.

When I got back to England I found out that my fiancée had married an American while I was away! Quite a shock I can tell you. So I went back to Germany with the Allied Control Commission. Eventually I met the girl who was to become my wife, so it all turned out OK!

F. K. Thornton, Heywood, Lancashire

I was born in 1930 in a little village nestled in the vales of Salisbury Plain in Wiltshire. It was called Imber, and is now known as the 'ghost village'. When the war began life changed for me like everyone else. There was always a lot of military activity on the plain as there is today, but as the war progressed this increased, with long convoys of lorries passing through the village. As children we found this quite exciting as it brought the village alive for a while. We would shout and wave to the troops until the last vehicle had passed through, and then once again a hush would fall over the village.

We had many scares as bombs were always dropping around the village. We were surrounded by army camps. Fortunately none hit the village, but one night we were hit by incendiary bombs and I remember one of the villagers swearing when a bomb fell in the pen where he kept his cockerel that the Germans were out to get his Christmas dinner! Then in 1943 the Ministry of Defence dropped its own 'bomb' on our beautiful village. All adult residents were called to a meeting at the village school. I sat at home with my two brothers awaiting my mother's return. She came home in tears. They had been told that everyone, without exception, had to leave the village within six weeks. It was to be used solely for military training.

Everyone in the village was totally devastated. Most of them were from families that had lived there for generations. In my family Imber had been our home since the time of my great-grandmother. A few days later everyone received a written notice to quit the village with a promise that we would be able to return after the war. That was not to be. We had to leave by 17 December, less than eight weeks after the public meeting. How could we do that? Men had to find new jobs, accommodation had to be found. A rural community was being destroyed in just a few weeks.

I remember that as we were packing my mother was taken ill with the flu but we still managed and we moved out on 16

December 1943. Grandmother and Grandfather left the same day. Grandad was the village blacksmith and he was heartbroken at having to leave. He was the last person to leave Imber – and the first to return. He died six weeks after leaving. His doctor said it was of a broken heart and his last wish was to return to Imber. All military training was stopped for the day to lay him to rest in the little cemetery at the beautiful fourteenth century church, which still stands on the village hillside. Everything has been removed from inside and taken to other churches in the area.

When we moved from Imber we moved to the village of Roundway near Devizes and I remember my mother sat and cried for days. We didn't celebrate Christmas at all that year as she was so unhappy. My father cycled to Devizes to get our meat ration for Christmas dinner and when he told the butcher of our plight he gave us a lovely big piece of beef, much bigger than our ration allowance! What a kind man. He felt so sorry for us all.

There was always such a happy atmosphere at Imber – you could almost breathe it in the air. It was such a pretty village with thirty-five cottages, a pub (The Bell Inn), a chapel, a beautiful church, a vicarage, three farms and Imber Court, also known as Imber Manor. Most of the village activities were held there, such as fetes and celebrations. I remember the Jubilee of King George V and Queen Mary was celebrated on my fifth birthday, 5 May 1935 and we had tea in a big barn. And everyone always joined in the fun like one big happy family.

It is so sad to return to the village now and see the devastation. Many people have tried hard to get the village back for us but to no avail. That was the final blow for the Imber people. My mother never did settle anywhere afterwards. She is now back at her beloved Imber lying in the cemetery with my father. That is the only way we can go back for good. I still have very happy memories of my childhood days and I will treasure them for the rest of my life. Then I too will return to Imber for good like my mother and father and grandad and grandma. The village is now opened for one day each year, always on the first Saturday in September. The church, now surrounded by barbed wire, is also opened for two services one at midday and the other at 3pm. There are not many of the Imber

people left now but always a large crowd gathers for the open day.

We wanted to do our part to help in the war and although it broke our hearts to leave we did so without trouble because we knew it was the price we had to pay for what was to be the invasion of Europe. I know thousands of young men made the supreme sacrifice and many wives, mothers and fathers knew the pain of a broken heart as a result. But if we had to leave in 1943, and we went quietly, couldn't the Ministry of Defence have kept its promise and allowed us to return to our homes and our village? It broke its promise and it broke our hearts in the process. So when I remember D-Day I remember the sacrifices made for us all in Britain. But I also remember the price that was paid by the people of a lovely little village called Imber that ceased to exist as a result.

Doreen Charles, Chippenham, Wiltshire

I was one of the thousands that went across to Normandy on D-Day. I remember the first sight we saw from a good distance out at sea was all the houses along the coast road ablaze, and then as we got in nearer land there was an ambulance floating in the water – an early casualty. This was about 10am with the tide half out. I was in the 73rd

LAA Regiment of the Royal Artillery and went over in a Jeep with my colonel, a driver and a wireless operator. My motorcycle, a 125cc James, was tied on to the back of the Jeep.

We were the last off the landing craft and fortunately we had a dry landing thanks to the skill of our captain. Those in the craft alongside had two feet of water to wade through. Not a good start, so we were lucky. I can remember that as soon as we were off the craft my colonel walked up the beach just as if he was going for a game of golf!

We were soon off the sands and digging in on the land side of the coast road near Luc-sur-Mer and Hermanville, about six miles from Caen. One thing I shall always remember is a Jeep ploughing through the surf when suddenly it went into a pothole in the sand and the water was up to the driver's waist. Coming out of the pothole the front wheels were spinning in the air like a prancing horse but the driver carried on flat out and eventually got out of the hole and the beach commander commended him over the loud hailer for his wonderful piece of driving – it really was marvellous.

Later that day a Jerry plane flew over and bombed our petrol dump but was shot down by our gunners and crashed. It was in that same area that I remember having a shower outdoors using a biscuit tin when some locals strolled by and I was still in my birthday suit! They took no notice!

I also remember our bombers going over and towing the gliders and the whole lot looked like a flock of crows there were so many of them.

Jack Newby, Maidstone, Kent

I remember D-Day 6 June 1944, as a petty officer engineer aged nineteen years serving on board one of the many landing craft (LCI 391) taking part in the invasion of Normandy.

At 7am we were just off the Normandy coast having threaded our way through what seemed like endless miles of shipping – battleships, cruisers, destroyers all firing shells towards the shore. The noise was unbelievable and one wondered who could survive under such a barrage.

After standing off for about one hour we were ordered to land our troops. The sea by this time was choppy and a heavy swell was running. Everything went fine, we beached OK, the two landing ramps went out and troops started to move off. Hardly had this started when another landing ship came alongside and collided with our port side, which in turn carried our ramps away. This was the moment our troubles started. By the time our troops had disembarked the tide had receded and we were high and dry with no hopes of refloating until the tide returned.

We landed on Sword Beach near the entrance to the Caen Canal. The German resistance at this point was still formidable and there we were exposed to German shelling on an open beach. It was at this time our captain Lieutenant Jack Haughton decided to abandon the ship. It did not take long for the crew, just twenty-two, to carry out his order. It was a race to the cover of the ruined and burning houses. From here we could see how vulnerable the ship was with shells exploding near. However, after some little time the German guns were silenced and miraculously the ship had escaped damage.

Even at times like this there was a bright moment. One of the crew realised the rum ration was still on board! There was no need to ask for volunteers to return to the ship to collect it. I well remember the lad who went was cheered enthusiastically as he returned to safety with it. At this point a wit in the crew made the classic remark: 'Never in the history of the Royal Navy has a ship on operations been abandoned and none of its crew even got their feet wet.' However it was not all fun and games, especially with the sight of dead bodies and thinking it could be you – a chilling thought, despite the rum issue.

The small town, which was situated just beyond the beach, was just like a ghost town. Where was everyone? I never did find out but I did recall the barbers shop, less front door etc. Everything was intact – clippers, scissors and aprons, even yesterday's hair – isn't life funny. I remember so clearly thinking why didn't he clear up before he went home last night.

The tide by this time was returning and the skipper decided to return to the ship. We were soon back on board and within a short time re-floated and pulling off the beach, the ship and crew undamaged. As I recall these events in 1993, I think how young we all were! Our captain Jack Haughton was twenty-two years and except for one of the crew (he was twenty-eight years) he was the oldest. What responsibility and what a fine captain. As the newspaper article about us in the *Daily Mirror* dated 17 June 1944 said: 'Boys led by a Boy'.

By late evening we were once again at sea and somehow order had been restored, and we had joined a small convoy of ships returning to England. However, the day had not finished as we now found ourselves being attacked by a small number of German aircraft. There was a considerable amount of gunfire and our seaman gunners claimed to have destroyed one enemy aircraft. Being an engineer I was not in a position to witness much of this action, but some few hours later I was called on deck to assist in trying to save some

survivors seen floating nearby. The ship moved out of convoy and scramble nets were lowered, but despite heroic efforts to save these men they were swept away. This was possibly the lowest point of our feeling during the whole operation and so sad and frustrating to be beaten and unable to save these young men. By dawn of D-Day plus one we were back in port preparing to return. Boys possibly grown into men...

Charles F. Gray, Southrepps, Norwich

I was eighteen years ten months old and a Stoker 1st Class serving on LCG(L) 831 for the D-Day landings. LCG is the Naval term for Landing Craft Gun. There were very few LCGs in the Royal Navy, I myself never saw any more than three. The armoury of LCG 831 consisted of two 4.7-inch guns, which were manned by Royal Marines and thirteen Oerlikon anti-aircraft guns. All anti-aircraft guns forward of mid-ship were manned by Royal Marines, all anti-aircraft guns aft of mid-ship were manned by Royal Navy personnel. We also carried small arms such as rifles, Sten guns, revolvers etc. The crew consisted of twenty-two Royal Navy Officers and Royal Navy Ratings, plus twenty-three Royal Marines. So you can imagine how small our living and sleeping quarters were. For these cramped conditions we were paid one shilling and sixpence a day, hard layers money.

We were ordered to action stations around 3:30am, D-Day 6 June 1944. I was on duty at the engine room control table, when I received a signal on my telegraph for emergency ahead, the time around 5:40am. At the same time our 4.7-inch guns started firing. The vibrations from the four-point-sevens shattered most of the electric light bulbs (this always happened even on firing tests), so the light in the engine room was pretty dim. The next signal after about five minutes was for emergency astern. As I was reacting to this signal, waiting for the revs of the main engines to slow down to idle, before I could change gear from forward to reverse (astern), I could hear machine gun bullets hitting the starboard side of the engine room. At the same time an enemy shell went through the exhaust stack rupturing the exhaust pipes and the engine room filled with exhaust fumes. At action stations we always carried our lifebelts and gas masks, so I put on my gas mask, which I had to wear for about three-quarters of an hour, during which time all my signals were either emergency ahead or emergency astern. My feelings and thoughts during this time were as follows: I felt anxious, although I was not frightened as such, and my thoughts wandered to home, my mum, dad and family, my girlfriend Hilda, who all lived in the beautiful village of Tadley in Hampshire, and of the lads on the upper decks. Had any been wounded or killed? How were things going? It seemed an eternity before I received the signal slow ahead, the time about 6:40am. All our guns stopped firing. After about ten minutes I received the signal to stop. At about 6:55am a Royal Marine messenger came into the engine room and told me to fall in up forward on a gun deck. When I fell in I could see we were about two hundred yards off Arromanches and the activity going on had to be seen to be believed, with no enemy fire on our troops landing on the beaches.

The lads told me how things had gone during our engagement with the occupying enemy. One marine had been killed on B-gun and B-gun was put out of action. The young Royal Navy signalman on the bridge was very badly wounded. That was the extent of our casualties on D-Day morning. They also told me they had knocked out nine eighty-eight millimetre guns and that the Germans ran for their lives across the fields, fired on by our small arms, so the way was really well cleared of the enemy for the army to land. During our engagement with the enemy, Jerry riddled us with eighty-eight millimetre shells. We were in so close fighting that most of the shells went right through our LCG and out into the sea! It took a LCE landing craft engineer three days to weld plates over the shell holes.

At Arromanches was a lovely church with a steeple and in the middle of the steeple was a shell hole. All who landed at Arromanches on D-Day and after noticed and spoke of this shell hole in the steeple. The rumour went around that a sniper had been active up in the steeple; I even heard Sir Harry Secombe talking on television on the forty-fifth anniversary of

D-Day at Arromanches that a sniper was holding out in the church steeple. I can honestly tell you that this was not the case. What happened was that when the firing ceased on D-Day morning the captain of LCG 831 said to the gun crew on A-gun, 'You see the steeple of that church, with one I round only, if you can put a shell through the middle of that steeple I will give the order to splice the mainbrace.' That is the truth and that is why we spliced the mainbrace at Arromanches on D-Day morning 6 June 1944.

Maurice 'Blackie' Black, Newton Abbot, Devon

On the 5 June 1944, the day before D-Day, I was stationed at an RAF Operations Training Unit at Market Harborough; we were flying Wellingtons. I had not started my operational flying on Lancasters at that time, that doubtful pleasure was yet to overtake me, but the Powers That Be decided that we were to be pressed into service to fly to the French coast to drop leaflets, warning the French population (in the areas to be defined by Bomber Command) to stay away from strategic points, e.g. railway sidings, bridges and all places that would come under attack when the invasion – soon to come – would take place.

There were seven members in my crew, including myself as Wireless Operator/Air Gunner. I was only a lad at the time, the youngest in the crew. I am now a sprightly sixty-eight – I was about eighteen at the time. We were piloted by Sqdn Leader Bretherton, whose father was a minister of the church; I never knew his peace-time occupation. He has recently died. We had three Canadians – a Flying Officer Hill who was our Rear Gunner, Flying Officer Kendal was Mid-Upper Gunner and Flying Officer Carney as Bombardier – I believe he was something to do with his father's motel in Quebec called Dinty Moores. I never knew the occupations of the other two. The navigator was F/Officer Peters who had been an insurance agent in Wolverhampton. The engineer was F/Sgt Dickinson who lived in Lincoln. He later became Secretary of our Memorial Flight of a Spitfire, a Hurricane and one of the only Lancasters left flying which takes part in various flying exhibitions around the country. He has also recently died.

We took off at about 1am on D-Day and set course for Brest, stacked as far as possible with leaflets and stacks of

Back row: Carney, Dickinson and Hill. Front row: Alfred Smith, Bretherton and Kendal

window. Two other aircraft were bound for St Malo and Rennes. It was a little windy that night so we unloaded the leaflets down the flare chute. I had to stand at the chute and push out bundle after bundle of leaflets – disbursed with bundles of window. These were strips of tin foil, the same as housewives use to cook the Christmas turkey. This was to put the radar beams out of focus so that they could not give correct readings.

This was one of the hardest night's work I can remember in all my missions, including the thirty I made after D-Day. We turned ten miles off the coast, as the wind was strong enough to carry the leaflets on to the targets. This gave us a better chance of dodging night fighters etc. Fortunately, the wind dropped and the seas calmed before the invasion started, helping our troops no end. In fact, the invasion was in doubt until then. Whether this calm was brought about by the same magic as the one before Dunkirk must be left to the imagination.

After what seemed like an eternity, we turned for home and I shall never forget the sight of the invasion fleet sailing to the Normandy coast. I had the most shaky feeling in my legs and stomach and I said to my Bomb Aimer, who had been helping me to drop the leaflets, 'Look, Earl, let's say a prayer for all those lads down there, that they may be kept safe until the job is done.' My heart goes out to all the people who lost their men in that gallant effort to rescue our country from that madman, Hitler.

Alfred 'Smithy' Smith DFC, Orpington, Kent

In December 1943 I was awaiting a draft to sea from the Royal Naval Signal School, in Glenholt near Plymouth, with three of my pals with whom I had trained for over a year to become a Wireless Telegraphist.

My three pals were delighted to land a draft to Simon's Town, South Africa whilst I was to stay behind and miss what appeared to be a very glamorous posting. I therefore went to the Base Regulating Officer to try to volunteer to go with them only to be told that I was already on a draft designated 'special party foreign', which turned out to be a spurious name for the training for the assault on Fortress Europe.

I'm writing this to suggest that if anyone would have liked to bet on who would survive I'm certain none would have placed their bet on me. Sadly all three of my pals lost their lives within a few weeks of leaving me, drowned in the sinking of the convoy leader SS *Khedive Ismail* off West Africa, while I went on to survive the assault on D-Day, 1944.

My draft turned out to be LCH (Landing Craft Headquarters) 275 which was a converted LCI (L) redesigned to carry a large communications staff plus the DSOAG (Deputy Senior Officer Assault Group) whose job was to control the forces engaged in the storming of the beachhead. Our landfall was the beach section King Red on Gold Beach, close to the small village of La Riviere where we put ashore the tanks of the Westminster Dragoons 79th Armoured Division and Infantry of the 50th Northumbrian Division, the 1st Hampshire, 5th East Yorks and 6th Green Howards Regiments. We commenced our journey to the beaches on the night of 5 June 1944 from the Solent, where thousands of craft were gathered in really foul weather, it being so bad that we had to tow an LCA (Landing Craft Assault), which had apparently broken down. I commenced my watch at 20:00 hours reading Niton radio (the transmitter on the Isle of Wight).

Sitting alongside me in the wireless cabin was a shipmate reading the fleet wave. Also in the wireless cabin was a Royal Marines captain who had taken refuge in the office to grab a few hours sleep before H-Hour. Unbeknown to me my shipmate's wave had closed down for a few hours so he had gone to his bunk for some sleep, but the marine captain had slipped into my shipmate's chair alongside me and dropped asleep.

On completion of my work reading Niton radio I turned to see this shock of curly hair alongside me, identical to my shipmate's hair, and reached out to shake the sleeping figure awake. As I shook his head I was horrified to see that I had in fact grabbed a captain of His Majesty's Royal Marines by the hair and was violently rocking his head back and forth! He came to and in fact apologised to me for his lapse, while I almost curled up. I must be the only naval rating to have not only got away with such an act but actually received an apology in the process! Sadly the telegraphist whose head I thought I was shaking was killed exactly twenty-four hours later at 22:00 hours when the Luftwaffe bombed our beach section.

I returned back on watch at 04:00 hours on 6 June, and was then asked to quit the wireless office and continue reading Niton radio using an army portable set on the bridge of my ship. While setting up this equipment I asked another shipmate to climb up the mast and secure my aerial up there. This he did, but while he was up there the RAF commenced their carpet-bombing at the same time as the big guns of the Royal Navy opened up. Within a few seconds, and within one thousand yards of us, there was suddenly this massive pyrotechnic display.

My shipmate almost fell from the mast with shock and in fact he was in such a state that in his anger he actually accused me of knowing it was going to happen! I eventually did calm him down and convince him that I had no contact with the supreme commander and was just as shocked and surprised as he was at what had happened. My banishment from the wireless office to the ship's bridge turned out to be a real blessing as it enabled me to watch the actual landing in our beach section of King Red from a distance of only two hundred yards instead of being locked away in the wireless office where nothing could be seen.

I felt as if I was watching a film as the tanks, followed by the infantry, stormed ashore, but as they went I felt especially sorry for the army lads who had suffered seasickness after a rough night on our ungainly landing craft, then got a thorough soaking as they went ashore, and then had to go on and meet, and defeat, the enemy. My heart went out to them.

The bombing of our landing craft on the night of D-Day caused three deaths. Bomb shrapnel holed our fuel and water tanks, which meant we had to drink water that tasted of fuel for the whole of our twelve-week stay.

After a couple of days we were allowed to beach our craft to repair shrapnel and bullet holes along the hull. While this was taking place some of us went along the beaches to take out cigarettes to the men of the Pioneer Corps who had the fearsome job of clearing the beaches of anti-personnel mines. Weren't they pleased to see us! We saw the hastily dug graves of British soldiers with no apparent identification on them and also found the temporary grave of our shipmate Richard Wilby, Telegraphist Royal Navy, with his ID in a little bottle stuck into the soil above him.

The food situation got quite bad during the period we were there and for approximately three weeks I existed in the main on four Mars bars a day, which we could obtain from a little NAAFI store aboard ship. This must be a good advert for Mars but it certainly kept me going!

The dreadful storm that blew up on 19 June, lasting approximately three days, did enormous damage to the Mulberry harbour pontoons we had seen being erected, completely wrecking the American section at Omaha and doing considerable damage to the British sections. My ship seemed to have no place to hide from the weather and for most of that three days we steamed up and down our area, almost turning turtle at times as the storm raged.

The old ships that had been sunk to try to form some sort of breakwater for the landing area codenamed Gooseberry did not seem to afford the protection they were designed to do but on the other hand things would obviously have been much worse without them! I still have a ship's bell taken from one of these old ships as one of my war souvenirs.

During the period that Caen was being heavily bombed by the Allies, we saw a Lancaster bomber in trouble above us and, after the crew had baled out the plane, it went into a dive, crashing into the sea in an area thick with ships and craft of the landing forces. Fortunately it missed them all and we all joined in to gather up the aircraft crew but we never did find out if the pilot survived. He had obviously steered his aircraft clear of the ships as it came down. A brave man indeed.

During the actual assault period we witnessed the eruption caused by one of the ammunition and fuel barges taking a direct hit and filling the surrounding area with tiny black pieces of debris that seemed to take hours to clear. I well remember hanging from the propeller guards of our ship gathering up five-gallon jerrycans of petrol, which were bobbing about all over the place. Some of these went on to provide fuel for our mid-shipman's car, a birthday present from his wealthy parents!

A very poignant sight during this period was the survivors of infantry battalions forming up on the beaches to sing out their names when read out. Many of these battalions of seven hundred to one thousand men had been reduced to approximately two hundred and thirty men and made me realise how fortunate we had been.

After the collapse of the German army at Falaise we returned to Southampton Royal Pier to be greeted by the Wrens boat crews who we found out had believed us to be sunk! As our skipper was married to one of these ladies it made our homecoming that much happier. During the weeks that followed we re-grouped on another LCH to take part in the battle for Walcheren Island in November, 1944 where our force took rather a battering with seventy-five per cent losses both in men and ships.

Raymond 'Shiner' Wright, Burton-on-Trent, Staffordshire

I was in D Troop, 431 Battery, 147th Field Regiment, The Essex Yeomanry. Aboard our LCT we had four twenty-five-pounder SPs and as the light improved we were ordered 'take posts'. The 'run in' shoot in support of 231 Brigade, Tyne Tees Division would soon begin. Believe it or not, this brigade comprised of the Hampshire, Devon and Dorset Regiments. Three hundred rounds of HE would be fired on and beyond the beaches from each of the four guns, firing salvos. Soon the assault craft carrying the infantry and marine commandos (who were attached for the landing) were going through our lines. Small craft these, lowered from assault ships some way out, and crewed by Royal Marines, they were cheered on and wished 'good hunting' by the gun crews.

We had little or no sleep during the night, due to excitement and seasickness. Then it came, orders to lay and load and everyone was on his toes. We had to shoot those boys onto and beyond the beaches and we'd do our best. 'Fire' was given and all hell broke loose. The navy guns behind us, the rocket craft just ahead and our own guns began belching fire and smoke onto the beaches.

We opened fire about two and a half miles out and continued until 'ceasefire' came. The beaches were now clearly in sight. Heavily laden infantry struggling up among Bren carriers and DD tanks, which had swum ashore from two or three hundred yards out. During this lay off period between ceasefire and actual touch down we reloaded with ammo, carried on the deck of the LCT. The chains securing the SPs to the decks were released and everything prepared for the 'run in'.

Now, for the first time, we looked around us. Assault craft were still going for the beach, wreckage was everywhere, ships were being hit. At this point we passed a sailor bobbing up and down in a lifebelt yelling at us to give the b******s hell. We wonder if he lived. We saw the stern half of an assault craft with three or four men clinging, obviously sinking, but we had orders: hit the beach and give the infantry all the support we could. Reluctantly, we could only wish them good luck.

We turned for the beach and began the run in. Turning, we could clearly see the obstacles ahead. Steel fences set pointing out to sea with teller mines on the top, waiting for us. About now, the craft dropped anchor on a loose hawser, which it would use to winch itself off the beach. We crunched onto and through the fence, we could see the mines bobbing along the side of the craft, but they must have been filled with sand and water, because none exploded. We uncrossed our fingers! We felt the craft shudder on the seabed and down went the ramp. The guns began to move forward, this was it! Into the sea and keep going up the beach. No. 1 was clear, No. 2 stopped, No. 3 stopped, I had to stop on the ramp. Each SP was towing a sledge full of ammunition, which was under the sea out of sight and No. 3 had run onto No. 2 sledge. They soon cleared themselves and went ahead again.

We went off in about five feet of water, each SP having been waterproofed to take off in eight feet. Drivers were actually below water level and were guided by the No. 1 standing behind them. Up the beach, onto the road and into action again, but fast. The infantry assault troops had cleared the beaches and were moving inland. They suffered considerable casualties, so bad we heard they had thrown in the reserve battalion. First aid points were established and

the wounded were being attended to and loaded onto craft returning to England. There were dead men lying on the beach and washing at the edge of the sea.

Landing ships infantry had now hit the beach behind us and were disgorging men down ladders either side of the bows into the sea to struggle ashore. In front of us was a barbed wire fence hung with signs saying 'Achtung Minen'. In order to bring the guns on line the GPO's staff had to enter the field beyond and set up their director. This they did without any trouble and we thought this must be one of Jerry's bluffs until someone spotted a half buried teller mine. It was real enough.

We continued firing at targets as and when needed. While this was happening members of the gun crews opened the sledges and broke out the ammunition, which we were using at a fast rate. One of the regiment's LCTs had broken down during the night and so missed the run in shoot. The LCT was now lying stranded on the beach and we were able to collect its ammunition. We took ashore ammunition to last the first three days. Such was the need by the infantry that this was almost used up and so without that stranded LCT what would have happened?

Towards evening we set off, out of the bridgehead, towards the Americans on our right. We were to support the Marine commandos in their efforts to capture Port-en-Bessin. By now D Troop were out on a limb in No Man's Land, and it was a queer feeling! Port-en-Bessin was captured. We supported 231 Brigade in their attack on the enemy battery at Longues and we 'stood to' all that night.

Percy Page, Woodford Green, Essex

I was No. 92527, L/Cpl. Snook, JWHHQ Platoon, 118 Company RASC, 49th West Riding Infantry Division, 'The Polar Bears'.

We were not in the first wave of the D-Day landings, we were support troops, but we were there, and my recollections are as follows.

Our three-tonners were loaded onto the tank landing craft, the SS *William Carson*, at night, in the London docks. We awoke next morning at sea, no land in sight. We were surrounded by ships, and more ships, simply hundreds of them; whichever way that you looked there were ships, riding the waves, what a magnificent sight it was. I shall never see the like of it again.

The SS *William Carson* nosed onto the beach, her ramp came down with a rattle of chains, and within seconds, the first Bedford was down the ramp, and into the sea, and with the sea over her bonnet, she drove up and away between the marker lines, heading for the sea wall above. My turn came, and with the sea up to the windscreen, I put my foot down and away I went, following the truck ahead. We just went like crazy, the engines roaring their heads off, what a thrilling feeling, pulling out of the sea and up that beach, I shall never forget it...

We joined a stream of vehicles pouring inland, tanks, trucks, guns, Jeeps and motor cycles, all under a cloud of red dust; we could only breathe through the muslin taken from our first aid packs. We stopped, finally, and were ordered to de-waterproof our engines and to dig slit trenches, as we were under sporadic mortar fire. We had no idea where we were except that we were in the Caen area. There was barbed wire, with 'Achtung Minen' signs of skull and crossbones all around us.

But miraculously, in all this frenzy of noise and confusion, and a battle raging nearby, a French farmer had his cows tethered to posts driven into the ground, and they were grazing happily.

We asked the farmer for a supply of his milk as he came out with his bucket, but he refused, point blank. He would not even look at our invasion French francs! Would you believe such awkwardness! But next morning, I was out before him, with a bucket and a box to sit on, to milk his lovely cows, and for us to have a lovely cup of tea, at his expense.

Our division, the 49th, sadly lost two thousand men, killed in the campaign, many of them around Rauray, and Fontenoy. Some of our battalions at that time were losing two hundred men a day. There are Polar Bear men buried in each of the five permanent cemeteries around Fontenoy. May they rest in peace. We owe them our lives and our liberty...

Jack Snook, Llangadog, Dyfed

Claude and I were twin brothers and both members of No. 2 Platoon, 249 Field Company of the Royal Engineers, attached to D Company of the Ox and Bucks Light Infantry, which was incorporated into the 6th Airborne Division. On D-Day we comprised one hundred and eighty men in six Horsa gliders and our job was to capture two bridges over the Caen Canal and the River Orne approximately five miles inland. We were under the command of Major John Howard, Ox and Bucks, and Captain Jock Neilson, Royal Engineers.

Gliders 1, 2 and 3 would land on the Canal bridge, and Gliders 4, 5 and 6 on the Orne bridge. Claude and I were both in No. 6 glider – I'll bet there weren't many twins in that position that night! With blackened faces and hands we got aboard. The doors closed and then we heard the increased power of the engines of the Halifax and then the jerk of the towrope and we were off! The gliders left at one minute intervals into the night sky. Thirty men in each glider, five of whom were Royal Engineers.

For most of us this was our first time in action and I remember there was almost no conversation in the blacked-out interior of the glider. No lights at all were permitted. We flew at six thousand feet with fighter-aircraft escort and crossed the French coast a few minutes after midnight. Tuesday, 6 June 1944. Suddenly we felt our glider being released and then seemingly in minutes we had landed with grunts and groans from both our bucking plywood aircraft and ourselves!

I had previously been detailed to check that after we landed everyone had left the glider and so I jumped out from the rear-side door, ran a few yards and flattened myself on French soil. And nobody else was there! Just a few staring cows four or five yards from me and otherwise complete silence. Where had all my mates gone and where were the other two gliders? For a second I thought I might be a one-man invasion force and so I moved ahead of the glider and found to my relief a bunch of men kneeling by a hedge. 'Scout section,' I whispered. 'Shut up,' came the reply. So I moved ahead and there found the others from my glider and we all moved off at a fair pace, down into a ditch, up the other side and onto a road and there straight ahead of us was 'our bridge'.

One shot was all we heard from the enemy and one of our men threw a smoke bomb and in the same instant we charged across the bridge. As we did that the sappers were checking for electric wires that would lead to explosive charges as intelligence reports had stated that the bridges had been prepared for demolition. Guns were now firing on the Canal bridge four hundred yards away but all I heard from the defenders of our bridge was the sound of running feet down the towpath! But before anybody mocks, I suggest the sound of thirty pairs of British Army hob-nailed boots rushing around in the darkness was enough to scare the bravest hearts! But how far would they have gone and where to?

I went under the bridge to the water's edge and in the patchy cloudy moonlight saw a huge dark object right under the centre of the bridge. A barge filled with explosives? A continuation of single width scaffold boards had been laid through the girders into the darkness. 'That's where the explosive will be,' I thought. 'Phew.' So I called for support and lo and behold my twin brother appeared alongside me. Apparently while I was under the bridge all other personnel had moved off. So we went to investigate. Crawling through the girders with rifle and backpack was no joke, and the water rushing below me was not inviting either. The 'dark object' turned out to be a huge brick pier containing the bridge opening equipment and, thankfully, no explosives. They were discovered next day in a nearby shed.

While under the bridge we heard running feet above us. Hopefully from the other gliders, but we weren't going to check! I put out my torch and waited and when it was silent Claude and I climbed back onto the road. It was thirty minutes since we had landed and as we got onto the road we saw the first paras dropping, and then amazingly, from somewhere in the distance, the 'all clear' sounded. They didn't know we were there! Claude and I made our way cautiously to the Canal bridge, which had by now been captured and waited for the inevitable German counter-attack. But all we saw before dawn was a German foot patrol, staff car and motorcycle, which were quickly finished off by the infantry on the river bridge. A sole German tank approached the Canal bridge but that was quickly destroyed with a Piat bomb.

Early dawn saw a number of Lancaster bombers twisting and turning very low over a coastal gun battery prior to an attack by the 6th Airborne, and a naval bombardment could clearly be heard. Daylight now and we saw and learned of our casualties. One officer killed, one drowned, six wounded and one glider (No. 4) missing. Our Glider, No. 6, had been the first to land at the river bridge – hence my being on my own initially!

Then we saw two German naval craft cautiously approaching upstream to the Canal bridge and we opened fire. From my slit trench I only managed to fire one round at the wheelhouse before my gun jammed. I had managed to get grit into and over my rifle bolt! But it caused no problems. The boat grounded and the crew surrendered and Claude went aboard to check everything out. The second craft managed to turn back but I presume would have been finished off shortly afterwards by the beach landing troops.

A little later in the morning now and we were getting problems! There were German snipers in the trees and the church tower and buildings were in use by German troops. The fire was becoming heavy and accurate. We had limited heavy equipment, but the Ox and Bucks had got hold of a German anti-tank gun together with ammunition and started to use it with some success against the church tower. While we were now getting some heavy fire on the bridge I

remember seeing Allied fighter aircraft flying overhead quite unmolested! Very frustrating!

A little after midday now. Then sweet music in the air – bagpipes! A company of commandos, with a piper at the head and their officer next wearing a white pullover, had reached us from the beach. What a joy for us all – temporarily. For as they crossed some of the lads were hit by the snipers. We buried one by the bridge next day. I painted his name on an improvised cross – Lieutenant Campbell. I can't recall where I got the tin of paint and the brush – probably from the café by the bridge.

Evening now and the sky suddenly filled with a vast number of gliders and aircraft dropping supplies in the bridge area. A most welcome sight. We knew now that we had tanks and mobile guns with us and more comrades. A plane was hit by German anti-aircraft guns and came down in flames crashing in a nearby field. For us sappers by the Canal bridge it now meant an all night guard duty. Certainly a very long and eventful day.

On D-Day plus two a German fighter-bomber flew in low and dropped a bomb on the Canal bridge. I was stretchered onto a French resistance lorry and taken almost instantly to a beach first aid station. In due course I was told I was to be taken back to the UK. Inside this huge tank landing craft many stretcher cases arrived – I was one of the first batch delivered. I wasn't sure what had happened to Claude. I asked an attendant if someone like me, as he was my twin brother, had arrived. 'Yes,' he replied, 'He was in the last load aboard.'

Hospitalised together for a couple of weeks with plenty of humour and care from the nurses and then I was moved on alone for a further two months to another hospital, and we both re-joined our 249 Company of the Royal Engineers in September.

Cyril Larkin, Lowestoft, Suffolk

HMLCT 898 was a Mark IV Major Landing Craft. A strange monster which behaved like a crocodile on the shore, half in and half out of the water and like an elephantine boot box at sea! She was my first command, and I was very proud of her.

No commanding officer could have been blessed with a more loyal and hardworking crew. A/B Porter my Signalman had become my good and valuable companion through many a middle watch on the bridge. The Seaman Gunners A/B S/T L. Batty and A/Bs G. Wells, J. McKinnon and R.V. Hood had honed themselves into superlative gunners with Oerlikon, Tommy guns, Sten and Lancaster and also with the rifle, and could give a good account of themselves in unarmed combat. In Leading Seaman G. Tyson I was fortunate in having a well-trained and experienced coxswain from general service.

In the engine room department again I was fortunate in having my namesake P/O M/M W. Flynn in charge, ably assisted by Stoker A. Hutchings and Stoker William Swordy. I sat down with my first lieutenant S/Lt Willis and looked at all these young expectant faces. 'Well, I began, 'This is it. We are off tonight and we beach tomorrow morning at Lion-sur-Mer at 08:15 hours.' Stabbing my finger at the chart laid on the mess table I said, 'I don't want any heroes. Our job is to get the army safely there, beach them dry-shod, get the tanks off and get back here for more tanks to support the poor bastards who will be fighting for their lives.'

The daylight hours came and went and soon it was time for 'main engines, coxswain on the wheel, gun crews close up' and all the hustle and bustle of a ship alive and underway. It always gave me a thrill of excitement and never more so than on the night of Monday 5 June 1944. We were on our way – 6 June was to be D-Day.

Aldis lights flashed as fleet numbers were exchanged and craft manoeuvred for their correct position in the embryo convoy. For the purpose of the initial assault I was to form part of the 41st LCT Flotilla, and land at Sword Beach on Queen Red Beach by Lion-sur-Mer.

I had no illusions about the Germans. Although they fought for an idiot's evil regime they were a brave, resourceful and cunning enemy and Rommel a superb general. We were in for a hard day. All was going well. Dawn had come and by the growing light everything seemed in perfect order. I was on the bridge with A/B Porter and two army officers. Breakfast had just been placed on the chart table when suddenly there was the most almighty explosion. A wall of cordite impregnated seawater erupted from the port side, ascended to a height of about fifty feet and then came crashing down on the bridge and my still untouched breakfast! I looked around – there wasn't an army officer to be seen! The engine room reported that the shell had blown in the sea inlet suction valve and they

would do everything they could to get it right before we beached. Enveloped by a continuous deafening roar, which marked the tumultuous sounds of the bombardment, we reached the assault area and formed into line abreast. Then the group commander in his HQ ship chose this very moment to steam east to west which meant he was going right across the front of the now advancing landing craft each doing 'emergency full ahead'! I was on the extreme right of the flotilla and it became plain that unless I altered course I was about to ram him amidships! Reluctantly I reduced speed and altered course to port and gave him sufficient sea room to take avoiding action. The headquarters ship at least had the courtesy to signal 'thank you!' As a consequence I fell astern of my next in line so that when the German battery of 88mm guns opened fire the shell hit another ship in the area where I would have been. Sadly I saw that three of his tanks had been set alight.

I went in between two of Rommel's beach obstructions – steel tripods with a teller mine set at the apex – but unavoidably hit the next. I signalled on the klaxon for the winch crews to close up. I looked at the chronometer – it was exactly 08:15 hours. Everything was still going smoothly until simultaneously with the bow ramp dropping a shell entered obliquely from the starboard side and blasted its way through the port winch house. The crew of the winch house sustained shrapnel wounds but nevertheless remained at their posts. Two near misses starboard side aft now swamped the bridge and did further damage in the engine room. The 70-ton pump was sufficient to prevent serious flooding, but we were starting to get in serious trouble. Then another direct hit from a German mortar shell on the port winch house killed A/B S/T L. Batty, seriously wounded A/B G. Wells and wounded A/B J. McKinnon. Meanwhile, amazingly, the tanks were going ashore miraculously unharmed into the midst of all this mayhem.

Another near miss forward had caused shrapnel to enter the starboard winch house injuring my first lieutenant S/Lt E. R. Willis. By this time there remained only one tank to go ashore. I had sent A/B Porter below to assist the first lieutenant with the wounded and so I was now alone on the bridge. I had to make a strong effort of willpower to stand on the raised duckboard and expose the upper part of my body over the parapet of the bridge in order to encourage the remaining tank to get off so that I could un-beach. This accomplished, another near miss caused damage to the superstructure on the quarterdeck, shrapnel entering the wheel house wounding the coxswain Leading Seaman G. Tyson but he nevertheless remained on the wheel. It was now 08:22 hours – all this had taken just seven minutes! To add to it all I observed the army major on the beach unbelievably walking about with his walking stick surrounded by his tanks. His officers were literally screaming at him to mount his command tank and get moving!

I signalled to Hutchings and we were able to raise the ramp sufficiently to un-beach. At 08:34 hours the one remaining winch wire and the anchor cable leading from aft gave under the dead weight and the bow ramp now hung directly from its hinges. It acted on the ship like a sea anchor. Progress was slow. The first lieutenant, assisted by A/Bs Hood, Fowler and Porter were treating the more seriously wounded in the army shelter on the tank deck. Amputation of two of A/B Wells' fingers had to be carried out there and then using scissors. At 10:58 hours I requested permission to go alongside the hospital ship HMS *Princess Astrid*. I transferred the dead body of A/B Batty and the seriously injured A/Bs Wells and McKinnon but retained on board the first lieutenant and the coxswain. This was my first opportunity to speak to A/B George Wells. Although seriously injured and pumped full of morphine he remained cheerful throughout and was concerned only for his mess mates. I took this opportunity also to visit the engine room and found that Stoker William Swordy had stripped and was in the bilges attempting to stem the inrush of water with materials supplied by and with the assistance of Stoker A. Hutchings and P/O Flynn.

The following morning, 7 June, at 08:35 hours, the port engine broke down but we got it repaired. I finally reached Gilkicker Point, Portsmouth at 13:10 hours when my first lieutenant and coxswain were taken ashore for hospital treatment. The return journey had taken twenty-nine hours – truly the longest day! I was alone when there came a knock on the cabin door. It was A/B Fowler. 'Sir, I have been chosen by the remainder of the crew to thank you for getting us back.' After he had left I laid my head in my hands on the wardroom table and wept.

A/B G. Wells was deservedly awarded the Distinguished Conduct Medal and Stoker W. Swordy and I were Mentioned in Despatches. Finally, may I add a tribute to A/B S/T Laurence Batty, the rating who was killed. He was a senior rating of great character who had refused all offers of further advancement in order to remain part of the ship's company.

He was a Sheffield lad who demonstrated all the true grit of that great county and a true patriot.

Charles Flynn, Croydon, Surrey

I was a trooper in the 4th Troop, B Squadron, 4/7th Royal Dragoon Guards. I was co-driver of an amphibious tank in 8th Independent Armoured Brigade. We were roused while it was still dark, stowed our equipment and made last minute checks to see that everything was in order. All loose gear inside the tank was checked to make sure it was safely fastened down and in its proper place. Rations, personal kit, chocolate, biscuits, cigarettes, all were checked. Including those special extras we all had, a seven-pound tin of cocoa saved from a recent pre-invasion exercise! Ammunition all in its proper place and readily accessible. Make sure the ammo is not jammed and the release catches for the 75mm main armament shells are operating freely. Check the outside of the tank; nothing must foul the canvas screen to stop it inflating. All outside decks free of loose equipment and ropes. All safe and stowed away.

Dawn was beginning to break and the coast of France could be seen ahead, like a low cloud on the horizon. There was a heavy sea running, but what I remember most was the vast armada we could now see in the lightening day. I felt a sense of awe. It seemed the whole might of the Allied navies was there to make sure we got ashore! Battleships, cruisers, destroyers, minesweepers and landing craft of all shapes and sizes. The whole sea seemed to be covered in craft and yet they were clearly in allotted positions ready for the assault which was obviously about to start.

At 6am the naval bombardment started. It was the most spectacular thing I have ever seen. The shore, which could now be clearly seen, suddenly erupted in a mass of smoke and flame as shell after shell went home. The noise was terrific and as we got nearer the shore shells began to fall around us, but it was only a desultory reply. The rocket launchers in particular gave a staggering display of fire-power. These were LCTs fitted out with rockets on their flat decks. There were three or four a short distance from us, and when they fired a salvo it seemed that the whole craft exploded!

The time had now come to get into our tanks. I settled into the co-driver's seat with the other four crew in their positions. Driver to my left. Gunner, wireless operator/loader behind, and tank commander in the turret behind and slightly above me. The co-driver operated the front machine gun, which was mounted on a free moving fixture and was used independently from the main gun turret arma-ment which comprised a 75mm gun and a machine gun. We raised the canvas screen on the tank ready to go. Finally the order came 'start engines' and we knew this was it. The moment we had been waiting for. What would we find ashore? All the crew were keyed up and waiting to go, and I remember thinking, 'If I survive today I'll go through the rest of the war without being killed'.

Suddenly with a crash the ramp of the LCT was dropped and immediately the tank in front of me moved its thirty tons slowly forward and down the ramp at an angle of about forty-five degrees. We followed. I remember looking at my watch. It was 7:10am. Down the ramp we went – first gear and foot off the accelerator otherwise we would have shot to the bottom. I scanned the shore through my periscope during the few seconds we were on the ramp but could not pick out any targets. We suddenly floated clear of the LCT and after about twenty-five yards we touched bottom. Immediately we deflated the screen, which dropped in a couple of seconds and I saw the beach stretching ahead of me. The tide was out and exposed on a wide sandy beach were an array of various beach defences. Some were iron spikes constructed so that at high tide they would tear the bottom out of a boat. Most of them also had an explosive device attached, which wouldn't have helped either! After advancing through some of the obstacles we engaged a gun in a concrete emplacement directly in front of us. The navy was supposed to have knocked all these out and so we had a double surprise. It was still in action and it wasn't on the aerial photographs we had memorised!

Rapidly we placed half a dozen rounds of HE through the slit and silenced it and then moved on, firing at the targets that had been allotted to us. We put down a blanket of fire for about twenty minutes when the infantry started to land and pass through our positions. They went up the beach and into the slit trenches beyond. Fire was still coming at us and an infantryman to our front was suddenly somersaulted through the air, either through shell blast or treading on a mine. I don't know which. The beach to our immediate front was very narrow with a concrete sea wall about four or five feet high. The only way we could get off the beach was to turn right and through a hole that had been blown in the wall.

To perform this manoeuvre the tank had to reverse whilst half-turning and then complete the turn in a forward direction. We started to reverse and after a few feet came to a halt, unable to make any headway backwards or forwards. We were stuck in the sand and four feet of water and every minute the incoming tide made it harder to move. I told the commander I would get out and fix a towing hawser if he could call up the troop leader to tow us out. I quickly dismounted and instantly became aware of the sounds of battle all around me! These were not audible inside the tank, what with the noise of the engine, our guns, and radio messages flashing back and forth.

My first reaction on hitting the water was to get the screen inflated again and float the tank off, but the canvas screen had been torn to ribbons. A shell had landed a few feet behind us, wrecked the screen and made a crater and we had backed straight into it! The troop leader's tank had now arrived and I attempted to fasten the towrope to our front shackle but this proved impossible as it was under water and the sea kept washing me away from it. Eventually I managed to do it by telling our driver Cliff of the other tank to hold me under water by standing on me while I secured the towrope as it needed two hands to fix it to the shackle. He obliged! The tow tightened as the tank pulled away, but then it became obvious that the dry sand would not support the new tank without it shedding a track. We were well and truly stuck, with the tide still rising and the Germans not being very helpful either! I unhitched the tow and the tanks moved off through the breached wall. We were now on our own. Salvaging equipment from our tank before the rising tide covered it now had to be carried out quickly. With bedding rolls, rations and sundry other items of equipment we struggled out of the tank, through the sea and through the sea wall time and again dumping our gear by the side of the gun emplacement we had recently knocked out.

My next thought was to put some dry clothing on! I had started the day dressed in my one-piece tank overalls and I had salvaged my uniform dry and intact. The hours were now passing and I knew at 3pm our A1 echelon were due to land with the first line supplies of petrol and ammunition for the squadron. I decided to make a recce along the beach to link up with any other squadron tank crews who may have come to a sticky end. I found an infantryman's discarded bicycle and rode off along the track parallel to the beach. I found three crews who had experienced similar disasters. It was now past midday and the tide had covered the tank except for the top of the turret but as the sea receded we tried to recover some of our gear but it was all ruined. While doing this a photographer took a picture of the gun emplacement and I have obtained a copy because it shows two of our crew, my overalls spread on the sea wall to dry, the bicycle and our bedding rolls etc. The tank isn't visible as it was on the seaward side of the gun and hidden by it.

The two crew are the driver and the gunner (who was called Stan Moffatt) and the driver Cliff Ford. In the photo Cliff is second from the left and Stan third from the left. They are both in 'tank' helmets – no brim. Stan was killed in Belgium in early September and the driver, Cliff Ford, was wounded in October. I believe he died some years ago. By mid-afternoon we saw the wheeled vehicles coming ashore and so I clambered aboard an ammo truck and we set off inland to the harbour for the night. I must say I remember feeling very vulnerable and defenceless sat on that ammunition! We stopped at a farm that night and our crew set to work to make a base for the tanks that had survived. Ammunition, petrol, rations – they were all manhandled off lorries and stacked as unobtrusively as possible around the orchard. We worked until it was too dark to see anymore and then we found a meal had been prepared – were we ready for it! It was tea and hard biscuits! When my guard duty ended I turned into my blanket under the trees in the orchard with petrol and ammunition heaped all around! One good shell among that lot and it would have been 'bye-bye' with a vengeance! We were too tired to bother! Out of a total complement of nineteen tanks the squadron lost nine on the beach and in the fight inland on D-Day. In view of the difficulties and opposition we faced I felt that this was quite a remarkable achievement. So D-Day ended for me. We had been on the go for twenty-two hours in a highly charged situation and when I put my head down all thoughts left me and I lost myself in the sweet pleasure of sleep!

Wilf Taylor, Llandysul, Dyfed

It cannot have been more than a month after my sixteenth birthday, when I awoke one late June morning to the sound of my mother moaning. It was more like the cry of a wounded animal as she sat rocking to and fro at the bottom of the stairs.

I heard the mattress creak in the bedroom next to mine, as my grandmother threw herself out of bed and hurled remarkably quickly downstairs to comfort her child.

Fear had paralysed my limbs but eventually I leaned over the bannister to view the scene below.

There was my mother's silver head bent low and gran had enveloped her in a huge bear hug. Her immense bulk filling the tiny entrance hall of our three-bedroomed semi. If mother's hair was silver, gran's was as white as driven snow, as it lay around her shoulders like some ancient matriarch.

My mother clutched in her hand the dreaded missive from the War Office. Hope had been dwindling in her heart for the last three weeks, but here it was: 'We regret to inform you that your husband Cpl A. Surtees 13115148 serving with the Pioneer Corps has been killed in action.' This of course had been in the Normandy landings on D-Day. I can't remember if her widow's pension papers were enclosed, but at any rate they followed shortly. The War Office didn't stand on ceremony to let you get used to the idea.

Mother and gran seemed immersed in one another, while I felt vaguely embarrassed by this unwonted display of emotion. We had never been a demonstrative family.

Catherine with her brother Jim

I went to do the only thing I could think of; boiling the kettle for a strong cup of tea. I was destined to make many more before that long summer's day was over, for the news spread like wildfire throughout the district, as bad news always does. So there were a number of callers to weep and offer words of condolence, pity for the boy of eight, my brother, 'A boy needs a father', but in the same breath my father was, 'Lucky to have Mary, such a sensible lass'. It seemed I had been hearing myself called that since ever I could remember.

It always made me feel like kicking over the traces, but I just didn't know how, so I remained sensible to the end.

My poor thirty-nine-year-old father had given his life for his country, he'd gone before he'd begun to live. Mother had nothing to look back on but years of trying to make ends meet during the Hungry '30s.

Why is that day stamped so indelibly upon my memory? Firstly, it was the most dramatic thing that had ever happened in our humdrum lives, but more importantly I had reached a turning point. I could no longer escape into that realm of childish irresponsibility; I had not wanted to grow up, not just yet awhile at any rate. But with the news of the death of my father, I'd had adulthood thrust upon me.

Catherine Mary Surtees-Robinson, Eastbourne, Sussex

It was D-Day, one hour and forty-five minutes after H-Hour and our LCT 593 was heading towards a section of the Normandy coast not far from Ouistreham, carrying four self-propelled guns, three Sherman tanks, four half-track vehicles and eighty British soldiers of the 3rd Division. I was first lieutenant to the CO, Lieutenant J. F. D. E. Jones. We were in company with five other LCTs.

We fired several hundred rounds from our self-propelled guns as we approached the beach and could see obstacles sticking out of the water, many of them with shells and mines attached. We managed to avoid most of them, hitting the beach at maximum speed. By this time bullets and shrapnel were flying in all directions and the noise was deafening.

After landing our men, tanks and vehicles in about two feet of water, we turned the LCT and set off for home. No sooner had we set course at 'full ahead' when the mechanic appeared, reporting that we were holed in the engine room and taking water fast.

I dashed below with the mechanic and found the engine room flooding rapidly. Jagged beach obstacles had holed us in two places. The pumps were working to full capacity and we endeavoured to plug the holes with spare kit and about one hundred and forty blankets. Unfortunately, the pressure of water was too great and as it poured in one of the engines seized up. If the other did the same it would be only a matter of minutes before we sank. However, it kept going. Following instructions from the bridge we closed all watertight doors, and I returned to the bridge. By now the stern was gradually settling lower in the water, making accurate steering impossible. Return to the UK in this condition was out of the question. The CO decided to beach the craft. It was the only option, but it was the beginning of five very uncomfortable days marooned on Sword Beach.

The rest of D-Day passed surprisingly quickly being occupied with securing the craft, digging a trench on the beach and finding something to eat. It took our minds off snipers in the houses along the front, firing at us whenever the opportunity arose. We had only two Oerlikon guns but we used them to good effect. During the evening we had a fright. A thick mist came rolling along the beach. Our first thoughts were that the Germans were using poison gas! We donned our gas masks and took cover, wondering what sort of gas it might be and how it would affect us. After ten minutes, taking note of the indicators on board, we were relieved to know that it was a harmless, chilling sea mist!

We did not get much sleep during the night of D-Day and as dawn broke on D plus one any rest which we did get was quickly shattered by the arrival of enemy aircraft, six Junker 88s. One was shot down by a Bofors gun on the shore road, and a member of our crew, Ordinary Seaman Townsend, hit another and set its starboard engine on fire. Later in the day men from the salvage ship *Northland* came aboard to see if they could be of assistance. They decided to return to our stricken LCT the following morning, with cement to fill the holes.

D plus two brought further troubles. We had such command of the air that enemy aircraft didn't worry us too much. It was the shelling from Le Havre which was so devastating. It came without warning, and on the beach there was nowhere to run, nowhere to hide. The shelling was intermittent and during one attack three of our crew and two salvage men were wounded. Stoker Tom Beatson died later that day from his wounds. The holes were slowly being filled with cement, the salvage men worked hard. It was a difficult job because every time the tide returned fresh cement was dislodged.

D plus three was busy. We were more or less watertight and the *Northland* pulled us off the beach by a length of cable almost half a mile long. The salvage vessel could not come any nearer to the shore for we were still being shelled.

We watched the slack being taken out of the line. It was agonisingly slow, with shells bursting every thirty seconds in the water around us. At last the line appeared above the water and it began to take the strain. We moved slightly and a shell just missed the bows. We started to swing and another shell missed. We all expected the next one to be a direct hit but we were

towed a good distance from the shore and told to drop anchor. We were now out of range of guns at Le Havre.

D plus four was a day of disappointments. It was impossible to start the engines and there was no one who was keen to give us a tow back to the UK. We had to spend the night at anchor.

D plus five brought the offer of a tow. We set off but towing with a long line was not successful. The thick wire hawser quickly frayed and we were worried. If it parted we would drift into minefields either side of the Channel, which had been swept for us as a highway to the beaches. We sent desperate signals to the towing craft, and it was decided to take us alongside. This was not an easy exercise, an LCT is a cumbersome craft. We had another sleepless night keeping close watch on the cables, renewing and repairing the protecting canvas where necessary.

D plus six found us in the broad stretch of water separating the mainland from the Isle of Wight. We dropped anchor and breathed a sigh of relief. We had been lucky. Many of our friends in similar craft did not return. The obstacles on the beaches took their toll.

Our efforts were not in vain. Following a week's leave we returned to our repaired LCT and made more trips to the French coast. On one occasion we brought back the fuselage of one of our planes, which had been shot down. The salvaged metal was vital to the war effort.

Robert J. Pollard, Hythe, Kent

I was a regular soldier, serving with the Hampshire Regiment and during the war I was with the 1st Battalion. After service in the western desert in Egypt we saw action in Sicily and Italy, and if that wasn't enough we were then selected as an assault battalion for the landings in Europe along with the other two battalions in our brigade, the Dorsets and the Devons. With all the replacements we had received over the years to make up for our losses I suppose we were now about two-thirds veterans and one-third 'new boys' who were going to be thrown in at the deep end. There was a very heavy swell so none of us slept much that night and about 4:30am there was breakfast – for those who fancied it! A lot of us ate it even though reluctantly because we knew it could be a long time before we got another meal. For some it would really be their last.

At 5:30am we went up onto the main deck to be lowered into the flat-bottomed infantry assault craft, banging away on the davits. It was still fairly dark. In the craft we sat one behind the other, in three rows, one man's chin practically resting on the pack of the man in front. We were lowered down, but as soon as we were on the water the craft was going up and down on the swell as though we were in a demented lift. We had to try to hold position until all craft were in formation, and before we headed for shore we were in our craft for one and a half hours, thoroughly miserable, drenched by the spray, and feeling not a little seasick! It only needed one man to be sick and it would spread throughout the craft. We had one! It was the only time I was ever seasick in all my years of service.

It gradually got lighter and when we were about three miles from shore the navy ships started their own bombardment. It took our minds off our miserable conditions and made us feel a lot happier knowing the enemy was on the end of that lot! But as we got nearer the shore the enemy added his own fire – only this time in our direction! A hell of a lot of stuff was falling around us with other landing craft being hit. We grounded, quite a way out because of the waves sweeping in, and the front ramp went down. The craft never stayed grounded because one wave would sweep us in and the back surge would drag us out. Then back in again and so on, mostly at a nasty angle to the beach. A number of men were lost by craft coming back at them while they were in the water, knocking them down and going straight over them. The officer I was close to in the craft jumped in, was either knocked over by a wave or slipped, so I followed him and gave him a hand up. Fortunately for both of us a big wave literally picked us up and carried us ashore. Our instructions were to get off the beach as quickly as possible – stop for nothing. With the flak that was coming we didn't

need any second bidding! We set off at a run, not easy after being cooped up in the assault craft and loaded down with equipment. I remember going up the beach, between the 'hedgehog' defences set in the sand, each with a mine on the seaward side. They would be covered once the tide came in. On my left as I ran was Corporal Bill Winter, already the holder of the Military Medal. He would be wounded within half an hour. On my right was Private Monty Bishop.

Bullets were flying everywhere but strangely with the noise of the bombardment, the wind and the sea you didn't hear them! You didn't realise anyone had been hit until you reached the sand dunes. It was only then as I looked back that I saw our men lying wounded and dead on the beach. When we reached the sand dunes we went down into a kneeling position, grateful to get our breath back. Another platoon that had just landed was trying to sort out the pillbox to our front. I noticed that Monty was leaning heavily on my right shoulder and I thought that like me he was 'puffed' and pleased to have someone to lean on. But when we got orders to move forward and I got up he just fell forward on the sand. He was dead.

A bullet coming down the beach from the sanatorium on the seafront at Le Hamel, just to our right, must have hit Monty as we waited. The sanatorium, the main defence position in the area, should have been taken out by a low level air attack just before we landed, but because of the low cloud none of the concrete-bursting bombs found their target and the place was still bristling with guns of all types. Another thing that made our job difficult was the absence of armoured support. During 'rehearsals' for the landing we had the support of swimming tanks. These were Sherman tanks fitted with an inflated skirt which kept the tank afloat until it got to the beach where the 'skirt' would be deflated and the tank revert to a conventional tracked vehicle. However, in our case the first wave of tanks launched from the craft were immediately swamped by the heavy seas and sank. No more were launched from the craft until tank landing craft could get in and conventional tanks could get ashore.

After a great deal of hard fighting we achieved our objectives, capturing the town of Arromanches at 9pm in the evening with an attack from the landward side. It hadn't been an easy day by any means. Our casualty list was one hundred and eighty-two men killed and wounded out of about five hundred and fifty who had set out that morning. The commanding officer was wounded twice in the first half-hour. When the second in command came ashore he was killed almost immediately so the company commander of C Company took over command of the battalion. During the morning of D-Day the wind eased up, the sky cleared and by the afternoon the sun was shining. A completely different scene to when we had landed just after 7am that morning.

D-Day of course was just the start of some severe fighting in the bocage of Normandy. After five weeks of almost continuous action against the best the German army could put in the field, only myself and two other men remained of the ninety or more men of my company who had landed that morning. The others had been killed or wounded. But before too long we were part of the chase through France and

Belgium, the highlight being when we were the first infantry to liberate Brussels. A couple of days of pure heaven after what we'd been through! Why and how did I survive? I'm afraid I shall never know the answer to that!

Stanley 'Chalky' Chalk, Faversham, Kent

My name was Phyllis Laura Carley then and I lived in Sidley at Bexhill-on-Sea. I was almost thirteen when D-Day took place. My bedroom had a view of the sea and all my life it seemed the lightship had shone across the sea and onto my bedroom wall. Of course, in wartime we had no lights that I can recall. All we had was blackout. Anyhow on this particular night I'd heard little hoots and noises and could see flickering lights. Mum suddenly came into my bedroom and opened the window. I sat up in bed.

'What's the matter?' I said. 'Something's happening,' said Mum. 'What?' 'I think it's started,' she said, and I didn't understand! 'What has?' 'The invasion.' I shot out of bed. 'But I thought we were all right now.' Mum looked at me in frustration! 'Not the Germans – us!' she said, 'I think it's begun.' I couldn't sleep with excitement. I think they were moving troops and equipment to Portsmouth or along the coast. At least that now explained why all those convoys of lorries had been coming down our High Street.

A few days earlier my young sister Eileen (almost nine) had nearly caused a major accident as the convoys went through. Eileen, me and my other sister Jean (aged eleven) were waiting to cross the main road. Mum was across the road going to the chemist. The noise of the tanks and lorries was earthshaking and mum didn't see or hear us. Suddenly Eileen shot across the road in front of a tank – which only missed her by slewing round sideways! The commanding officer was following on in his Jeep and was beside himself with rage he was so furious. He stood up like a general reviewing his troops and waved his stick at us. The convoy was split in half and the soldiers were all looking out of the lorries, and my mum was so frightened and upset she was giving Eileen what for with whacks around the legs. And then I got the same when we got home and it wasn't my fault!

The day after the night of noises from boats etc. I awoke to the noise of aircraft. I will never ever forget that day. I've never seen so many planes in my life. Bombers – low. Probably Lancasters but I don't know the names of planes much. Spitfires, of course, but hundreds of silver shapes high in the sky. We tried to count the formations of heavy bombers flying low overhead but it was hopeless and the

noise was terrific! They were still crossing overhead when we went off to school and I can remember the children dancing and running along the streets cheering them on as they flew overhead. We yelled our heads off and waved frantically in delight. It was just so exhilarating. It seemed to go on forever and I tried to picture my dad over the other side. I prayed to God to bring him home to us.

Dad had gone over with the Inns of Court Regiment. He was in armoured cars, one of Monty's men. He used to tell us that there was only one black beret with two badges on it and he and Monty had had a fight over it and Monty won! So that was why Monty was a General and not my dad. Do you know, we believed every word of it! After D-Day we used to look every day in the papers for the map showing how things were going because mum said that dad was the 'arrowhead' of the regiment and so we faithfully looked up each day to see where dad was. It was the arrowhead, wherever that was. We were quite confident that no German would DARE fight our dad. After all he'd nearly become a general! But we worried just the same. He was at Neimegan at the time of the Battle of Arnhem and met my cousin Kenny Oaten aged eighteen only an hour before he was killed by a shell in the face. He's buried at Neimegan. When dad came back we had become a houseful of women. Poor dad! We all had to adjust but we were so glad to have him home with us again. And at least he came back. Many other poor souls didn't and I grieve for those who lost their loved ones.

With all the activity of D-Day the 'in' game became wandering around looking for spy hideouts because we were all convinced they were there – somewhere! I once led my friends into what appeared to be an empty schoolhouse and there on the wall was a map with flags on it. This was it – we'd stumbled on a spy hideout! Suddenly a deep voice asked us what we were up to. There was a US army captain with his Sam Brown belt on. We were chucked out double quick! I now live only a few yards from that school and it still brings back memories of that day whenever I pass it! Another time we entered an empty house and in the fireplace someone had burned maps and things relating to France and Germany. A lot of things I remember had 'Ypres' on them and I remembered had I read that name before. Of course it was from World War I but we were only kids, the invasion of France was happening on our doorstep and we were hell bent on assisting by capturing our very own spy! We collected the 'evidence' to take it to the police station but halfway there we realised we'd then have to own up to entering the house. So self-preservation got the better part of patriotism and we abandoned it! Anyway, we convinced ourselves the spy was probably miles away by now seeing as he'd burned his papers! I laugh at it now but we were very serious then. That's my memory of D-Day and the effect it had on us. But the best part was that Dad came home safely to us.

Phyllis L. C. Bestley, Bexhill-on-Sea, Sussex

I was an Amphibious Vehicle Mechanic in 299 DUKW Coy, RASC, part of the 3rd British Division. With a full complement of DUKWs, equipment and personnel on board LSTs 213 and 214, we sailed to a rendezvous in mid-Channel. At the break of dawn I decided to go up on deck and, to my amazement, ships of every size and description had assembled overnight in preparation for the D-Day invasion. The quiet was shattered by ear-splitting crashes as salvo after salvo was fired at the coastal defences. I felt a sense of security being part of such a massive fleet, supported by air cover overhead. The noise was deafening and the faces of my comrades told their own story. It was nearing time for us to disembark. At twenty years old, it suddenly dawned on me that I was a bit young for all this, although I was fully trained in beach landing. I was feeling sick and, I don't mind admitting, scared as well. As the battleships *Warspite* and *Ramillies* sailed past the LST, all hell was let loose. This was no place for a rookie! The coastline of Sword Beach was almost visible.

After calling us to the lower decks, the padre conducted a short service. Afterwards, our OC Major Person briefed us on the day ahead and added, 'God bless you all and may you reach the Normandy coast safely.'

We climbed aboard our DUKWs as the huge doors of the LST opened. Each DUKW in turn moved forward slowly and went down the ramp into a very rough sea. I didn't like the look of the sea but I tried to remain calm as we tossed around like a cork in the water.

I felt really sick and I removed my haversack and the remainder of my kit, thinking I would eventually have to swim to survive. Visibility was deteriorating along the foreshore because of smoke pouring from houses along the beach, which were set on fire by the assault. As we approached the last hundred yards or so, still chugging along, I could see the difficulties ahead.

The 6th Airborne Division were providing plenty of air cover – not an enemy in sight – as they dropped thousands of troops over a wide area of the Normandy beachhead. The troops from the initial assault, by then tired and hungry, must have thought this a Godsend. Reinforcements were always welcome. The planes returning from the dropping zone, flying low over the housetops, were picked off one by one by sniper fire. One plane landed along  the water's edge, another crashed into the sea on our port side, with no survivors. A few planes crash-landed into the shallow waters and a rescue launch manned by the RASC was there in a flash to pick up any survivors.

After approaching the beach cautiously I could see enemy soldiers assisting the Royal Engineers, Pioneers and the beach clearing units to tow the large metal objects, with teller mines attached, out of the way. A flail tank was detonating as many mines as possible, so we followed it for the remaining thirty yards before we reached sand. A temporary track was being laid on the sand dunes directly in front of the entrance to Hermanville.

I could not believe what I saw along the dunes. The beach was littered with dead and wounded, wrecked vehicles and many other craft which had beached. There was chaos everywhere. This was a sight I would never forget. I can assure you that my comrades and I were sickened and upset at seeing the loss of so many lives. On reaching the sand, I immediately jumped out of the DUKW – why, I don't know! Dazed and shell-shocked, I wandered round until I found the DUKW control post. Many dead soldiers were laid on a large tarpaulin; some had drowned before reaching the beach. Tank crews were lying beside their wrecked tanks. There was worse to come as I zigzagged over and around the dead bodies who had perished in front of the Hermanville strongpoint. One soldier lay dead with his accordion by his side. Another in a crouched position with his rifle holding him in balance, but dead. Feeling sad and desolate I suddenly remembered the words of hymn 581, 'The Sands of Time are Sinking'.

The complete length of Sword Beach from Ouistreham to Lion-sur-Mer was a sitting target for occasional air attacks and shelling. To ease the tension barrage balloons were erected to shield us from further attacks. Large duplex drive tanks, which were causing congestion on the beach, were towed aside to make way for us. An entrance to Hermanville was now ready to use, so cautiously we moved onto a rugged track. I remember saying, 'Thank God we got off the beach.' It was a real boost to all of us. A few houses by the roadside were still sheltering snipers who immediately attacked us. Fortunately, a group of commandoes appeared with bayonets at the ready and forced their way into the buildings. A few shots were fired then a yell or two. Afterwards a commando instructed us to move on to the unloading depot.

After unloading their cargo, the DUKWs returned to the beach and started to ferry the wounded to hospital ships anchored in the bay. Many vehicles were damaged by mines during the evacuation. Trees and hedgerows were almost non-existent owing to the continuous bombing and strafing during the assault. Now and again we encountered a few civilians. Many stayed in hiding to await the outcome of the day. The noise of battle was never-ending as the infantry fought to consolidate the land along Perrier Ridge. The enemy were still holding on around Lion-sur-Mer.

We were now at Hermanville where we commandeered the local farmyard to set up a temporary workshop to repair and service the DUKWs as required, to keep them seaworthy. In a field nearby were about thirty dead cows but the bull was still alive. As it did not attempt to get up on its feet I assumed that it was shell-shocked. Intermittent firing from the church spire accounted for the loss of many soldiers who were drawing water from a tap in the square. As a sniper could not be located it was decided, after consideration, to remove the spire by shellfire.

The first burial ground was opened in a field adjoining the workshop. A continuous convoy of lorries brought in the dead for burial. I watched the padres removing identity discs and personal belongings which they placed in small individual containers. After the bodies were laid to rest, side by side, a service was conducted. All this was very disturbing and depressing, but made us all realise that we had survived the first ordeal. I remember saying, 'Thank God for sparing me during the first day on French soil.'

The farmyard buildings were made of stone and mortar. The yard contained a dwelling house, byre, implement shed and a few other barns, all in poor condition. The farm buildings survived the D-Day bombardment with little or no damage. We had a feeling that we were unwelcome probably because the farmer felt the army was responsible for the loss of his entire herd of cows. He showed no appreciation for the freedom we had brought to Normandy. It was almost dusk.

Tired and hungry, my comrades Billy and Staffy assisted me in digging a trench to secure our safety for the night. With sweat pouring from our faces we opened our emergency packs and with apples from the orchard and cider from a barrel in the farmyard shed we had an appetising meal before we decided to kip down for a well-earned rest.

At midnight a despatch delivered to OC workshop informed us that the DUKW control post on the beach received a direct hit killing the entire HQ staff. This was our saddest moment of D-Day.

No wonder it was later called 'The Longest Day'.

Jack Patterson, Kirkcudbrightshire, Scotland

I was Platoon Commander in B Company, 2nd Battalion, The East Yorkshire Regiment. We made the initial landing at H-Hour on the left flank pivot of the invasion at a place called La Brèche.

02:00 hours: I stir from a fitful, all-too-brief sleep, to the uncomfortable awareness of being one of some thousand fully armed and equipped men crowded aboard an infantry landing ship. I pick my way through the human sprawl to the fresh air of the boat deck; in the semi-darkness Bert Shaw, i/c 12 Platoon, reckons the small flight of planes he's heard pass low overhead were towing gliders... we exchange hardly a word during the next half-hour of eerie quietness until another wave of aircraft throbs over to conjure out of the darkness miles ahead a desultory display of flak... going below I find my own platoon mostly awake, tense but quiet.

04:00 hours: I'm drawn back on deck to watch the cold grey light of dawn gradually revealing the immensity of this armada, stretching as far as the eye can see – at least to starboard and stern. That the navy is somewhere out there protecting our port beam is suddenly brought home to us by the unnerving sight through the haze of a destroyer with bows pointing skyward... in another hour the ever-increasing roar of an invisible armada overhead is supplemented by a naval bombardment from behind.

05:30 hours: All minds are suddenly concentrated by the call to boat-stations. The ticklish job of loading thirty-six fully armed men into our sardine tin of an assault landing craft, being swung out from davits and lowered into a tossing sea, is accomplished with fewer hiccups in routine than hearts in mouths... with a minimum of jockeying by our Royal Marine navigator up front (surely, only months out of school!), we slip into station, one of six puny craft abreast as the first wave of the battalion's assault formation.

06:00 hours: With ninety minutes and seven miles to go to H-Hour touchdown there's no turning back. The sight of this vast bobbing fleet with its hundreds of men within hailing distance should be good for morale – but I bet every man Jack of the three dozen packed in this craft has never felt lonelier in his life... pity the sea is running so high: five-foot waves can't be ignored in this cockleshell and a feeling of nausea is already growing... another half-hour and I can't fight it any longer – our marine engineer sympathetically indicates a lifted board amidships and several of us get shot of last night's meal into the scuppers rather than chance our heads over the side.

Another retching half-hour (keeps one's mind off the war!) and a shoreline gradually emerges: amazingly the sparse hotchpotch of boarding houses along the beach tallies exactly with the low-level air-recce photo with which we have been briefed – can this be just another training exercise? No! The roar of our divisional artillery firing low trajectory over our heads is for real; and some angry explosive crumps alongside are grim proof of an impending hostile reception.

07:25 hours: A last snatched look towards a sloping beach barely one hundred yards ahead. A fleeting prayer that our young navigator steers clear of those partly submerged beach obstacles – a grating crunch as we hit shingle, and THIS IS IT! – the ramp falls and I lead out our charge into (thank God) only two feet of water and the blessed feel of firm land on which my leg muscles can take over from my stomach muscles!

In the hectic rush to deploy to the scanty protection of sand dunes one hundred yards above water line and exchange fire with an unseen enemy, my mind begins to register in a rapid succession of camera shots: to the right one flail tank hammering away at a beach exit with another heeling over; an amphibious tank burning in tragic end to its gallant two-mile swim as others waddle ashore; seaward over my right shoulder an obvious hit on our HQ ship; behind me, crawling up the beach, with shattered leg, our company sgt major whose pallid face asks merely to be pulled above the fast rising tide; and successive boatloads of battalion colleagues threading their way through the

confused mass of armour towards beach exits on our right – but where, oh where, on my left is Bert Shaw's platoon? ... 'Don't think his boat made it, Sir,' mutters my young sergeant. Two conflicting thoughts race through my mind; so my LCA was the extreme left-hand boat to land of the whole blessed invasion (!), but what about my exposed left flank?... Hell! My batman is missing, too, and with him our 38-set radio link with company HQ... My fears are eased: a boatload of commandos lands to strike off left along the beach without obvious trouble; and a message from company HQ orders me to leave to our follow-up company the trickle of enemy troops now emerging in sorry-looking surrender from houses in front of us, and to join 10 Platoon through a cleared beach exit on to the first road.

Between the houses we cross the main coastal road to face completely open country stretching inland for some one thousand yards, first empty marshland, then cultivated fields rising gently to a skyline of copse – but, before we can begin to deploy, a dyke some fifteen feet across and ten feet deep threatens to bring us to a more dangerous halt than the beach itself... well done, corporal, wherever you scrounged those lengths of rope! Thankfully we negotiate the open ground without harassment from an enemy whose observation and fire is obviously concentrating on our armoured vehicles streaming inland on the only road half a mile to our right... and how well they're doing their clearance job for us to have reached the comparative shelter of this next lateral road one mile in from the beach – comparative because, like any road, it is being accurately ranged by enemy mortars – still, we can use the concealment of this coppice for a quick reorganisation of company structure necessitated by an inevitably growing casualty list.

12:30 hours: In an unexpected liaison role I'm continually adding to my album of mental snapshots as the battalion edges forward from one hamlet to another; I've observed C Company's successful assault from the rear on one strongly fortified gun emplacement that we'd bypassed earlier; in the same arc of view over the beach I've marvelled at the unexpectedly large silhouette on the horizon of a Royal Navy battle cruiser and ducked at the terrifying, express train scream of its heaviest shells hurtling low overhead; and now, two villages later, I'm looking across to the small twin bridges over canal and river, and more particularly at the six gliders, now crumpled and forlorn, that had passed over us in the dark early hours to secure those bridges for our paratroopers. I keep telling myself I'm seeing history in the making – but here, well in from the beaches, with the farmsteads not that much knocked about, there is a mellowness about the afternoon air; and some of the morning's tenseness is slipping away as our follow-through battalions assume the immediate responsibility of pushing ahead. This dangerous sensation of bemused detachment is hardly dispelled by the sight of a woman appearing out of nowhere and walking out ahead of our men to collect her few cows still standing – the milk of human kindness, if you like!

17:30 hours: I'm back to normal platoon routine as we reach our likely limit line for the day; we now hold the left-hand end of a ridge, some two and a half miles inland and the highest ground between the beach and that town, hidden in the river valley barely six miles ahead, which is the division's ultimate objective. But such higher planning is not our present concern; we concentrate on the self-preservation exercise of digging well-sited slit trenches against a possible early hours counter-attack... I withdraw a third of my platoon at a time, to a hedgerow on the reverse slope where a hot stew meal miraculously appears in hay boxes from Battalion Rear HQ – together with the news that our CO has been wounded and evacuated; I find I can't face the meal – but I gratefully grab a mug of tea, with the sober thought that, apart from one boiled sweet, it constitutes my only sustenance this whole, long day...

23:00 hours: With two-hourly duty rosters arranged, my sergeant tactfully indicates a deep furrow in this field of corn standing four feet high; in the enveloping darkness I flop into this funk-hole – the corn enfolds me like a tent – I try to marshal the details of this eventful day; I suppose we haven't done too badly – I hope it's all worthwhile. I wonder what they've heard back home – I pray she hasn't been too worried; Dorothy, devotion, dedication, D-Day! 'My heart aches, and a drowsy numbness...'

S. J. B. 'Jack' Pearse, Amersham, Buckinghamshire

I was a Wireless Operator, K Section 50 (Northumbrian) Divisional Signals and Personal Signaller to Brigadier Sir Alexander Stanier, in 231 Infantry Brigade. We embarked on HMS *Nith* on 4 June and the following day were given a final briefing. We learned that H-Hour was to be at 07:00 hours on 6 June. Wireless sets were to open at H minus sixty and wireless silence was to be broken at H minus thirty unless emergency arose.

As dawn was breaking I could hear formations of heavy bombers passing overhead, slowly the visibility improving. At first I could only see ships near ours, then the outline of the coast and finally line upon line of ships of all sizes and shapes from cruisers and destroyers, sleek and lean, to the landing craft, squat and cumbersome. By this time the LCAs and smaller assault craft had been lowered from their parent ships. Landing craft were circling around an LSI not far from us, while further away flotillas of LCA carrying the infantry were in formation.

The coast was now receiving the attentions of the Royal Navy and squadrons of planes and was soon covered by a pall of smoke. The cruiser HMS *Orion* was one ship in our task force. She was firing her broadsides not many hundred yards from us. My brother was on this ship but little did he know that I was so near and yet so far from him.

I got on board my LCM and unfastened my small pack and stowed it on the Jeep. As we approached the coast we came under light shelling, and on looking over the side of the craft my eyes met a sight that I shall never forget. The shore was about eighty yards away, the beach seemed crowded with tanks and a few carriers, but not one appeared to be moving although there were one or two burning. Between the shore and our craft were rows of formidable looking obstructions. There were long poles about seven inches thick embedded in the sand at an angle pointing out to sea with mines attached.

I saw five or six men clinging to what looked like a telegraph pole; they were being tossed about unmercifully and the wash of various craft attempting to land added to their discomfort. I hoped that some naval craft had been set aside for picking up such men as these.

I received a message saying that the reserve battalion had landed and I knew that we were scheduled to land about the same time. This latest information was reported. On reaching the place I had found for myself behind the Jeep I was shaken by a violent explosion. My steel helmet evidently got tired of waiting to land and jumped overboard deciding to fend for itself. In a flash I realised we must have hit a mine. My thoughts of a dry landing faded into the background and I was more concerned about the depth of the water in front of us. Our craft had stopped and as the ramp was lowered 'written message for you' came over my set. Hastily taking my pad and pencil from my pocket I accepted the offer and proceeded to take the message. The message was surprisingly long. I read it through and acknowledged it. On looking up to see to whom I could hand it I was amazed to discover that I was apparently alone. The remainder of the party I observed, through the open end of the craft where the ramp had been, were strung out in a line making for the shore. The nearest person was quite some distance from the craft and the water was almost up to his chest. I could see that the handcarts were floating. I then intimated to all out-stations by code word that I was about to land. I folded the message I had just received, put it on top of my set and tied the waterproof bag round it.

I heard a voice, which I immediately recognised as Cpl Davidson's, coming from the carrier. I climbed on the front and looked inside and saw Cpl Davidson and Cpl Gunning who were making an officer comfortable. I observed that the latter's hand was more or less smashed, and heard afterwards that this had been done when we hit the mine. The officer had been blown overboard, but had been hoisted back aboard almost immediately. Knowing Cpl Davidson would try to land the carrier, I volunteered to stay on the front and give him steering instructions, because he was unable to see from his driving seat. Before starting, I drew his attention to two mines on a pole slightly to the right of the craft and about eight feet away. To avoid these I told him to bear left when he felt himself on the ramp, or when I should tell him.

Cpl Davidson started the engine and we began to move. I stood on the front, with my back to the carrier. As we were moving onto the ramp the carrier hit the side of the craft and I felt myself falling sideways. For a split second I did not know what had happened, and I felt myself being dragged along beside the carrier. We were now making for the shore. My fingers pained me intensely but I realised that if I attempted to move them I should, to say the least, lose my tow ashore. My right hand was free and I brought it across my chest and held the set above the water, at the same time kicking my legs.

Cpl Davidson stopped when he got into shallow water and I stood up and disengaged my fingers. He looked at me and said that he thought I was dead, and wanted to know what had happened. He could hardly believe it when I told him. Neither of us to this day can say how close we must have been to the two mines. They must have been barely inches away.

I called up my group and was relieved to be answered by the three battalions. I did not receive a reply from the Brigade Major's party or the Main Beach Signal Office despite repeated calling. The two sets in the handcarts were not working, as water had leaked in through the waterproof bags. The operators unloaded two spare sets from the carrier but before they had time to effect a complete change, the brigadier decided to move off the beach. The crater blocking the coast road was being filled in by Royal Engineers, beach parties and tank crews, who were waiting to drive their tanks off the beaches.

Soon after the tanks started coming through, 47 Royal Marine Commando came along. They had been heavily shelled when coming in to land and had lost a considerable part of their equipment. They had picked up and armed themselves with British and German arms and ammunition. The colonel spoke to the brigadier and shortly afterwards the commandos moved off. Meanwhile the signal officer had arranged for the commandos to net a twenty-two set to my set to replace the one they had lost.

While in this location I received a message saying that one of the battalions was encountering heavy opposition in Le Hamel from snipers. The snipers were being mopped up but it was taking longer than expected. Another message said that the Germans had expected an attack in this area, but not on that particular day. The brigadier decided to have a recce up to Le Hamel himself. Our little recce party consisted of the brigadier, the colonel and adjutant of the field regiment supporting our brigade and his wireless operator, Cpt Wheaton and myself. We made our way along the coast road past the enemy pillbox with a dead German sitting outside it on guard. The pillbox had been hit by a near miss from a shell or rocket, but was not badly damaged. Many of our infantry had paid the extreme penalty along that road. They had all been covered by gas capes or ground sheets. A few wounded were being brought back on stretchers to the beaches. Our progress was not very rapid because we walked half crouched to be below the level of the banks on either side of the road. We did not know how thoroughly the adjoining fields had been cleared of snipers and we were not taking chances.

Our progress was very slow because of other transport, tanks and infantry on the road. As we rode along I was able to see the effect of some of the naval shelling and RAF bombing. Houses were mere heaps of rubble. More notices were displayed disclosing the presence of mines on either side of the road.

I arrived back from the last visit of the day in time to do 'stand to'. It was getting dark and for the first time I saw German planes. They were attacking our shipping but the flak did not give them a very pleasant welcome and I saw two shot down in flames. After 'stand down' I ate the remainder of my box of rations, and borrowed a box ready for breakfast. I borrowed some blankets, as I had lost my own, and all my kit had been in the Jeep which we had lost in the LCM.

My clothes had dried on me during the day and I slept with them on. Before going to sleep the events of the day passed through my mind and I could not but think that at last we could say that the war was entering its final phase.

The day closed as I had begun it with a prayer. Very tired I soon fell asleep knowing that at 05:00 hours I should be preparing to do some more visiting with the brigadier.

Lewis 'Taffy' Richards, MBE, MM, Bedwas, Gwent

I was a sergeant of the 7th LI Battalion, Parachute Regiment in the 6th Airborne Division seated in the fuselage of a Stirling bomber. D-Day was a few minutes old. As we neared the French coast, anti-aircraft shells started bursting all around the plane causing it to rock, but the pilot flew straight towards our target area near the village of Ranville. Suddenly, a red light appeared near the rear of the aircraft, which denoted twenty seconds to the commencement of the drop. The tension could have been cut with a knife; we were all as taut as bowstrings. The red light changed to green and as the despatcher shouted go, the first man disappeared through the hole in the floor, swiftly followed by others who were shuffling towards it, until it was my turn at number seventeen. I stepped into space, but just as I did so the plane rocked and I hit both sides of the hole during my exit, breaking my army watch which I later found had stopped at 00:36 hours.

I now had a few seconds to look around and get my bearings. Many searchlights trying to locate our planes were lighting up the area, while the tracer shells and bullets wove a beautiful pattern in the night sky. Then in the distance I saw a church with a detached tower, which I instantly recognised as Ranville Church, so very good had our briefing been back in England. I was in the right place at the right time, a thing that had bothered many of us. I heard a thump as my kitbag hit the ground denoting that I was about to land myself, which I did almost immediately. Then for a full minute, I was violently sick, which I can only put down to the sudden release of tension, as I had never been airsick in my life! I released myself from my parachute harness, then gathering my kitbag I turned my back towards Ranville Church and ran forwards and slightly to my left where I knew I would find the road that led to the bridges now known as Horsa and Pegasus bridges. Soon we had made a group of twenty or thirty parachutists, one of whom was a wireless operator who was trying to contact the glider troops that had landed just before us near the bridges, and who we hoped, had captured them intact. We were about two hundred yards from the first bridge when the wireless operator shouted 'ham and jam' the signal that the glider troops had captured the bridges intact. I immediately threw away my kitbag containing the dinghy which would have been used to cross the water obstacles had the bridges been demolished by the Germans. We raced onwards and as we approached the Canal de Caen bridge, I saw a number of dead bodies lying in the roadway. On the other side of the bridge there appeared to be a mighty battle in progress but this turned out to be ammunition exploding in a German tank that had been destroyed by the glider troops.

The others and myself were part of A Company, 7th (LI) Battalion of the Parachute Regiment, who having crossed over the captured bridges turned left at a T-junction into the village of Bénouville. Slowly we crept through the village until we came to the large iron gates of the Château de Bénouville, which was situated on a minor crossroads.

It was here that one of our party, Private McCara, climbed over a hedge and was (we believe) knifed to death by two Germans waiting on the other side. A No. 36 hand grenade with a four-second fuse was thrown over the hedge into the slit trench that the Germans had then occupied. We believe that the two Germans were themselves both killed by the grenade. A machine gun then opened fire from inside the chateau gates, wounding Private Whittingham who later died of his wounds, and a German stick grenade exploded near the head of our officer who started to bleed from his eyes and ears, which gave us the impression that he had a fractured base of the skull, and so we withdrew, taking our wounded with us.

We set up a defensive position on a bank of earth bordering a sunken cart track that was about ten feet wide. On the opposite side of the track and immediately in front of us was a seven-foot brick wall with a wooden door at one end. We were now on the seaward side of Bénouville. Our position enabled us to control any enemy movement along the main Caen/Ouistreham road, as well as preventing him from making any attack on the bridges from the western side of the village.

The night was taken up with small skirmishes between German and our own patrols who were constantly probing to locate the enemy. At about 10:30am, three large German tanks came rumbling along the main road from the direction of Caen. They stopped near the chateau gates, then the leading tank lowered its gun and fired a shell at the end of our position. Private McGee, who was near the main road, picked up his Bren gun then started to walk up the middle of the road towards the tanks firing the Bren gun from his hip. As one magazine became empty he replaced it with a new one, discarding the empty magazine on the roadside. We could hear the bullets ricocheting off the armour steel plating of the leading tank who immediately closed down his visor, thus making him blind to things in front! Corporal Tommy Killeen, realised what was happening and ran up the side of the road, taking two Gammon bombs from his pouches. He threw the first bomb, which hit the leading tank where the turret and body meets which nearly blew the turret off. He threw the second bomb but being further away from the second tank it fell short, landing against the tank's track, which was promptly blown off. This tank now tried to escape, but only having one good track it went around in circles, so the crew baled out and tried to escape. They were shot by McGee.

Next came an attack by a company of Panzer Grenadiers, but this was easily contained and they withdrew after losing a number of men. I was now with Sergeant Young guarding the right flank when we saw a section of about ten Germans break cover some seven hundred yards away on our western flank. We waited until they were  on an open flat piece of ground, then opened fire with our rifles, which were fitted with telescopic sights. We didn't see any enemy movement on that flank for the rest of the day. It was just after this event that I saw L/Cpl Davey lying in an orchard, his face covered with blood and I was just about to investigate when a German Panther tank appeared about forty yards from our position, quite near to Davey. It stopped, lowered his large 88mm gun, which now appeared to be pointing straight at me. I shouted a warning as I dived into a ditch, and the shell made a hole in the wall about three yards to my left but we suffered no casualties. It was later learned that Davey had realised that the Germans were all around him, so he pretended to be dead. In fact he made his way back to Pegasus bridge as soon as it was dark and was later returned to England with his wounds. After a period in hospital, he re-joined the regiment and survived the war.

During the many attacks made by the enemy that day (mainly by about a company strength), all were successfully dealt with at a considerable cost to the enemy, but our own casualties were now mounting. It was during one of these attacks that a German walked through the wooden door in the wall in front of us. He was just as surprised as us and immediately disappeared back through the door before we could react!

We had now been surrounded by the enemy since our arrival and so Sergeant Young and myself decided to try to get back to the canal bridge to find out the position. As we travelled along the ditch, with Sgt Young leading, a shot rang out and he shouted that they had broken his back. I pushed him down into the ditch and fell on top of him, then examined his wound, which proved to be a furrow right across his back but did not appear to have injured his spine. I gave him a morphine injection, which we all carried, and dressed his wounds before returning to our position.

By 16:15 hours we had gathered twenty-three German prisoners and L/Cpl Jackson volunteered to escort them down to the bridge for interrogation. He was killed by a sniper's bullet whilst returning to A Company positions.

It was about 21:15 hours when the 2nd Battalion of the Royal Warwickshire Regiment put in an attack on Bénouville in an attempt to get us out. This proved to be successful. We had been surrounded by the enemy for seventeen and a half hours but the very gallant A Company had held out. We returned to the canal bridge, later named the Pegasus bridge, in honour of the men who had captured it and held it against all odds. Here we managed to get a small meal from the rations we all carried. It was while we were doing so that we came under sniper fire from the church tower at Le Port. Corporal Tommy Killeen asked us to give him covering fire, then picking up a Piat (Projector Infantry Anti-Tank) gun and a case containing three bombs, he ran forward towards the church. When he was about twenty yards away he stopped and placed the butt of the Piat on the ground, then he placed a bomb in position, and guessing the angle, he lined it up on the church tower and pressed the trigger. We watched as the bomb soared towards its target then hit the tower quite near to the slits through which the German snipers had been firing. We ran towards the church to assist him and saw Killeen stop in the church doorway, remove his helmet and make the sign of the cross before entering! In among the debris of the church spire (inside the church) we found twelve dead German snipers. At 23:30 hours we were taken back to our DZ (dropping zone) as reserve company, where we all dug slit trenches. I lined mine with part of a discarded parachute that I found, then climbed into the trench pulling the remainder of the parachute over me and I fell asleep about 01:00 hours, 7 June. Private McGee was awarded the Distinguished Conduct Medal, but was killed later that day. Corporal Thomas Killeen was awarded the Military Medal, and in fact survived the war. The tasks given to the 6th Airborne Division on 6 June were all successfully accomplished. The left flank of the invasion area was held secure.

I must say that we had the most wonderful support from the Royal Air Force who were masters of the skies over Normandy, and the Royal Navy who shelled everything that was asked of them. Finally, the army personnel who fought to get ashore and advance through the enemy defences to ensure that we had the maximum support. They were all magnificent.

So ended D-Day, which for myself and many others truly was a very long day!

Edgar 'Eddy' Gurney, Thorpe St Andrew, Norwich

J.J.P.

Yesterday I met a man, who went in on D-Day on that
 Norman coast,
Who knowing of my visit, asked,
'Did they ever get them buried right?'

We couldn't stop; we left them where they fell, wrapped
 in grey blankets,
Some dying and some dead... rows on rows,
Just where the guns had mown them down.

I often wondered how many died, who needn't, of neglect.
It doesn't bear thinking of, all that...
And the bodies floating in the sea.

Drowned long before they reached the beach, tangled in
    their landing gear, or
Fallen off the lifeline beyond their depth.
And every officer dead before we topped that beach.

In the end we joined the Yanks, and went into the Panzers'
Arms in Cambey's Wood;
Panzers three sides, our naval guns behind,
And us lot caught between the two.

If the Panzers didn't get us, our own shells did. Whole
    Company gone, and Panzers too,
Boxed in that wood.

It doesn't bear thinking of, all that,
That nightmare long ago...

J.J.P. is Mr Pancott, a one-man builder and decorator, who one day listened to our talk of a holiday in Normandy. Then he spoke and what he said came out as blank verse. I let him go on – he was miles away, years back in the past to D-Day. I wrote it down straight away – as this is his memory. What  struck me was his disbelief that all those bodies could have been buried – there were so many. He's now retired and sadly I've lost touch.

Gloria Bennett, Oxford, Oxfordshire

I was in the 6th Battalion, Durham Light Infantry, and after spending six months in England on 3 June 1944 we were ready to embark for the invasion of the continent. But we didn't move until the morning of 4 June. Our carriers were waterproofed for water four-feet in depth. My mates were Ken as a gunner, and Arthur as a driver. But Ken had vanished. When we boarded the LCTs Arthur was behind me and Ken was on another boat. He was driving a carrier full of mines, gelignite etc. Phew. I wouldn't have liked that job. We sailed the next day and it was a rough sea. Quite a few chaps were sick, but I was lucky. Arriving off the coast of Normandy the next morning we were surprised that we were not under constant air attacks. Then we nosed into the shore, Gold Beach. I took the camouflage off the carrier and warmed the engine. I was thinking, will the water be shallow enough to take the carrier, or if the water is deep, will the carrier float? We knew the beach had been taken before we landed, and our job was to pass through La Riviere and push on inland. Our aircraft (Spitfires) were overhead, but one Spitfire caught the tail of another with his wing. One dropped and crashed. The other, with smoke coming from the tail, turned back across the Channel.

That day we had pushed approximately twelve miles inland. We had tanks on either side of us, a bicycle company, mixed in amongst the carriers, and planes above our head. Whenever we met any opposition our concentrated fire soon moved it. On the night we stopped and took up positions against counter-attack.

Three carriers had to go forward, on a recce. My section was chosen and it was dark when we set out. We had only gone one hundred yards when we came to a big gun burning in the road. Going over it I had a large piece caught in my track, and so had to stop. In the ditch near the gun was a wounded Jerry, and with him was a young Italian, about eighteen years old. We tried to fix the Jerry up but we knew he was dying. The Italian worked like a slave to remove the piece of metal from round my track (voluntarily) and when we went back we left him to look after his mate. That night we withdrew, as the marching troops couldn't get up to us that night. We laagered up in a wood and I was chosen to do a stag and I did my two hours with Arthur. The next morning we again started off on the column, and everything went OK until we reached our final objective, when, as we were moving up a side road, a corporal dashed up to us and said there were some Jerries coming towards the crossroads.

Being the leading carrier I started to go up. A motorbike dashed past with two Jerries on. A corporal stood at the crossroads, and fired his Sten at them as they went past, then a truck towing an anti-tank gun came across and the corporal fired again and the truck stopped. I was only five yards away then. My crew baled out. In trying to swing the carrier round, I got stuck on the bank. It was then that our anti-tank gun hit the Jerries' truck, and set it on fire. Being only five yards away from it, I baled out and lay behind my carrier. I looked round and saw everyone had fallen back, about a hundred yards. As shells etc. (from the truck) were flying quite close I decided to stop where I was! I heard another truck pull up and saw a Hun walk across the road. I

wished I'd had my rifle with me. On the arrival of our tanks the Jerries surrendered. We threw a roadblock across the road and cut off a lot more Boche. Our carriers then carried on with my carrier leading, and we turned down the road, the same way the Jerries were going before we stopped them.

About two hundred yards down, we came to a crossroad (Jerusalem Crossing), our final objective. Some French civilians came out and gave us some wine. Our planes had been flying about all the time, but one suddenly turned and faced us. Smoke came from his guns and canon and everyone dived for cover, bar the French who were too horrified to move. I threw myself over the gear lever and waited. Being the first carrier I took the brunt of the attack and as I was lying there I suddenly felt someone sticking red hot needles in my back and side. Then I felt warm and wet, and putting my hand to my side and back, I pulled it away covered in blood. Expecting him (the Thunderbolt) to come back, I baled out and ran into a house. I saw my sergeant lying against the wall with his legs peppered with shrapnel, the French in a heap on the floor, two dead and one with his leg off. The lads got a carrier and sticking the serg and myself on, they dashed us back to the RAP. After being dressed, we were passed back from one dressing station to another until we reached the beach. The same night I was taken down to the beach on a Duck, but owing to the congestion on the beach we could not board the ship. While we were wedged between the traffic, some German planes came over and strafed the beach. So we were taken back to the dressing station. The next morning, we were again loaded onto the Ducks and this time when we got to the beach the way was clear, so we went straight into the water. After floating around for a while, we drove straight onto the LST. It is marvellous how they do this loading of ships at sea. I was lifted onto the floor (still on my stretcher), then I was put on a rack against the other racks full of wounded (including German). After landing in England, being transported by train and army ambulances, we arrived at Royal Gwent Hospital, Newport.

My future wife was just going to post my twenty-first birthday cards when she was told I was missing, so she took them back home! But next day my father told her I was wounded but OK.

Ron Bennett, Birmingham, West Midlands

All through May 1944 our thoughts and hopes revolved round the increasing signs that the invasion across the Channel was imminent. The bombing of French railway marshalling yards and, by mid-May, news restrictions in England obviously hiding the build-up of forces, were clear signs.

Of course, all official information was controlled by the German occupation authorities; radios had been confiscated. Well, most people had handed in an old set and hidden a working one! Newspapers were only read for the lists of food coupons, some local news and the latest in oppressive measures. But clandestine information sheets and our hidden radios kept us informed. The oppression had been growing after an initial uneasy period after the overrunning of the Netherlands in 1940. We had been told we were a Germanic brother people, but this and other forms of propaganda were met with ridicule. We got rations which kept us lean, a little hungry, but fairly healthy. But soon the executions of Resistance fighters had started and so had the first measures against the Jews. This closely concerned me, because about one third of the pupils in my class were Jewish. Then young men were called up for work in the German war industry; many refused and became 'onderduikers', literally 'submerged': no identity papers, no food coupons, liable to be rounded up or apprehended at surprise checkpoints. Worst of all was the fate of our Jewish friends, although nobody, including them, realised the truth. Barred

from public buildings initially, forced into ghettoes, then herded into the camp at Westerbork before – as was published – being sent to work on collective farms in Poland. The sinister thing was that at that point we lost all contact, all correspondence ceased. In 1943 the rumours got strong that they were being killed, but in 1944 there was hope that German defeat would be in time to save some, apart from those who had gone into hiding with incredible risk to them and the people who hid them. So many people's hopes hinged on the invasion.

I had been in hiding since early 1943 when the Germans had tried to get the universities in their grip. I had helped organise student resistance, had narrowly escaped on my bike in the darkness from a surprise checkpoint with the list of sympathisers in my pocket (the kind of stupidity that cost many lives in the early phases of resistance). I had lived in hiding in various places, being confined for a year in a small room initially. Now I lived in my parents' home, with a hiding-place twice the size of a coffin, which I could reach and close up in twenty seconds. As my father on one occasion was able to hold three Germans up for two minutes with a magnificent display of grammatically perfect German (he was a teacher), this was adequate. The radio set was there, too, the same one my father had listened to each morning during the Battle of Britain; I still remember him lifting his headphones: 'They're still fighting.' Now it was our link with Normandy and on 6 June, every half-hour, we listened to the BBC. Of course the communiqués were in guarded tones but we became aware of the size of the undertaking; that afternoon it was clear that footholds had been established securely. All the time we were aware of human suffering out there. All our hopes lay in the troops going ashore and how the Normandy fighting dominated our thoughts is perhaps best illustrated by an incident in our family. In August that year my grandmother (eighty-four) collapsed and was obviously dying. After a week in a coma, two of her daughters sitting by the bedside, the old lady woke up and spoke her last words: 'Has Cherbourg been taken?'

On 6 June we knew that the door to liberation had been wrenched open. Not a year has passed when my wife and I have not stood by some grave of an Allied soldier, sailor or airman, read his name, and asked ourselves why the privilege of a full life had been granted to us and not to them.

Mr Dijkstra, De Bilt, Holland

During the time of the 'invasie' (invasion) as we used to call it, I worked at a bank in Amsterdam. As a language student I had had to sign the famous 'declaration' requested by the Germans, that I would not undertake anything whatsoever against them, which of course I refused to do, just like the greater part of Dutch students. Therefore, I was called upon by the enemy to serve as a 'postwoman' in their post office. My father got furious at the idea and managed to get me a job in one of the Amsterdam banks. My boss, who was in charge of the bank's staff, looked for someone whom he could trust and who would help him in keeping as many staff members out of forced labour in Germany by providing them with (faked!) official German papers stating that they were

indispensable for the economic life in the Netherlands. I also was given one of these declarations and so was left in peace by the Germans for the rest of the war. One of the employees in this bank had a radio set (as indeed many people had) and listened to the BBC news every morning. He took a tremendous risk and knew that he could face the death penalty if caught. This man took the news down in shorthand and after writing it out he handed it over to me.

I, in my turn, typed it out using carbon paper, and on my way home delivered these copies here and there at 'reliable' addresses, hiding them between the linings of my shoes, naive and inexperienced as I was. (A silly thing to do as the Germans soon discovered the trick, but I never got caught.)

The carbon paper was torn into small pieces and flushed down the toilet for fear of discovery. Every now and then a new supply of carbon paper mysteriously appeared on my desk. I assume my boss knew where that came from but I never asked him. In those days it was best to know as little as possible!

And then came the day of 6 June 1944. The usual routine: my meeting the 'man with the BBC news' in the hall at 8:30am. But this time he whispered, 'Wonderful news, they've landed.' No more. I could not wait to read the bulletin and there it was: the news we had waited for so long. I cannot say how it spread, but it became obvious in the course of the morning that these good tidings had been heard by everybody. Happy faces all over the place, but nobody speaking about it, afraid of betraying his source.

That is one of the things I think people who have never lived in an occupied country can hardly understand: how rapidly news can be spread by word of mouth only and what a tremendous power the BBC had in keeping up the morale of our people.

Willy Dijkstra, De Bilt, Holland

I was in the 12th Yorkshire Parachute Battalion. It was just growing dusk on the 5 June 1944 when we got in the aircraft – Stirlings, four engine jobs. We were all very quiet – the RAF came round with canisters of tea, but nobody wanted any! As we went over the Channel and over France I held my breath – the world seemed to stand still – THIS WAS IT – the start of everything. I thought of my wife at home. I hoped I would come through and I prayed to God, as many others did, and as I did at Dunkirk. He must have been listening to me and perhaps thought I still wasn't good enough to die! When we approached the dropping zone the plane was getting hit, it was like driving on a new road with the grit hitting the body work – it was only light stuff, but it still sounded fearful!

The red light came on and then the green light – this was the moment – we all had to jump through the hole in the floor. I had a kitbag with a Bren etc. It took one or two seconds to get through as there were more men with kitbags and equipment and the plane was going like hell – I think the pilot had his foot through the headlights!

I landed awkwardly with the kitbag rope wrapped round my boot. I thought I had broken my foot and I had wrenched my arm badly. I could still feel the heat of the plane's engine – and I still can! I also thought about the cups of tea we had turned down in the aircraft. I carried a Bren gun and when I reached our rendezvous we found Jerry giving us heavy fire from his armoured cars. Then a Jerry started to machine gun us – we did a flanking movement and went round behind him. Then the lads went in with the steel. That finished that problem. After forming up we started to move to our objective – Bréville. Its capture was essential – it was to be done at all costs. It was on high ground overlooking a valley through which the Germans could percolate at any time into the bridgehead, which was to be established unless we took it.

We formed up in an area only three quarters of a mile from Bréville and came under terrific mortar pounding from the Germans. As darkness fell our artillery opened up in support of us and soon the night was lit up by tracer and the deafening din of artillery from the Allied lines, and counter-fire from the German mortars. As we stormed up towards the village one after another of our men fell on the way, but we went on, determined to do the job we had been given. Despite the killed and wounded we eventually fought our way into Bréville where the battle raged on at close quarters until Jerry was driven out.

Then we started our next job with no respite – digging in frenziedly to await the inevitable counter attack from the mortars! We were not disappointed. Within a quarter of an

hour the inferno began and the entire village seemed to be ablaze. The Germans knew its importance as much as we did. But we clung on, despite everything. I remember at the height of the bombardment we lost the sergeant major and our colonel. The colonel was dashing about rallying everyone and shouting, 'Dig in you... or die.' Shortly afterwards he was killed – and many of our lads and my comrades did die. One lad was lucky – he had his helmet blown open just like a tin can – he was wounded, but he was lucky to be even alive after a hit like that.

Throughout the long night we waited for the German counter-attack against what was now a shambles of a village – not with mortars now but with infantry. It never came. Not until prisoners were interrogated later did we learn that we had given them such a hammering that they had neither the strength nor the will to make another effort. But we didn't know that at the time and so through the next day and night we stuck it out and after two days, very tired and weary, we were relieved. Incidentally I carried out the lad who had his helmet blown off and took him to a Jeep to get him out of the line of fire. But when I got to it I found the rear tyre was ablaze and I had to put it out by smothering it with horse or cow manure. Things were too hectic for me to take much notice which it was! It was at this time that I realised I had been wounded in the leg – I hadn't had time to notice until then! By this time the church and everything else was on fire. Shells from our own artillery were hitting us as well because apparently the officer directing the shelling had been killed and so we got both lots – British artillery and German mortars.

When we were relieved I was taken to the Royal Navy and so back to England where my report from the hospital at Blackpool gave my problem as 'leg wound and exhaustion'.

One incident that shows how fate plays a part; one of my mates dropped his fighting knife just before we set off and cut his foot. We dressed it for him and said nothing because he didn't want to be left behind. But he had trouble in walking once we got there and so he was left to look after the equipment when the shelling started. He was promptly hit by shellfire in the lower head and neck.

When General, later Field Marshal, Montgomery held a Field Investiture for officers and men of the Airborne Division, one DSO went to the colonel, and one MC, two DCMs and four Military Medals to other officers and men of the 12th Yorkshire Parachute Battalion. Only one was present at the investiture to collect his award – the rest were either killed or wounded. That about says what it was all about.

Charles R. Pearson, St. Ives, Cornwall

I was in the 7th Armoured Division and I remember as we moved up the lane a German Staff car came down towards us! Everyone opened fire at once and it turned over and crashed. What it was doing there I'll never know. When I passed it again later in a Bren carrier I didn't even bother to look at its occupants. There were going to be plenty more in the next few weeks that was certain.

In Villers-Bocage I was sent out with four others to patrol the immediate area when suddenly I saw a tank fire from a farmyard. This was followed by a barrage from others in sheltered positions, immediately setting fire to our tank, trucks, and Bren carriers in the narrow sunken lanes, where only minutes before our troops had been drinking tea as if on a Sunday afternoon picnic.

The scene was one of fire, smoke and continuous explosions. It was all too evident that the Germans had been waiting for us and had picked the right moment to strike, which they had done with a vengeance! It was discovered later that they were Panther and Tiger tanks of a Waffen-SS Heavy Tank Battalion, which included a German tank 'Ace' with one hundred and nineteen 'kills' to his credit on the Russian front.

In the mayhem and confusion everyone began destroying their equipment to stop it falling into enemy hands. I began by smashing up our radios and finished by throwing my Bren gun into a pond, minus its firing pin. I then took cover under a fallen telegraph pole. I kept low enough to hide from a couple of Germans who were by now only yards from me, surveying the scene of their successful ambush from their side-car motorcycle, but still ready with their heavy machine gun.

I could have 'popped-off' both of them easily, but knowing that I would almost certainly be captured if I did I decided not to do anything. There was still total confusion everywhere else – I was hidden behind my pole in an island of comparative quiet by now. But I could hear my sergeant shouting orders and calling out, and I even saw others of my platoon flag down a Tiger tank thinking it was one of ours arrived to help them! Shortly afterwards word had obviously got back to HQ because the area began to be bombed by British and American

aircraft, so I and a couple of mates who had also been hiding made a break for it and got away. After a couple of days continuous walking we managed to get a night's kip, which was a blessed relief I can tell you. The trouble was that when we woke up we found ourselves surrounded by German troops and trucks. Hundreds of troops! We had obviously been walking in the wrong direction and were now well behind the enemy lines thank you very much!

I tried to make another break for it but a German sentry, a very big chap as I remember, spotted me and fired from about one hundred yards. The bullets just seemed to riddle the ground in front of me at which point I decided it might be better to stand still! I can particularly remember raising my hands and for some inexplicable reason shouting, 'Mum, Mum, Mum!' A reflex action I suppose, just like when you were a kid and got hurt!

Before he searched me the sentry motioned with his gun in a threatening manner, and I became even more nervous than I was already! Then suddenly the penny dropped. He wanted me to discard what I had in my hand. To him I suppose it could have been a grenade, but all it was unfortunately was a pair of gloves rolled up!

Anyway my part in the fighting came to an end there and then. I was a POW for eleven months in various Stalag and work camps in southeast Germany. I suppose it is something to be able to say now that I fought in the Normandy invasion, but it wasn't as if I had much choice at the time! But then it was the same for everyone – the luck of the draw so to speak. You all just got on with it – no matter where or who you were.

George Benham, Southbourne, West Sussex

I was in the American 508 Parachute Infantry Regiment and I must say here that one of my major criticisms of all our detailed briefings had to do with hedgerows. We were told that there were hedgerows but no one explained in detail how they were to affect us. We all pictured hedgerows as dividing two fields but something that one could push through easily. This is not so. Each of the fields in this area of Normandy are not more than fifty yards square and are outlined on all four sides by hedgerows which consist of a berm of earth about three feet thick and about three feet high. From the top of this berm there are thick bushes growing to a height of six to ten feet. In addition, each berm of earth has a drainage ditch on each side about two feet deep. What you have is thousands of little fields, each one an island unto itself. Men could be fighting and dying in one field and people could be taking a break in the next one.

It was 2:30am on D-Day when the green light came on and I was out some four hundred feet in the air above the Normandy countryside falling into that sea of tracers. Fortunately for me, I landed right in the middle of one of those fifty-yard square fields. As soon as I hit the ground I heard this German, I didn't know what he was saying but I could tell by the pitch and loudness of his voice that he was really excited and that he meant business. I knew that I had to get out of my chute and away from it as soon as possible. We were loaded down with extra equipment plus having a harness that snapped around each leg at the groin and across the chest with a snap fastener. In order to minimise the opening shock these straps were very tight and under all the other equipment that we carried. Because of this and what I knew would only be a short time to get out of my chute, I used my razor-sharp knife that was attached to my jump boot to cut my way out of my harness. In my haste I also cut my way through my rifle sling. If I didn't have enough problems already, I was also confronted by a cow right next to me with a bell around its neck. It stood looking down at me moving her head and ringing the bell!

I was fortunate to be able to get out of my harness and slither about ten yards away toward the opposite corner of the field from the Germans. Suddenly I heard the very distinct 'pop' of a Very pistol and I knew that in a few seconds the whole area would be flooded with the white light of a parachute flare. I got as low to the ground as possible and faced the chute. As soon as the flare came on the area was flooded with light and a hail of bullets came from the German position on the corner of the field. I saw my parachute and equipment being shot to pieces. The firing continued for the whole time the flare was lit (about twenty seconds). It seemed like an eternity to me. The only thing that saved me was the fact that I had gotten a little distance away from my chute and that my hands and face were blackened and that I was hugging the ground. When the flare went out, they didn't fire another one.

For whatever reason, they did not come into the field after me so as soon as the flare went out I started to crawl to the far corner of the field. There I ran into another pathfinder who was lost. We almost shot each other before we realised who was who! The two of us proceeded along the hedgerow into the next field when we heard the sound of German voices coming toward us. We ducked down into one of the drainage ditches along the hedgerow and waited for them to pass. Unfortunately for us they didn't pass by. Just on the other side of the hedgerow from us I heard the unmistakable sound of a machine gun being set up. The snap of the trails being extended and the sound of the bolt going back and forth as the belt was fed through. It appeared that we were in the middle of a German platoon position. We could hear them talking quite clearly just on the other side of the berm of earth. What to do...? There was no way to throw a grenade through that hedgerow. We had to whisper very quietly. I thought that we could sneak out of

Henry Le Febvre, front row second from left

our position but the dry brambles and weeds would crackle loudly and we would hear 'vas is los?' and we would freeze.

I recalled from our briefing that the force landing by sea on the Normandy coast would relieve us by D-Day or D plus one so I figured that we could just stay put until the Germans were forced to move. Unfortunately for us, the seaborne invasion didn't make it to us as planned. My pathfinder friend almost got his hand stepped on by a German who was apparently going out to the platoon outpost on our side of the berm. My friend's hand was on the edge of the ditch in which we were hiding and suddenly we saw these two legs go by us... Our days and nights were spent huddled together. Each move in the ditch caused a lot of noise because of the dry brambles and weeds. I was sure the Germans would be driven out by our forces momentarily so we waited. We lived on a little water and D-Day ration chocolate bars. It was three nights before we finally heard the Germans packing up to leave.

After checking my compass for an easterly direction we started out and shortly ran into our own forces. It was a tense confrontation as everyone was jumpy. I parted company with my pathfinder friend and never saw him again. I, along with many other 508ers who were scattered, began rejoining the regiment with many stories of firefights, escapes, and individual exploits of courage and determination. But only five of my platoon were present for duty.

Henry Le Febvre, Balboa, California, USA

I was with the 5th Royal Tank Regiment, 7th Armoured Division on D-Day. As we approached the coast we passed through the lines of naval ships, which were carrying out the covering bombardment. Battleships, cruisers, destroyers, rocket ships sending salvos of shells and rockets onto the land. It was at least ten times louder than our barrage that we had passed through at El Alamein!

It was impossible to hear any reply, but great splashes appeared in the water and a merchant ship near us was hit and fell behind in a pall of black smoke. As we approached the beach, our patrol vessels and aircraft dropped smoke flares to screen us as we landed, but the strong wind blew it away. All the landing craft were jockeying for a place to beach. Each division had sent ahead beach parties to mark the landing area and also the exit from the beach. Our craft charged the beach and as the ship shuddered to a halt the large door was lowered. Our troop leader was first, we were second. Before we started up, the instructions had been repeated. The troop leader's tank moved out, through the water and onto the special wire mesh laid out on the beach. But the driver made the error of going too near the edge of the mesh and the tank turned over on its side, and threw the left track.

After clearing up pockets of resistance that had been by-passed by the infantry of 50 Division we pushed on down the road towards Saint-Paul-du-Vernay. The road, with cornfields on each side had no hedges and as we left Trungy there was no cover for about five hundred yards. Our troop was in the lead with Sergeant Cook in his Cromwell being point tank. We moved cautiously along the exposed road trying to see what was in the trees where the road disappeared in the distance. We were about halfway along the road as Sergeant Cook's tank entered the trees when there was a terrific explosion. The tank literally disintegrated and the Sergeant was thrown onto the road. We moved forward and fired four AP shells into the area where we thought the shot had come from. Sergeant Cook staggered back down the road and was helped behind our tank by two infantrymen but he died later.

A Company of the Essex Regiment later arrived in support. They were all spic and span and looked newly arrived from home. Not at all what we had expected. They prepared for the attack as if on the 'square'. When the arranged artillery barrage began, they began to move forward, but in open order carrying their rifles at the port position. We could hardly believe what we were seeing.

In just a few minutes the line was massacred. The ones that were left fell back. They formed up again as an officer came running up shouting, 'Send them in on their bellies.' This time they made use of the waist-high corn, as the enemy flamethrowers moved forward. It took the remainder of the day and most of the night to clear the woods as the enemy counter-attacked time and again. Enemy tanks came up in support, and enemy infantry were attempting to attach grenades to the side of the tanks. Two enemy tanks were put out of action by the infantry with their Piat guns. In the darkness, one enemy tank commander passed through our lines and destroyed two of our reserve tanks before he was disposed of.

We left the infantry to carry out the final clearing up when we were due for replenishment. Forming up on the road

where we had previously lost Sergeant Cook and his crew, we made our way to the rendezvous. As we turned into the area where the replenishment lorries were gathered, a sniper shot Sergeant Major Knight as he stood in the turret of his tank.

Without rest, but with a little breakfast, we moved off leaving the Essex Regiment to clear the area and the nearby village of Ellon. We had been ordered to try to expand the bridgehead by moving down some secondary roads which would lead us to our objective which was Villers-Bocage.

With the element of surprise we passed through several small villages overcoming the opposition, despite the noise made by the tanks as they approached. We had travelled twelve miles before we encountered serious opposition. As we entered the village of Livry, an anti-tank gun opened fire from the side of the square.

We were carrying some infantry with us. It was necessary to dismount them and mount an organised attack on the village and we attacked from all sides. The anti-tank gun was knocked out and several enemy taken prisoner. We stayed in the village for the night, awaiting replenishment, and infantry patrols made contact with the American army on our right.

The lead was now to be taken over by the 4th City of London Yeomanry, one of the other two tank regiments in our brigade. As we moved along towards the main road to Villers-Bocage, 4th CLY passed by us and we then followed them. We were now moving out of the enclosed bocage country, and as the 4th CLY entered Briquessard, we moved off across the open fields to be on their left flank as they attacked Amayé-sur-Seulles.

We took up positions along the top of the hill, and around midday received a message that the 4th CLY had reached their objective and had entered Villers-Bocage. But around 14:00 hours, firing was heard and the air became full of messages! The enemy, who had been constantly delayed by our air attacks, had at last arrived and were endeavouring to make Villers-Bocage their headquarters!

Our leading column, who had earlier reported that they were in charge of the town, had found that the enemy tanks had allowed them to pass, and when all the tanks were in the town, had fired on the infantry half-track following behind, completely blocking the road. The last message received from the 4th CLY Squadron Commander was that his squadron was completely surrounded by enemy tanks and infantry, and that he would have to surrender.

Despite fierce fighting we were in fact finally able to relieve the 4th CLY who came forward to help with supporting fire and the Germans finally decided to call it a day. But it was touch and go.

It was to be 30 June before we were pulled out of this front line for the first time since we had arrived over three weeks earlier.

S. Storer, Barwell, Leicestershire

I was a sergeant in A Troop, 322 Battery, 103 Regiment of the Royal Artillery. We landed on Sword Beach at 7:45am and as our Rhino transport dropped the ramp I suddenly found the water coming up round my legs! By the time I was off the ramp it was up to my waist and I remember the chap with me was standing on the seat with his head out through the trap shouting, 'Keep her going serge or we'll all bloody well drown.'

We followed the space between the white tapes that amazingly were already in place showing where it was clear of mines and made it quickly to the road that ran parallel to the beach where we had to wait while the Sussex Yeomanry got into action with some German tanks on the high ground behind Hermanville. I must say they soon sorted them out, but it was terrible to see a tank catch fire. You still have feelings whether it's the enemy or not.

Other vehicles of our troop were arriving but we couldn't take up our proper position as it was still in enemy hands; so we didn't hang about but put the gun legs down where we were, ready for action just in case. It was just as well we did because we'd only just finished when the bombardier shouted, 'Enemy aircraft!' and we were attacked. We had to engage them through open sights but we hit a JU88, which blew up and crashed on the beach. Shells were also falling around us by this time from the German guns inland. We couldn't respond to that because we had no information of where to fire so we ran for cover.

Two of us ran for a trench left by the Germans and I remember seeing the chap with me run into it and then get straight out! When I looked to see why I found it was full of German troops who had been occupying it – all dead. No wonder he got out so quick!

So we sheltered behind a high wall where we saw the Royal Marine commandos carrying their dead and wounded out of the firing. I heard a sergeant say, 'We don't want that one, he's a bloody German,' and they just left the body – that's what war does to you. They'd all been caught by mortar fire, which was still striking the wall.

Later we got back to our vehicle and gun and it was then that we saw the first German prisoners of war coming in. There were a lot and they seemed to be mostly young boys and old men, but perhaps they weren't old. Perhaps they'd just been through an awful hammering that made them look it. I know what we went through was bad enough but I certainly wouldn't have wanted to be on the end of what they'd had!

About midday we moved on to Colleville where we suffered from snipers which in many ways was the worst of the lot. But then a plane came over and bombed us and without thinking I dived for cover under my lorry. Fortunately the bombs missed and no one was injured but the covers on the vehicles were torn to ribbons. It was only then I remembered that my lorry was half-loaded with petrol so if we had been hit there wouldn't have been much of me left!

Insofar as the landing itself is concerned we had no end of trouble. Regimental records show that A Troop was dive-bombed on our LST and the lift was jammed causing delay in unloading. The regiment landed as and when it could and not always according to the timetable arrangements. In some cases the guns had unloaded and landed before the recce parties had arrived! The records show that at the time, when sixteen guns should have been ashore, there was only one gun and one radar – such were the opposition and problems. But we persevered – and we made it!

W. A. 'Bill' Rogers, Deal, Kent

Acknowledgements

The authors wish to gratefully acknowledge the support so willingly given to us by the following Cross-Channel Ferry Companies: Brittany Ferries on the Portsmouth/Caen route. P&O on the Portsmouth/Cherbourg and Portsmouth/Le Havre routes, Stena Sealink on the Southampton/Cherbourg route.

This ready assistance has helped ensure we raise the maximum funds for all the veterans of the Normandy Campaign.

Index

Entries in *italics* indicate photographs.

Index of Contributors

Entries in *italics* indicate photographs.